INDIGENOUS KINSHIP,
COLONIAL TEXTS,
and the
CONTESTED SPACE OF
EARLY NEW ENGLAND

A VOLUME IN THE SERIES

Native Americans of the Northeast

EDITED BY

Lisa T. Brooks and Jean M. O'Brien

INDIGENOUS KINSHIP,
COLONIAL TEXTS,
and the
CONTESTED SPACE OF
EARLY NEW ENGLAND

—⁂—

Marie Balsley Taylor

UNIVERSITY OF MASSACHUSETTS PRESS
Amherst and Boston

Copyright © 2023 by University of Massachusetts Press
All rights reserved
Printed in the United States of America

ISBN 978-1-62534-725-1 (paper); 726-8 (hardcover)

Designed by Sally Nichols
Set in Adobe Jenson Pro
Printed and bound by Books International, Inc.

Cover design by adam b. bohannon
Cover art by William Hubbard, *A Map of New-England*, extracted from
Hubbard's A Narrative of the Troubles with the Indians in New-England (Boston, 1677).
John Carter Brown Library JCB D677 .H876n1. CC BY-SA 4.0

Library of Congress Cataloging-in-Publication Data

Names: Taylor, Marie Balsley, 1981–author.
Title: Indigenous kinship, colonial texts, and the contested space of early
New England / Marie Balsley Taylor.
Other titles: Native Americans of the Northeast.
Description: Amherst : University of Massachusetts Press, [2023] | Series:
Native Americans of the Northeast | Includes bibliographical references
and index.
Identifiers: LCCN 2022051863 (print) | LCCN 2022051864 (ebook) | ISBN
9781625347251 (paperback) | ISBN 9781625347268 (hardcover) | ISBN
9781685750190 (ebook)
Subjects: LCSH: American literature—Colonial period, ca.
1600–1775—History and criticism. | Indians of North America—First
contact with other peoples—New England. | Indians of North
America—Kinship—New England. | Indians of North America—New
England—Government relations—To 1789.
Classification: LCC PS191 .T39 2023 (print) | LCC PS191 (ebook) | DDC
397.3578—dc23/eng/20221118
LC record available at https://lccn.loc.gov/2022051863
LC ebook record available at https://lccn.loc.gov/2022051864

British Library Cataloguing-in-Publication Data
A catalog record for this book is available from the British Library.

Portions of chapter 1 originally appeared in "Recovering Indigenous Kinship: Community, Conversion, and the Digital Turn," in *Afterlives of Indigenous Archives: Essays in Honor of the Occom Circle*, edited by Ivy Schweitzer and Gordon Henry (Hanover, NH: Dartmouth College Press, 2019). An earlier version of chapter 2 appeared as "The Sachem and the Minister: Questions, Answers, and Genre Formation in the New England Missionary Project," *Early American Literature* 55, no. 1 (2020).

To Nate

CONTENTS

List of Figures   ix

Acknowledgments   xi

INTRODUCTION
Indigenous Kinship, Colonial Texts
1

CHAPTER ONE
Kinship, Captivity, and Diplomacy
Locating Wequash in the Indigenous Conversion Narrative
17

CHAPTER TWO
Questions, Answers, and Treaty-Making
Cutshamekin's Influence on John Eliot's Political Imagination
60

CHAPTER THREE
Corn, Community, and Cassacinamon
Indigenous Science in John Winthrop Jr.'s "Of Maiz"
91

CHAPTER FOUR
Treaties, Reciprocity, and Providence
The Role of Indigenous Justice in Daniel Gookin's Doings and Sufferings
124

EPILOGUE
Remembering and Forgetting
163

Notes   167

Index   197

vii

FIGURES

FIGURE 1. Title Page of *New Englands First Fruits*, 1643. 26

FIGURE 2. John Underhill's 1638 drawing of the Mystic Massacre, "The Figure of the Indians' Fort or Palizado." 35

FIGURE 3. "Turkie corn" from John Gerard's 1633 *Herball.* 99

FIGURE 4. Native American Sachem (1681). 113

FIGURE 5. "A map of New-England, being the first that ever was here cut, and done by the best pattern that could be had, which being in some places defective, it made the other less exact: Yet doth it sufficiently show the situation of the country & conveniently well the distances of places." William Hubbard, 1677. 144

FIGURE 6. Gookin's manuscript of *Doings and Sufferings* (1677), showing the names of the English present at the signing of the 1644 treaty. 151

ACKNOWLEDGMENTS

Writing about kinship constantly reminds me of the many kinship and communal networks within which I am embedded as a scholar, as a teacher, as a community member, as a relative, as a spouse, as a mother, and as a friend. It is out of these networks that this book has been produced. Any errors that remain are my own. This project developed out of my PhD dissertation, which I completed at Purdue University under the direction of Kristina Bross. Kris is not only a model scholar but a wonderful mentor. She worked through all of the early ideas with me, provided careful feedback, and has continued to support this project in the ensuing years. At Purdue, I am also grateful to Nush Powell, Christopher Lukasik, and Derek Pacheco, as well as the members of the Early Atlantic Reading Group, especially Rebekah Mitsein, Helen Hunt, Mary Beth Harris, and Stacey Dearing. When kinship moved me to Minnesota at the beginning of my dissertation, I found myself among another network of scholars, and their insights and advice have deeply shaped this text. At the University of Minnesota, I was welcomed with open arms by the members of the American Indian and Indigenous Studies Workshop. At many key points along the way, Jean O'Brien pushed me to think differently about this project, provided careful feedback, and grounded me in Indigenous studies approaches. At the American Indian and Indigenous Studies Workshop, I am also thankful to David Chang for his wisdom and encouragement and to Akikwe Cornell, Katie Phillips, Kasey Keeler, Rose Miron, Jimmy Sweet, Joe Whitson, Bernadette Pérez, Sasha Maria Suarez, and John Little for their friendship and support.

At the University of Minnesota, I was grateful to be welcomed by members of the Early Atlantic Workshop, where I am especially thankful for the scholarly advice and encouragement of Katharine Gerbner and Kirsten Fischer. As a postdoctoral research associate in the University of Minnesota's Center for Early Modern History, I was able to partake in numerous workshops and talks that helped me develop my project. CEMH facilitated my participation in the Folger Institute's 2018 "Digging the Past" seminar, led by Frances Dolan, which laid the groundwork for many of the ideas that eventually developed into chapter 3 and the Folger

Institute's 2019 seminar "Early Modern Iroquoia," led by Scott Manning Stevens. The readings and discussions provided by Professor Stevens and my workshop colleagues helped me better map northeastern Indigenous diplomatic ties. In Minnesota I was supported by an independent reading group of close friends and scholars who encouraged me as I figured out how to manage childcare, writing, and completing a PhD in absentia. I am eternally grateful to Lydia Garver, Wes Burdine, Luke Freeman, and especially Jennifer Awes-Freeman, who understands the demands of teaching, research, and motherhood better than most.

Participating in the Society of Early Americanists has given me the opportunity to expand my knowledge of both early and Indigenous America. Many SEA members have read parts of my work, provided insightful conference feedback, or offered other means of support. Included among them are Laura Stevens, Kelly Wisecup, Caroline Wigginton, Joy Howard, and Cassie Smith. It was also at SEA where I had the opportunity to meet Lisa Brooks. Her scholarship has long been an aspirational model for me, and her support for this project has been a gift to me. I am also thankful to Adrian Chastain Weimer for her comments on chapter 4. Joanne Jahnke-Wegner has been a constant source of support and encouragement. She has read all of these chapters at one point and has encouraged me as both a scholar and a friend. Samantha Majhor and Agléška Cohen-Rencountre have been wonderful friends and scholars who have keep me going in this project and others. At the University of North Alabama, I am thankful to the English Department and the College of Arts, Sciences, and Engineering for their support of my scholarship through course releases and funding. I am grateful to the guides at the Mashantucket Pequot Museum, the Tomaquag Museum, the Tantaquidgeon Museum, and the Mashpee Wampanoag Museum for sharing their knowledge and for the work they do at these important sites. At the University of Massachusetts Press, I am also thankful to Brian Halley, Rachael DeShano, Sarah C. Smith, and the other editors who patiently walked me through the publication process. I am thankful for the insightful feedback provided by the reviewers. Drew Lopenzina's carefully considered comments were especially generative in the final stages of the process.

While academia has been an important part of my life, the inspiration for my writing and my teaching comes from my family. My mother, Marsha, and my late father, Steve; sisters, Clair, Karen, and Elaine, and their spouses; my parents-in-law, Dan and Jayne; and my sisters-in-law, Annie and Julie have all encouraged me, watched my children, and continually reaffirmed the importance of family. My kids, Maeve, Abraham, and Esther, bring me amazing joy and remind me to think of the next generation. At the end of the day, though, none of this would have been written without my rock and my biggest fan, Nate. Go Team Balsley-Taylor.

INDIGENOUS KINSHIP,
COLONIAL TEXTS,
and the
CONTESTED SPACE OF
EARLY NEW ENGLAND

INTRODUCTION

Indigenous Kinship, Colonial Texts

—ɷ—

The story of the Puritan mission in New England often begins with the arrival of the Winthrop fleet in 1630. On the morning of June 12, 1630, after two and a half months at sea, Governor John Winthrop's ship the *Arabella* anchored off the shore of Cape Ann, north of the Salem settlement. Not long after, English colonists started rowing out to meet him. Winthrop was the representative appointed by the Bay Company to establish and govern the Bay Colony, and his arrival was a diplomatic affair. John Endecott, the English colonial governor of the settlement, and Samuel Skelton, pastor of the Salem church, arrived by shallop to formally welcome the new leader. After their arrival, Winthrop writes in his journal that he "returned with them to Nahumkeck." While on shore, the colonial leaders "supped with a good venison pasty and some good beer."[1] Despite their meager living conditions, the English settlers at Salem received Winthrop with formal fanfare. After their meal, Winthrop returned back to the boat for the evening.

As his journal entry indicates, Winthrop knew that he was in an Indigenous place from the beginning. What we might today call Salem, Winthrop was first introduced to as Nahumkeck, or Naumkeag, which in Wôpanâak translates to "the fishing place."[2] In the summer months, the land and waters around Naumkeag drew Wampanoag families and their extended relatives from neighboring communities together to gather food and fish. The Indigenous communities who spent their summers near the shore also watched the *Arabella* arrive. Like the settlement leaders, they also prepared to meet Winthrop. As Winthrop returned to the *Arabella* after his dinner on shore, Indigenous leaders began to arrive for a second round of diplomatic protocols. As he writes, on his first night "an Indian came aboard us, & lay there all night." The man Winthrop describes was likely a diplomatic representative sent to assess the colonial governor and his party and prepare for the impending arrival of the Pawtucket leader, or sachem, Masconomet. In the morning, Winthrop writes that the diplomatic protocols continued as Masconomet, "the sagamore of Agawan[,] and one of his men came abroad our ship and stayed with us all day."[3] Winthrop leaves out the details of the meeting. While Masconomet's visit may have been friendly, it was political in nature. Masconomet was an established sachem of the lands around Cape Ann, where the *Arabella* had anchored.[4] Confident of his authority and unafraid of capture, the Pawtucket sachem embarked upon the *Arabella* to let Winthrop know from the start whose lands the English were upon. Furthermore, Masconomet boarded the ship to open up talks and establish alliances—or in other words, he visited Winthrop to bring the newly arrived English leader into the establish governing systems that held the region together. In subsequent years, Masconomet would continue to engage in talks with Winthrop, and later with Winthrop's son, John Winthrop Jr. In their negotiations, the Pawtucket and colonial leaders would discuss land use, shared governance, and the military protection necessary to maintain the security of the region.

Masconomet's visit provides further evidence of what Native people have always known, and of what many scholars have reminded us in recent years—early America was an Indigenous place, shaped by the decisions, practices and beliefs of Indigenous people. When Winthrop disembarked at Naumkeag, he stepped into a political world structured by the alliances and treaties made among the many Indigenous nations on the coast. While treaties maintained the balance among communities, the communities themselves were sustained by the careful planting and cultivation practices of Indigenous women. Indigenous diplomacy permitted the early English settlers to arrive, and Indigenous corn kept English bodies alive during the settlers' first years on shore. Though leaders like Winthrop would try to downplay their dependence on Native people, their numerous records of encounters, negotiations, and treaties with Indigenous leaders conclusively indicate that English leaders understood the central role Indigenous communities played in structuring English colonies and sustaining English lives.

Indigenous Kinship, Colonial Texts, and the Contested Space of Early New England focuses on the ways Indigenous diplomats and Indigenous kinship shaped the early writings of the Puritan colonial mission. Though Masconomet was one of the first leaders Winthrop met on his arrival in the Northeast, subsequent accounts of Winthrop's landing and settlement almost entirely omit any reference to the sachem and his visit. The historical narrative instead centers Winthrop's work, building up the mission as he attempted to establish his "City on a Hill." Yet even a surface reading of the journals, letters, and histories written by early New England Puritan leaders reveals numerous references to Indigenous leaders visiting, teaching, and treating with the arriving English. As part of long-standing Indigenous diplomatic practices, these Indigenous leaders actively instructed the new arrivals how to live within the established governing systems, find local foods, and practice local customs to ensure that the arriving visitors provided for the well-being of the whole.

In recent years, scholars of early America and Indigenous studies have begun the necessary work of uncovering Indigenous presence in the colonial world and moving Indigenous narratives to the fore. In this book, I build upon this growing body of scholarship by asking what it means to see colonial texts as deeply influenced by the actions and teachings of Indigenous leaders. In other words, what does it mean to see Indigenous people as coauthors of early colonial texts? Throughout the book, I return to several important diplomatic exchanges between arriving colonial leaders and established Indigenous leaders to reframe our understanding of Indigenous-colonial exchange in the early years of the Massachusetts Bay Colony. After their arrival from England, the Bay Colony settlers were few in number, lacking food and resources, and oftentimes at the mercy of the more powerful Indigenous nations. As such, colonial leaders mirrored Indigenous practices and attended to Indigenous instruction to ensure their own survival. Much of their instruction came from Indigenous community leaders. In the Northeast, there were many levels of leadership. At the head of the nation was a supreme sachem, or *saunkskwa*. Smaller bands or family groups were led by less powerful sachems or saunkskwas. As representatives of their communities, a sachem or saunkskwa was often the first figure with whom English leaders came into contact. They played a fundamental role in forming English conceptions about Indigenous people. However, Indigenous leaders at all levels worked to teach the English how to act in ways that would promote the mutual flourishing of Indigenous and English communities.

Both the encounters and the results of them can be traced through colonial texts. Colonial texts not only recorded events but shaped and defined colonial communities even as they attempted to interpret the significance of the colonial experience for a transatlantic audience. By focusing on the content of early colonial texts alongside the Indigenous-colonial relationships that facilitated the formation of these texts, we can see the influence that Native people, Native polities, and Native places had on the formation of New England colonial thought. Returning an Indigenous context to early English settler textual formation, we come to see that many early American genres were developed in response to the influence of Indigenous presence. Despite being written in English for European audiences, these genres were jointly created by Indigenous sachems and settlers in order to facilitate their acting together within the contested space of colonial New England.

Indigenous Nations in Colonial New England

Recognizing the influence and persistence of Indigenous diplomacy during the early years of settlement necessitates a broad understanding of the ways early settlement narratives were constructed. Penned out of a colonial mindset that worked to justify settlement, many early American documents minimized the existence of Native people and attempted to downplay Indigenous agency. In her work *Firsting and Lasting: Writing Indians Out of Existence in New England*, Ojibwe historian Jean O'Brien traces the process of rhetorical erasure within historical narratives. Focusing on local New England histories written in the nineteenth century, O'Brien points to the role of what she terms a "replacement narrative"—a rhetorical move in which history is narrated in a way that firmly cements English settlers as the harbingers of a "new modern social order" intended to replace a now-absent Indigenous one. As O'Brien points out, replacement narratives begin with a process she terms "firsting," in which Indigenous people are credited as the original landowners. However, in these narratives, Native people are depicted as passively giving way to a new social order in which settlers take over landownership and bring "civilization" to the "wilderness." As O'Brien writes, "the 'first' New Englanders are made to disappear, sometimes through precise declarations that the 'last' of them has passed, and the colonial regime is constructed as the 'first' to bring 'civilization' and authentic history to the region."[5] These historical narratives served to justify settler land possession by proclaiming the inevitable demise of Native people who could not survive in a "modern" world.

The rhetorical strategies O'Brien identifies in the nineteenth century are evident in earlier accounts as well. From their arrival, English settlers started "writing Indians out of existence" in their letters and documents. Like their nineteenth-century descendants, early settlers emphasized Indigenous land rights in order to claim that those rights were legitimately passed to the colonial arrivals. In the early years of settlement, English chroniclers were preoccupied with reprinting Native treaties and concurrent Indigenous acts of diplomacy to prove they had obtained "possession" of New England lands. This practice, as Jeffrey Glover points out, "led to a profound irony, one that powerfully shaped English colonial writing. When the English pointed to treaties with Native people as evidence of possession, Native words, gestures, and other ways of marking agreements suddenly became highly charged evidence in international legal disputes."[6] Yet once land possession had been claimed, colonists were eager to point out how Native people had disappeared.

English authors adapted their narratives of encounter with Native people to fit their intended audience. When writing to their English investors, colonial leaders emphasized the docility of Native people, or pointed to diseases or warfare as evidence that Indigenous people were either easy to conquer or absent.[7] Yet among themselves, the same leaders strategized how best to negotiate with the very present and established sachems and saunkskwas with whom they were in constant contact. Examples of these conflicting narratives abound in the letters and treaties written by Governor Winthrop himself. In a July 1634 letter to his friend Sir Simonds D'Ewes in England, the Bay Colony governor writes, "But for the natives in these parts, Gods hand hath so pursued them, as for 300 miles, the greatest parts of them are swept away by the small poxe. . . . So God hathe hereby cleared our title to this place." Of those that remained, Winthrop writes that they were subdued, having "put themselves under our protection."[8] In claiming that Native people have either been killed by disease or submitted to

English authority, Winthrop assures his friend that the colonial mission is justified in its land claims. Yet, only a few months later, in a letter to his son John Winthrop Jr., who was himself a part of many diplomatic negotiations between English settler and Native leaders in New England, the governor paints a different picture as he lays out the complicated negotiations he was undertaking with Pequot and Narragansett leaders.[9] Whereas his description for D'Ewes was intended to update his friend on the progress of the colony's land claims, his letter to his son is part of an ongoing conversation between the two on how to secure colonial interests and obtain Indigenous lands from the very present Indigenous leaders.

Even today, despite the proliferation of scholarship on the Indigenous Northeast, Winthrop's claims of Indigenous absence and submission are more often repeated than are his many references to Indigenous presence. Whereas colonial accounts were once touted to celebrate colonial conquest, today they are referenced to mourn a lack of Native presence.[10] While disease and warfare were certainly devastating to many Indigenous communities, they in no way resulted in Native absence. In the aftermath of the Pequot War, those remaining drew closer to one another—in times of troubles, communities came together to sustain their living relatives and work toward rebuilding. Unfortunately, the narratives of absence coined by Winthrop and others continue to undermine historical accounts of Native people. When one comes to the documents expecting that there is nothing to find, one often fails to really look.

While narratives of absence have often erased Indigenous diplomats and their influence from our analysis of the early colonial project, Indigenous converts have loomed large. Colonial leaders were anxious to erase Indigenous people as political agents; however, they were eager to tout them as religious converts. Claims of conversion are especially persistent in writings by Puritan authors whose colonial charter cited the desire to "win and incite the Natives of Country, to the knowledge and Obedience of the only true God and Saviour of mankind" as the "principal end of this Plantation."[11] In claiming Indigenous people as converts, Puritans were pointing to not only a religious transformation but a cultural one as well—for Puritan ministers, the two went hand in hand.

Like narratives of absence, claims of conversion also played a large rhetorical role in advancing a colonial mission. The figure of the Praying

Indian—the term used for Indigenous converts at the time—was deployed in colonial accounts to remind English authorities of the "spiritual" value the colonies could bring to England at a time when other colonial ventures were floundering. Amid the chaos of the English Civil War and interregnum, and alongside the uncertainties plaguing the colonial mission, colonists "found in Indian evangelism a reason for their continual colonization of America."[12] Among colonists anxious to employ Indian missions as a means of proving the value of the colonial endeavor, stories of Indigenous conversions proliferated to the point where "words outweighed deeds and textual production exceeded conversions."[13]

Taken together, these narratives of erasure bolster the idea that Indigenous people in the Northeast were killed by disease, displaced by warfare, or transformed by conversion. Importantly, not only have these narratives of erasure predetermined our understanding of Native people, but they also guide our interpretation of colonial settlers as well. In assuming that the colonial project was inherently successful from the start, we begin to accept that settlers were always already active agents working against passive subjects. Over the years, the story of colonial success has remained the same, though the merit of that success has changed. Whereas colonial leaders were once glorified for their "civilizing" efforts, they are now often criticized for their destruction—yet in either case, they remain the primary authors of the colonial story.

The Contested Space of Early America

Looking back through centuries of relationship between colonial settlers and Indigenous nations, it is not hard to see why the narrative of Puritan agency persists. Establishing a model for those to follow, the Puritans were some of the first to actively attempt to eradicate, transform, or convert Native people in an effort to displace them from their lands. Yet despite Puritan efforts, and the efforts of those who have followed in their footsteps, Native people and Native places have persisted. Even beyond persistence, Native people themselves have been agents of transformation. Though their efforts may be less visible in U.S. narratives, Indigenous people, including those who performed Christian conversion, were also working to shape the encounters that have taken place, and continue to take place, between settlers and themselves. In teaching the settlers how to hunt, fish, and plant, in instructing them in the governing practices of the region, in negotiating treaties to facilitate relationships, in teaching them how to speak their languages, and in advocating for the survival of family members, Indigenous people worked to transform the minds, bodies, and practices of the arriving settlers to conform to the relationships and practices governing Native space.

In recent years, the increased visibility of northeastern Indigenous community members and the increasing availability of scholarship by Native scholars, and scholarship using Native studies approaches, have given us the tools and resources to better access and theorize the voices of seventeenth-century Native people in colonial spaces. Building on recent developments in Native American and Indigenous studies and early American studies, this book answers recent calls for early American scholars to "engage in structural and substantive ways with the materials and methods of Native American and Indigenous studies."[14] To date, much of the scholarship on Native people in the early years of colonialism has focused on recovering Indigenous voices and experiences. Using this important recovery work as a base, I develop a multidisciplinary methodology that first locates Indigenous agency within the conversations and actions recorded by English settlers and second illustrates how, when incorporated into English tracts, sermons, and scientific treatises, these exchanges not only reflect Indigenous communal experience but serve to shape the beliefs and practices of the arriving English settlers as well. My approach illuminates the cross-cultural social exchanges at the heart of early American literary genres at the same time as it presents a nuanced portrait of colonial authorship. By centering the historical reality that colonial authors and their texts were susceptible to non-European, specifically Indigenous influence, I demonstrate the profound ways in which Native American and Indigenous studies approaches can facilitate more nuanced and accurate readings of many important colonial texts.

This book begins with two premises: one, that colonial New England was from the start an Indigenous place, and two, that settlers began their colonial endeavor from a place of uncertainty. As Abenaki scholar Lisa Brooks explains in her oft-cited notion of the common pot, New England's Native people conceived of their world as cooperative and interdependent.

This interdependence extended to the arriving Europeans: "As soon as Europeans settled on the coast, they became inhabitants in Native space. In the common pot, shared space means shared consequences and shared pain. The actions of the newcomers would affect the whole." To protect the whole, Native New Englanders sought a way to "incorporate the 'beings' from Europe into Native space."[15] Many of the voices and actions of Indigenous leaders captured in colonial texts depict Native people acting out of a common pot mentality—in essence, Indigenous peoples' interactions with Puritan settlers and other colonial leaders are often, though not always, evidence of their attempts to remake the whole.

The Puritan settlers arrived in the common pot with competing visions of what and how their colonial settlements would come to be. These ideological visions of colonial settlement quickly gave way to practical realities. As Kathleen Donegan writes, early English colonists "struggle[d] to construct an identity out of the incommensurable experiences of being English and living in the New World."[16] Though the English would eventually establish well-functioning colonial governing systems, the unsettlement of the early years meant that the English experience in seventeenth-century colonial New England was in direct contrast to that of the Native people they were attempting to colonize. As Cherokee literary scholar Betty Booth Donohue writes, "The infrastructure of American Indians provided the colonists with knowledge of the essentials of daily life—foods, hunting methods, roads, water routes, fighting techniques, medicines, land management, and democratic political structures. As colonists learned the tangible details of life in the New World, they also unknowingly absorbed the intangible aspects associated with the acquired knowledge and were subtly changed."[17] Despite the damaging effects of colonial disease and warfare, the Wampanoag, Narragansett, Mohegan, Pequot, and other tribal nations were confident in their status as the established protectors of New England lands and, as such, actively worked to bring the arriving missionaries into the existing polities and practices that governed the region.

The same process, I argue, occurred in colonial missionary texts. Although the New England colonists proliferated stories about their New England missionary project much faster than they created converts, their narratives were based on the lives of actual Indigenous people. As literary scholar Sarah Rivett writes, the missionaries were inherently observant of

Indigenous acts, which they copiously recorded, because they believed that "the evidence of God recorded on human souls could speak unequivocally as empirical verification that God's 'promise to his plantation' was finally bearing its fruits."[18] Interpreting the actions of Native people, Native leaders in particular, became a central way missionaries articulated the success or failure of their mission. Many of the mission's Indigenous participants joined after their own communities had been destroyed by colonial diseases or warfare, which means their actions were determined by fear and coercion. Yet, despite their challenging circumstances, they did not abandon the kinship ties and diplomatic aims that had guided northeastern Indigenous life for centuries before the arrival of European colonists. When they became part of the mission, they brought these concepts along. This interplay between Indigenous diplomacy and religion not only shaped the way in which missionaries wrote about their mission but also shaped their own conceptions of colonial diplomacy and politics.

This book focuses on the period when colonial uncertainty and common pot diplomacy intersected—the 1640s to the 1670s. It was during this time that New England writers developed many of the distinct genres and literary forms that have now come to characterize New England literary production. During this time, important New England and later American literary genres like the conversion narrative, the spiritual question, and the dying Indian speech were formed. At the same time, other genres like the scientific treatise took on a new significance as a result of their usage in colonial New England. Though scholars have discussed separately the role of unsettlement, genre formation, and Indigenous diplomacy in the colonial period, when put in conversation with one another, these three nodes of thought provide us a new portrait of colonial literary production in which Indigenous leaders played a profound and deliberate role in shaping the words and deeds of English authors.

While I clearly tread a well-worn path in writing about the New England missionary project and its founders, I aim to tell a new tale. By fleshing out our understanding of some of the Indigenous leaders who challenged, instructed, cajoled, and even inspired the New England Puritan authors, I show that the vision of leaders like Thomas Shepard, John Eliot, and John Winthrop Jr. was not as fixed as it often appears but was rather dependent on the participation and ideas of its Indigenous participants. By synthesizing historical, anthropological, and theological sources with close readings of tracts, letters, sermons, and other documents, I argue that English Protestant interpretations of Indigenous diplomatic practices often served as the central means by which early colonial leaders determined and articulated the success or failure of their own proselytization attempts. With a focus on English Protestants such as Thomas Shepard, John Eliot, John Winthrop Jr., and Daniel Gookin, and on their relationship with specific converts, I offer a new approach to several important early American literary texts by reading them as sites of cross-cultural negotiation rather than the sole product of Protestant missionary imposition. By understanding the colonial project and its textual production as beholden to the exchanges between Native people and English settlers, I reposition the New England mission as a movement created out of uncertainty—an uncertainty that required English settlers to work with Indigenous participants to craft a mission that both served English diplomatic aims and considered the sovereignty and customs of the local Native nations.

In pointing out the place of Indigenous influence on colonial people and colonial texts, I am not aiming to portray a more sympathetic colonist. As Joshua David Bellin, "It is dangerous to argue that violence can be compensated for by acts of sympathetic identification or creative appropriation."[19] In many instances, a colonizer's awareness of local Indigenous practices was later deployed to refine and enact a settler-colonial agenda. Knowledge of a person or group and sympathy for that person or group are not synonymous. The English Puritan leaders and their families prioritized self-protection and national advancement for the English first—oftentimes without considering the cost. They also inherently considered their own practices and ideas as superior to Indigenous ones. Colonialism came with devastating effect and its repercussions continue to this day. The process by which Indigenous ideas came to be present in colonial texts was often violent and devastating to Indigenous communities. Yet, settler colonialism was a slow-moving process that took place over many years; as Jean O'Brien terms it, it was "dispossession by degrees." To enact their colonial project, settlers had to work with Native people in Native places. Despite the impositions of colonialism, Indigenous people continued to govern their lands and instruct newcomers. The continued actions, teachings, and leadership of Indigenous people had an effect on colonial arrivals and these effects are evident in colonial texts.

Reconceptualizing the colonial project as one influenced by its Indigenous participants allows us to see the colonists themselves in a new light—as colonizers whose actions and writings, consciously or not, were influenced by the people over whom they attempted to exert power. I trace the sustained encounters between specific colonial leaders and Indigenous leaders to analyze the role that Indigenous thought plays in shaping a colonial writings over time. This approach not only provides a new context for a number of important New England colonial texts but brings to the fore many northeastern Indigenous leaders who have often been left in the background. Focusing on the Pequot/Niantic leader Wequash, the Mashantucket Pequot sachem Robin Cassacinamon, the Massachusett sachem Cutshamekin, as well as the Massachusett leader Waban, I show how these individuals used their relationships with colonial leaders to instruct the newcomers in common pot diplomacy at the same time as they attempted to protect their lands and communities.

Kinship and Recovery

The process I've used to recover the biographies of these sachems who have been overlooked by scholarship has relied on several disciplinary methodologies. While my recovery of the sachems comes out of close reading practices, my experience working with a number of Native studies scholars over the course of my writing means that my methodologies have expanded to include Indigenous studies methodologies as well. In their introduction to *Sources and Methods in Indigenous Studies* (2016), Jean O'Brien and Chris Andersen suggest some broad tenets for Indigenous studies methodologies. Quoting the Ojibwe and Choctaw author Clara Sue Kidwell, Andersen and O'Brien suggest that Indigenous methodologies may focus on "the central relationship between Indigenous cultures and land (or place); that historical relationship between Indigenous societies and settler communities were just that—relational—and as such, have to be told from both sides (which includes according agency to Indigenous history); that sovereignty is an inherent right of Indian nations; that language is the essential key to understanding culture and therefore requires preservation."[20] In this book, I have tried to be mindful of these adages in reconstructing Indigenous leaders' biographies.

Part of my indebtedness to Indigenous studies methodologies is that I have attempted to trace kinship ties to create a fuller and more authentic picture of the Indigenous leaders I detail. For the northeastern Algonquian leaders I address, kinship was a social, spiritual, and psychological reality. The kinship relationships that defined Indigenous communities in the seventeenth century served as both a "focus of identity" and a source of "affective ties" for the community's members. More than just familial relationships, kinship ties included obligations to extended family members and others whom the Algonquian had accorded kinship ties through marriage or diplomacy.[21] As the figure responsible for maintaining and creating kinship ties, a leader's familial, spiritual, and political duties were defined through their relationship to their community.

In his 2012 work *An Infinity of Nations*, Ojibwe scholar Michael Witgen concisely articulates the tie between kinship and national identity when describing the Algonquian people residing among the Great Lakes. As he writes, Indigenous nationhood was premised on "a set of relationships that bound Native peoples to one another. Political alliance was expressed as kinship. Trade, as a form of peaceful exchange, was the outcome of interaction between people who were related to one another. One shared with relatives, provided for their needs when there was want, and expected a reciprocal kindness in return."[22] While some of the systems guiding the northeastern Algonquian diverged from those practiced among the Great Lakes Algonquian, many of the kinship principles worked in a similar manner. A full picture of kinship within early colonial New England is found in Lisa Brooks's award-winning *Our Beloved Kin: A New History of King Philip's War* (2018). As Brooks details, Indigenous kinship practices adapted to the arrival of colonialism but still maintained their primary objectives—to grow and sustain one's community. In describing the powerful Wampanoag saunkskwa Weetamoo, Brooks articulates the many ways in which kinship guided Weetamoo's strategic alliances and her exchanges with colonial leaders. Weetamoo's actions were performed alongside "other leaders and their families to protect the many beings who depended upon them. Together, they steered a course of strategic adaptation to the colonial system that had begun to entangle itself in their roots."[23]

Kinship not only served as a guide for intertribal relationships but extended to intratribal relationships as well. As Colin Calloway explains, kinship was at the heart of northeastern Algonquian diplomatic practices: "Dealing with other peoples as trade partners required making alliances and turning strangers who were potential enemies into friends and even relatives. Native peoples extended or replicated kinship . . . to include people with whom they were not related by birth or marriage, bringing them into their community by adoption, alliance, and ritual. Forging and renewing relationships of cooperation, coexistence, and kinship with others was essential to survival in the pre-contact multi-tribal world."[24] When the colonists arrived, the Indigenous leaders I address acted toward the arrivals in a similar way as they had in previous diplomatic encounters—by extending kinship and reciprocity in exchange for new alliances.

Developing a Language of Diplomacy

I focus on the time period between the 1630s and the 1670s—namely, the period between the Pequot War and King Philip's War. This period encompasses the beginning years of the mission's formation. Consequently, this was also the time in which the majority of the founding documents of the New England mission were created, making it an apt time in which to observe the role Native people played in forming those early texts. Both the Pequot War and King Philip's War were devastating to Native communities in the Northeast, and they remain some of the bloodiest battles in American history. More than just instances in which Native people were forced from their homes, the Pequot War and King Philip's War were moments in which Native people reinforced their political ties and put their networks of diplomacy in place to protect, and later restore, their communities. It was as part of the diplomatic attempts that many sachems created ties with the New England mission. By focusing on the wars, their aftermaths, and the ways they connected (or distanced) sachems and missionaries, we can more clearly see the ties between sachem diplomacy and the formation of the Puritan mission.

Chapter 1 analyzes the conditions surrounding the conversion narrative of the Pequot guide Wequash, a leader who was also the Bay Colony's first claimed convert. Recorded in *New Englands First Fruits* (1643), Wequash's conversion narrative was lauded by Puritan minister Thomas Shepard as clear evidence of God's moving. Shepard also claimed that the account served as a catalyst for the mission itself. While English authors such as Shepard took great pains to define Wequash's actions as evidence of Christian salvation, Wequash's biography indicates that he performed conversion to facilitate the regathering of the Pequot in the aftermath of the Pequot War. In this chapter, I focus on how the New England conversion narrative format that developed from Wequash's narrative retained evidence of the Pequot kinship context within which it was originally performed.

Chapter 2 addresses the role Cutshamekin, a prominent Massachusett sachem and convert, played in instigating the post-sermon question-and-answer session, a literary convention usually attributed to John Eliot. It was intended by Eliot as a sort of catechism that verified the authenticity of Indigenous conversion. I argue that the post-sermon question-and-answer session was an adaptation of a post-treaty negotiation process used by Cutshamekin in both the Pequot War and the 1644 submission of the sachems. As the target of John Eliot's first missionary visit in 1646, Cutshamekin was the sachem responsible for forming many of Eliot's conceptions about Indigenous people and practices. Adapting Cutshamekin's processes, Eliot later incorporated the question-and-answer session into his own missionary dealings. Significantly, I posit that Cutshamekin's influence was not limited to Eliot's missionary practices but also influenced Eliot's political imagination. In the final part of the chapter, I point to several ways that Cutshamekin's influence can be seen in Eliot's later writings, most prominently in Eliot's *The Christian Commonwealth* (1651).

Chapter 3 focuses on the relationship between Indigenous knowledge and the development of European scientific discourses by paying close attention to Connecticut governor and colonial scientist John Winthrop Jr.'s 1662 treatise "Of Maiz"—the first scientific treaty to come out of colonial New England. Written at the request of Robert Boyle, "Of Maiz" describes corn cultivation in terms of Indigenous agricultural practice. By laying out Winthrop's complicated relationship with the Mashantucket Pequot leader Robin Cassacinamon, I illustrate Indigenous diplomatic and communal practices shaped early colonial scientific writing as Winthrop Jr. learned about corn planting while observing Cassacinamon replant Pequot lands as an act of sovereignty in the aftermath of the Pequot War.

Chapter 4 gestures to the broader ways in which sachem diplomacy became embedded into the language of the New England missionary project. I read closely Daniel Gookin's 1677 tract *An Historical Account of the Doings and Sufferings of the Christian Indians in New England* to show how Gookin makes an argument for Praying Indian civility through reliance on an Indigenous concept of treaties. Written as a defense for the Praying Indians during King Philip's War, Gookin's tract redefines civility. Challenging writers such as William Hubbard who argue that Indians, converted or not, are inherently savage, Gookin's tract defines civility as one's ability to honor one's covenants. He illustrates civility by including numerous examples of Praying Indians who have maintained their agreements with the English despite facing severe repercussions. At the center of his tract, Gookin reprints the 1644 treaty made between the Bay Colony and the Massachusett sachem Cutshamekin as a way of reminding Bay Colony leaders of their treaty obligations to Native people. In redefining civility as an act based on covenants and treaties, Gookin employs a concept of civility and nationhood that closely parallels that practiced by his Algonquian converts. I argue that this parallel is not merely coincidence, but the result of Gookin's almost twenty-five-year career as an Indian agent responsible for facilitating Praying Indian judicial systems. Gookin's adaptation of Indigenous concepts illustrates the extent to which missionary writers over time had—consciously or not—made Indigenous concepts central to their understanding and articulation of the Indian mission.

CHAPTER ONE

Kinship, Captivity, and Diplomacy
Locating Wequash in the Indigenous Conversion Narrative

—∿∿—

Wequash, the famous Indian at the Rivers mouth is dead, and certainly in heaven; gloriously did the Grace of Christ shine forth in his conversation, a yeare and a halfe before his death he knew Christ, he loved Christ, he preached Christ up and down, and then suffered Martyrdome for Christ.
—Thomas Shepard to Thomas Weld, 1641

The Pequots are gathered into one, and plant their old fields, Wequash and Uncas carrying away the people and their treasure, which belong to yourselves.
—Roger Williams to Governor John Winthrop, April 16, 1638

In 1643 the Massachusetts Bay Colony Puritans decided it was time to go public with their colonial missionary project. While in London, Bay Colony agents Thomas Weld and Hugh Peter published *New Englands First Fruits*, the first of several tracts describing Puritan missionary efforts among Algonquian-speaking tribes in colonial New England. As they claim in their introduction, the tract was intended to "declare . . . what *first Fruits* [God] hath begun to gather" among "those poore *Indians*."[1] Though the tract claims only one convert, Wequash, along with some other short vignettes illustrating the "sprinklings of Gods spirit, upon a few Indians," Weld and Peter enthusiastically promised that these examples indicated "a sure pledge . . . of a greater Harvest." By describing, or rather more accurately "invent[ing] . . . a policy of evangelism," the Bay Colony leaders hoped to assure their English supporters that they were (finally) fulfilling the aims of their 1629 charter to "win and incite the Natives of Country, to the knowledge and Obedience of the only true God and Saviour of mankind," which was the "principal end of this Plantation."[2]

The timing of *New Englands First Fruits* was strategic. In 1643 England was in the early stages of the English Civil War (1642–51). The urgency of the war and the general lackluster performance of the New England colonies meant that English support for New England colonial ventures had waned.

In response, many prominent Massachusetts Bay Colony stakeholders had shifted their funding to the West Indies, where they hoped to get a better return on their investments.[3] New England's appeal as a spiritual stronghold had also been shaken. Oliver Cromwell's rise to power promised a new status for English Puritans and challenged their earlier conviction that England was about to fall prey to Antichrist. Many of those who had come to New England with the intent of creating a religious refuge made their way back across the Atlantic to help usher in a Christian English utopia that had previously seemed impossible.[4] Hoping to stem the tide of loss, anxious Bay Colony leaders sent Weld and Peter back to England to try and drum up support.[5] While in England, the two men spent their time meeting with wealthy donors and politicians and gathering supplies. To help further their reach, the Bay Colony agents also entered the ongoing English pamphlet wars, publishing *New Englands First Fruits* in an attempt to spread the news of the colony's missionary success far and near.

New Englands First Fruits is not solely focused on Indigenous conversion—it also makes note of the "saving work of grace" in the heart of "a Blackamore Maid" living at Dorchester, lists potential future missionary settlements in "Virginia," "Barbados, Christophers, and Antego," and describes the early development of Harvard College.[6] However, the title page's proclamation that the tract includes the "conversion," "conviction," and "preparation" of "some of the Indians" makes it clear that Weld and Peter were convinced that their descriptions of Indigenous people would be the tract's selling point. More specifically, they hoped that the story of their only claimed convert, the "famous Indian Wequash," would have the strongest appeal to English readers. As they write, it was Wequash's story "of which coming into our hands very lately, was indeed the occasion of writing all the rest."[7]

In this chapter I focus on Wequash, the Pequot man at the center of *New Englands First Fruits*, and examine the ways his story has been told and retold. As the first claimed convert of the Bay Colony, Wequash's account in *New Englands First Fruits* marks the start of a new genre of colonial New England writing: the Indigenous conversion narrative. In uncovering the people and processes behind the writing of Wequash's tale, not only can we get a better picture of an often-misunderstood Pequot leader, but we can also more thoroughly understand the conditions within which the Indigenous conversion narrative genre developed. For Weld and Peter, the decision to use Wequash's story was both practical and calculated. Wequash served as a guide to the English during the Pequot War (1636–37). In this position he met with a number of colonial politicians and leaders both before and after the war. Among them were the Puritan minister Thomas Shepard. Present at Wequash's side a few days before his death, Shepard was moved by Wequash's performance of Christian faith. After Wequash's death, Shepard wrote an account of Wequash's final days and sent it to his good friend Thomas Weld. When penning Wequash's story, Shepard adapted the conversion narrative format, which itself drew upon an older Christian genre that employed narrative to chronicle a convert's spiritual journey. Conveniently, Weld received Shepard's letter as he and Peter were on their way to England to defend the colonial project. Weld transcribed Wequash's narrative in *New Englands First Fruits*, maintaining Shepard's conversion narrative format. Weld and Peter were so confident that Wequash's account served as clear evidence of missionary progress that they assure English readers that his narrative was "a sure pledge . . . of a greater *Harvest*."[8]

Only a few short months after *New Englands First Fruits* was published, Roger Williams challenged the Bay Colony's account of its star convert. In the introduction to his Narragansett-English dictionary, *A Key into the Language of America* (1643), Williams reinterpreted the story of Wequash. Like Shepard, Williams had visited Wequash a few days before his death. Yet he described the Pequot leader as paradoxically repentant and resistant to Christianity. Williams writes that the dying Wequash suffered from a "broken Heart" at the same time as he projected as "sence of inward hardnesse and unbrokennesse."[9] Countering Weld and Peter's confident claims that the Puritan missionary project bodes of future success anchored in Wequash's pious conversion, Williams adapts the genre of the Indigenous conversion narrative to implicitly frame the New England mission as lacking spiritual authority—a lack illustrated by the uncertain state of Wequash's soul.

In the years after *New Englands First Fruits*, colonial authors would follow the example set by the authors of Wequash's narrative and record their own tales of Indigenous conversion time and time again to "translate" the state of the colonial mission for a transatlantic audience. By providing relatable narratives of spiritual transformation, colonists used Indigenous conversion narratives to "prove" the authenticity of their work and claim divine sanction for their missionary endeavors. But more than just accounts of progress, Indigenous conversion narratives had a political aim as well—they were used to justify the removal of Native people from their lands. As the first step in church membership, conversion narratives instigated a "civilizing process" that attempted to sever Native people's ties with their home communities. For the colonists, an Indigenous person's performance of conversion signaled a shift in allegiance and indicated the convert's desire to become part of an English community. By extension, the colonists assumed that Native converts approved for church membership could no longer retain the same claims to their Indigenous communities, homelands, and families. Those converts who returned home or maintained visible kinship ties were looked upon with suspicion as colonists questioned whether they had "turned back" to their "heathen" ways. The use of conversion as a mechanism for displacement was not limited to colonial New England. In later years, Indigenous conversion narratives would be employed by settler organizations throughout North America to justify the breaking up of Indigenous communities and the taking of Indigenous lands.

When reading Indigenous conversion narratives, it is imperative to consider the role that settler colonialism plays in determining how a convert might tell the story of their soul. For this reason, contemporary scholars often interpret Wequash's conversion narrative as a well-timed work of missionary propaganda. The narrative's placement within a fundraising tract coupled with Williams's immediate challenge to the narrative's veracity have given rise to analytical readings that primarily cite Wequash as a "vehicle of meaning," or "a contested figure in the battle over who would frame the overall experience in the colonies."[10] Yet, while settler colonialism shaped the form of Wequash's narrative, the story itself is also a product of the Indigenous world out of which Wequash came and within which he remained. Indigenous archives, methodologies, and museums allow us to piece together very detailed and rich information about the Pequot world in the early seventeenth century, creating a new context within which to locate Wequash's story.[11] A closer look at the narrative itself, and the conditions within which it was formed, illuminates how the Indigenous conversion narrative genre also captures Indigenous interpretations of the Christian conversion process. Focused attention on the details of Wequash's life reveal that he was an important Pequot leader who lived the majority of his life outside of the English spotlight. By triangulating the missionary narratives, historical references to

Wequash, and what we know about Indigenous society at the time, we see that despite his performance of Christian conversion, Wequash remained dedicated to defending and sustaining the Pequot community in the years before and after the devastating events of the Pequot War. For Wequash, conversion did not signal cultural transformation but was rather another means of creating kinship networks and forming diplomatic alliances.

Knowledge of the real and very powerful relationships between Wequash, his Indigenous network of relations, and the English authors who penned his account provide us with a new framework for understanding the conditions within which the Indigenous conversion narrative genre was created. Not only was Wequash the subject of the first Indigenous conversion narrative, but the author of Wequash's narrative, Thomas Shepard, played a fundamental role in shaping the generic conventions of the New England conversion narrative. As part of his attempt to merge the visible church with the invisible one, Shepard carefully scrutinized the stories told by potential converts for clear evidence of God's call in their life. Between 1638 and 1645, Shepard recorded at least sixty-six conversion narratives recited by members of his congregation.[12] Long used in Christian practices as a genre for relating an individual's progress toward Christian salvation, the genre took on a new role within in colonial New England.[13] While scholars disagree about the particular ways in which the change was manifest, they agree that the primary stimuli instigating the changed narrative included a new location, colonial New England, and an altered function. No longer merely a testimony of faith, in New England conversion became a prerequisite for church membership, which was itself required for access to many colonial political functions. Shepard's recorded conversion narratives serve as the basis for much of our understanding about changing colonial Puritan literary forms and their subsequent development over time. Wequash's narrative contains numerous traces of Shepard's influence. Not only do the narrators of *New Englands First Fruits* emphasize the Pequot warrior's moment of conversion (which Shepard terms "justification"), but they also include descriptions of Wequash's contrition, humiliation, and vocation—the detailed steps Shepard claims are necessary to "prove" that a penitent had truly been called by God.[14]

Though Wequash's narrative follows many conventions of Shepard's other recorded narratives, it also stands apart. In 1642, when Shepard visited Wequash, the Pequot leader was on his deathbed having been allegedly poisoned by those he had attempted to convert. When writing to Weld, Shepard claimed that in death, Wequash had achieved the highest status available to a Christian convert—that of a martyr. In his letter Shepard writes that Wequash "knew Christ, loved Christ . . . preached Christ up and down," and in death, he "suffered Martyrdome for Christ."[15] For Shepard and the other Puritans, the category of martyr was one reserved for those who exemplified the highest form of Christian faith. Through their death, martyrs made Christ visible on earth. More than mere propaganda, Shepard's assured description of Wequash's salvation represents one of the few, if not the only, time in which Shepard records such a confident claim about another person's salvation.

What was it about Wequash's performance of conversion that spoke so convincingly to Shepard and the writers of *New Englands First Fruits*? I argue that the answer comes in part from Wequash's familiarity with the peoples and places of the Indigenous Northeast. In marked contrast to the many English settler conversion narratives Shepard recorded, Wequash is not a stranger in a strange land. Rather, his relationship to his ancestral lands, his ties to his community, and his Indigenous spiritual beliefs allow him to confidently and assuredly articulate his encounter with the Christian God. Though Wequash's performance of Christian salvation required him to abandon some of his previous practices and alliances, it did not necessitate a full-fledged cultural, spiritual, or political transformation. Even after conversion, the Pequot sachem continued to identify himself in terms of his relationship to his Pequot, Niantic, and Mohegan relatives, most prominently evidenced as he helped the Mohegan sachem Uncas replant Pequot fields and regather Pequot captives after the devastation of the Pequot War. Despite suspicions from English observers, Wequash did not "betray" the English by working with his relatives to build up his community. Rather, he interpreted Puritan conversion within an Indigenous spiritual framework. While the Indigenous conversion narrative genre was used as a mechanism for Indigenous dispossession, the conditions within which it was formed meant it was also shaped by Indigenous conceptions of kinship and community.

To chronicle Wequash's role in the development of the Indigenous conversion narrative, I turn back to the people, places, and communities named in *New Englands First Fruits* in order to reconnect the figure of Wequash with his Pequot past. In providing a new backstory for Wequash, I also provide a nuanced reading of his relationship with Shepard to illuminate the role Pequot practices played in the genre's development. For observing Puritans like Shepard and even skeptics like Williams, Wequash's kinship-centered approach to salvation was proof that the English God had traveled with them across the ocean and continued to act in their new land. As a result, Wequash's narrative became a blueprint for colonial observers of what conversion could, and should, look like within the unfamiliar space of colonial New England. When reprinted in *New Englands First Fruits* and challenged in *A Key into the Language of America*, English writers held up Wequash's narrative as a model for conversion in both New England and Old. However, in using Wequash's narrative as a guide, the colonial authors also forwarded a performance of conversion that was highly dependent upon Indigenous networks of relations, Indigenous spiritual practices, and long-standing Pequot relationships to lands. Though Wequash's story was told by a colonial minister and printed in London for English readers, it remains a Pequot story.

"Firsting" in *New Englands First Fruits*

Telling the story of Wequash's conversion requires more than a recitation of Wequash's biography. Rather, it necessitates a new framework within which to interpret how conversion functioned within the contested space of colonial New England. To understand Wequash's Pequot story, we must relocate Wequash within the network of relations within which Wequash made sense of his world. Kinship held together Wequash's Pequot world. Wequash and his relatives defined themselves through their relationships. Wequash's kinship network involved not only his relationships between himself and his relatives but also his relationship to the larger community, his relationship to the land, his relationship to nonhuman entities, and his relationship to the arriving New England settlers. As the bedrock of Indigenous identity, any understanding of Indigenous converts like Wequash requires us to see kinship and trace its influence.

Recovering kinship requires us to take apart texts that have been used in service to colonial advancement and reread them in the context of Indigenous relationships. Like other colonial texts, the authors of *New Englands First Fruits* largely ignore both Wequash's Pequot identity and his sustained ties to the Pequot community. This obfuscation of kinship ties was part of a larger colonial strategy on the part of the English authors. By placing Wequash's story within a colonial missionary tract, the authors take what otherwise would have been recognizable as a Pequot story and give it a biblical past, an English present, and a colonial future. This rhetorical strategy is exemplified in the tract's title. As the title boldly proclaims, *New Englands First Fruits* is intended to mark a new stage in the Bay Colony's Puritan colonial project. Comprised of two parts, *New Englands First Fruits* opens by describing some of the initial movements of the Puritan missionary project, then the founding of Harvard College. The coupling of these two events is not incidental. The Bay Colony's charter insisted that the first step in colonization was to ensure that the colony was "religiously, peaceably, and civilly governed"—which meant the establishment of churches, governing structures, and judicial courts. These systems were not only intended to create a peaceable and organized colonial society, but the settlers also believed that the establishment of civil structures was necessary to the advancement of the missionary project. Termed "the affective model" of missions, English settlers were convinced that their "good life and orderly conversation" would allow them to "win and incite the natives" to the Christian faith.[16]

Unfortunately, they quickly found that creating a working colonial system was much harder in person than it was on paper. Fortunately for the colonists, however, the Indigenous people upon whose lands they had settled had already established civil societies with governing systems and diplomatic procedures. The colonists' small numbers, lack of resources and skills required them work within an established Indigenous system—a system in which settlers were often dependent on Native people for food, trade, and agricultural knowledge. In the face of starvation, warfare, and internal dissention, the colonists were slow to establish any functioning systems of governance, much less a flourishing missionary project. Back in England, the Bay Colony's supporters had taken notice of the colony's floundering start. In response, the Bay Colony did its best to reframe the colonial narrative. Thus, the 1643 proclamation in *New Englands First Fruits* that the missionary project had begun was not merely a religious claim but was a signal from the colonial leaders to their English supporters that their colonial mission had finally progressed to the point that the Indigenous people were starting to take notice.[17]

Not only did the titular phrase "First Fruits" mark a new phase of the colonial missionary project, but it was also intended to signal the future religious and economic prosperity that the Bay Colony hoped to attain.[18] English readers well versed in biblical allegories would have recognized the title's scriptural allusion. The term "first fruits" referred to an ancient Israelite religious practice that required farmers to give the first of their harvest to priests or religious leaders, later known as a tithe.[19] The practice of giving first fruits signified both one's commitment to a religious community and served as a public act of faith—in giving away one's first harvest, one anticipated that a future harvest would come. In early modern England, the term was also a fiscal one. In 1540 the English government created the Court of First Fruits and Tenths. Not long afterward an Office of First Fruits and Tenths was established.[20] English clergy were expected to pay the first year of profit from a new benefice to the crown and a tenth of their subsequent yearly earnings in order to support clerical continuance. In the biblical passage from which the concept derives, the giving of first fruits is tied to land possession. Once the ancient Israelists have "possesse[d]" the "lande ... the Lord thy God giveth thee for inheritance," they are to "take some of all the fruite of the earth, and bring it out of the lande."[21] In using the titular term "First Fruits," the Bay Colony's authors metaphorically position Indigenous converts as a type of agricultural or fiscal commodity. Lacking money and resources, the converts stand in for the financial returns that colonial investors had anticipated.

Beyond its religious and fiscal implications, the term "First Fruits" also invokes a particular relationship between the colonial authors and their Indigenous subjects. Using O'Brien's concept of "firsting," the title and text of *New Englands First Fruits* assert that the Bay colonists "were the first people to erect the proper institutions of a social order worthy of notice."[22] Indigenous kinship networks, governments, and social functioning are all deemed deficient or peripheral to those being established as part of the English colonial order. While the colonists wrote *New Englands First Fruits* to provide evidence of New England colonial social order, the stories they tell come out of their location within an Indigenous world. Examining these stories closely, we find multiple storytellers involved and multiple audiences represented. These layers of meaning are all intertwined in the telling, retelling, and printing of the account. It is only by piecing together these webs of connection can we recover the story of Wequash and the role he played in the formation of the New England conversion narrative.

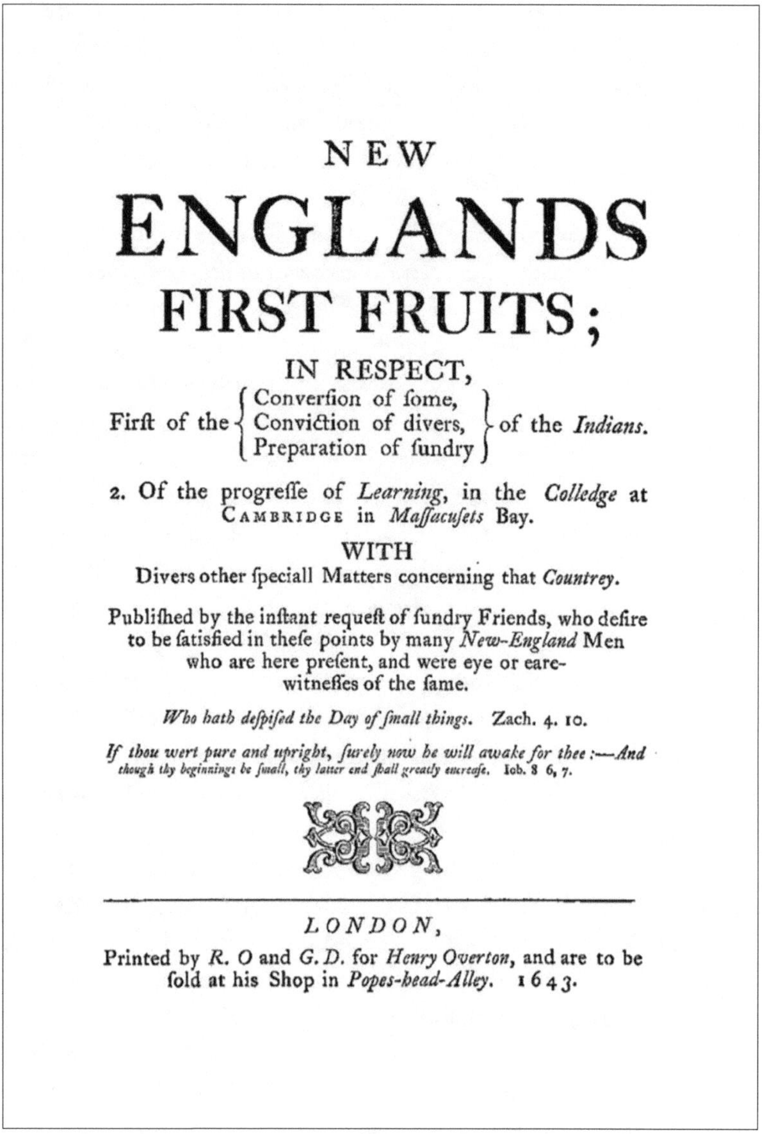

NEW ENGLANDS FIRST FRUITS;

IN RESPECT,

First of the { Converſion of ſome, Conviction of divers, Preparation of ſundry } of the *Indians*.

2. Of the progreſſe of *Learning*, in the *Colledge* at CAMBRIDGE in *Maſſacuſets* Bay.

WITH

Divers other ſpeciall Matters concerning that *Countrey*.

Publiſhed by the inſtant requeſt of ſundry Friends, who deſire to be ſatisfied in theſe points by many *New-England* Men who are here preſent, and were eye or eare-witneſſes of the ſame.

Who hath deſpiſed the Day of ſmall things. Zach. 4. 10.

If thou wert pure and upright, ſurely now he will awake for thee:—And though thy beginnings be ſmall, thy latter end ſhall greatly increaſe. Iob. 8 6, 7.

LONDON,

Printed by *R. O* and *G. D.* for *Henry Overton*, and are to be ſold at his Shop in *Popes-head-Alley*. 1 6 4 3.

FIGURE 1. Title Page of *New Englands First Fruits,* 1643. Courtesy of the Ohio State University Library.

A Pequot Backstory

Illuminating the Pequot roots of the Indigenous conversion narratives requires us to find a new starting point for Wequash's tale—one that is beyond the scope of the colonial texts. Both *New Englands First Fruits* and *A Key into the Language of America* tell Wequash's story through the recollections of English leaders whom Wequash met during the Pequot War and its aftermath. Both accounts prioritize Wequash's relationship with the English and his actions in the final years of life. Yet before meeting the English who would chronicle his tale, the Pequot leader spent the majority of his life as a diplomat and negotiator working to sustain and support his people. Wequash's story is inseparable from the story of the Pequot nation. As Mohegan author Melissa Tantaquidgeon Zobel writes, "the life of any one leader is inseparable from the story of the people as a whole."[23] Born sometime in the late 1610s, Wequash arrived in an Indigenous world held together by a tight, yet adaptable, network of kinship ties. More than a social structure, Wequash's Pequot kinship ties would serve as a guide for him throughout his life. Among the Southern New England Algonquian, kinship ties not only defined familial relationships but determined one's place in society, one's relationship to land, and one's responsibility to the community.

As a critical method, kinship also provides us with a means to reanimate Wequash's Pequot identity, which was deliberately erased through the narratives of conversion. While individual details may be hard to access, being Pequot meant (and still means) honoring one's kinship obligations. As Cherokee literary scholar Daniel Heath Justice writes, for many Indigenous tribes, "being a good relative itself presumes active and meaningful engagement—relatives aren't just static roles of states of being, but lived relationships."[24] The strength of these ties was embedded within the Algonquian language spoken by Wequash and his relatives. As Brooks explains, "Algonquian languages express kinship through pronouns like 'my,' 'our,' and 'his.'" However, "these terms do not denote possession, but rather evoke responsibilities and shared histories that bind people to each other and to the land. Every pronouncement of kinship invokes a bond." For Wequash to think of himself would have been to think of his place within a larger network of relations. Wequash's networks of relations defined his understanding of what it meant to be human and can be used as a guide to understanding the narratives he left behind.[25]

Wequash was born into a family of high status. Many of Wequash's family members had enacted their kinship obligations by serving as community leaders. Wequash's paternal grandfather was the Eastern Niantic sachem Saccious, and Wequash's father was Wepitanock, the sachem of the Eastern Niantic during the Pequot War. Wepitanock's brother (Wequash's uncle) was Ninigret, who would eventually marry Wequash's sister and become the primary Eastern Niantic sachem after the Pequot War.[26] Like their relatives and sometimes rivals the Pequot, during Wequash's early life the Niantic were rapidly becoming a powerful entity within the seventeenth-century Indigenous and colonial worlds. Before European settlement, Indigenous societies along the Eastern Seaboard were largely organized into villages composed mostly of family members and led by a hereditary sachem. For the most part these villages operated independently. As Europeans arrived in greater numbers and began to set up colonies, these smaller villages began to draw together into larger confederates run by powerful sachems. These consolidated groups controlled trade with Europeans and other Indigenous groups, collected tribute from smaller villages, and facilitated diplomatic relationships through diplomacy and warfare. During much of the early seventeenth century, Wequash's father and uncle were influential leaders among the confederation of tribes who governed the lands along the coast.[27] Though substantially smaller in number than the Narragansett or the Pequot, the Niantic were a powerful community—a power that came in part from their strong alliance with the larger and more powerful Narragansett.[28]

As the son of a sachem, Wequash, and his relatives, had alliances with a number of tribal nations. Many northeastern Algonquian leaders used marital relationships among their sons and daughters to manage alliances, consolidate power, and forge diplomatic relations, so the sachems of several Algonquian confederations and villages were closely related to one another by marriage and by birth, resulting in an interconnected network of leaders. The arrangement between the Eastern Niantic and the Narragansett was likely due in part to the strong kinship ties that existed between the two groups. On his father's side, Wequash was related to the Narragansett sachems

Miantonomi and Canonicus through both marriage and birth. Wequash's paternal grandmother was the sister of Canonicus, the elder of the two Narragansett sachems, thereby making Canonicus Wequash's great-uncle. Wequash's aunt on his father's side, the powerful saunkskwa Quaiapin, was married to Canonicus's son, Mixano, making Mixano Wequash's uncle by marriage.[29] Wequash was also related to the younger of the two prominent Narragansett sachems, Miantonomi, who was himself the nephew of Canonicus. Wequash's paternal grandmother was Miantonomi's aunt—meaning Wequash's father was Miantonomi's first cousin.

Yet, despite his father's clear identification as a member of the Niantic and his kinship ties to the Narragansett, in colonial records Wequash is almost exclusively referred to as a Pequot—an identification that seems to come from his mother's side.[30] In colonial records, his mother is only referred to as a "Pequot woman." Wequash's mother may have been a strong leader herself, perhaps a saunkskwa. In matrilineal communities dependent on agriculture like the Pequot and the Niantic, women were the life givers: they gave birth, they grew crops, they helped organized society. Their life-giving practices sustained their communities. Women leaders "were not uncommon," and many of their "oral traditions emphasized the power of women."[31] In a world where both women and men could take their place as community leaders, Wequash's responsibility to the Pequot and his later leadership role within the community may have been a result of his mother's status.[32] Choosing to remain beholden to their matrilineal kinship obligations, both Wequash and his brother, Wequashcook, identified as Pequot, remained on Pequot lands, and supported their Pequot relatives throughout their lives.[33] Regardless of her status, Wequash's mother would have assuredly been the one who taught him to plant, cultivate, and nourish the corn fields—skills that he would later use to rebuild his community after the Pequot War. Born into a high-status family and part of a large, interwoven Indigenous community, Wequash would have known the importance of communal responsibility and the significance of kinship ties from an early age. It was the obligations of kinship that would eventually lead him to the center of the 1636 Battle of Mystic Fort, better known as the Mystic Massacre.

A New Story of the Pequot War

While the start of the English Civil War provided the exigence for the English printing of *New Englands' First Fruits*, the tract's narrative is inextricably linked to the earlier Pequot War. Though the English settlers eventually won the Pequot War (due in no small part to their Narragansett and Mohegan allies), their victory did not gain them much support back home in England. English readers who read about the war's violence were skeptical about the colonists' motivations for attacking the Pequot. They were especially put off by accounts of war's central battle, the Battle of Mystic Fort. On May 26, 1637, colonial troops under the command of Captain John Mason and Captain John Underhill set fire to the Pequot fort and killed between four hundred and seven hundred Pequot—many of them women and children. For English supporters, the violence of the massacre seemed to run contrary to the settlers' claims that they were actively trying to build up colonial society and recruit Indians to join the cause of Christianity. "How," English readers wondered, "was the burning of Indian bodies facilitating the conversion of Indian souls?"

Aware of the damage that the war had done to their colonial reputation, Weld and Peter used *New Englands First Fruits* as a means of reframing the narrative of the Pequot War. As they explain, the war was a necessary, though unpleasant, part of their larger *benevolent* conquest that the English were deploying over the Indigenous people of New England.[34] Yes, there was violence, their tract suggests, but it was limited and done in an effort to create the peace that they now claimed to enjoy with their Indigenous neighbors. In a list providing evidence of the ways that New England's colonial actions have "thus farre wonne" the Native people "to look after the Gospell," Weld and Peter work to minimize the Pequot War as a short blip in an otherwise peaceful relationship. They write: "God hath so kept them, (excepting that act of the Pequits, long since, to some few of our men) that we never found any hurt from them, nor could ever prove any reall intentions of evill against us." And later, they explain: "God hath . . . giv[en] us such peace and freedome from enemies, when almost all the world is on a fire that (excepting that short trouble with the Pequits) we never heard of any sound of Warre to this day."[35] To further justify the Pequot War, Weld and Peter make the implicit argument that the violence of the Pequot War was redemptive as it instigated the "first fruits" of conversion that they go on to detail within their tract. More specifically, the tract cites the violence of the Pequot War as the catalyst for Wequash's conversion.

Scholarly observers have repeatedly cited Wequash's participation in the war on the side of the English, his performance of conversion in the aftermath of the war, and his inclusion in the "first major texts to come out of the colonies in New England" as evidence that Wequash was "someone who turned on his own people."[36] In references to Wequash following his death, Wequash is almost exclusively referenced by the moniker "Wequash the traitor."[37] Yet when we read Wequash's actions in light of kinship, neither Wequash's participation in the war nor his performance of conversion were acts of betrayal but were rather actions that the Pequot leader undertook because of his responsibility to his relatives. Wequash did not merely find himself in the middle of the battle by happenstance, or as part of a larger thirst for vengeance. He was present at the battlefield to fulfill his kinship ties.

The first clues we have regarding the kinship ties that drew Wequash to the Pequot War come in a 1637 letter written by Roger Williams to Bay Colony Governor Henry Vane and Deputy Governor John Winthrop.[38] In his letter Williams informs the Bay Colony officials that Wequash has aligned with a cousin, the Narragansett sachem Miantonomi. Wequash was likely a member of Miantonomi's "ahtaskoaog," or group of principal advisers who help a sachem to make decisions for the community.[39] After being banished by the Massachusetts Bay Colony authorities in the winter of 1636, Williams had established diplomatic relations with the Narragansett sachems Canonicus and Miantonomi, from whom he acquired land from to set up his small Providence settlement. Despite his exile, Williams retained many of his alliances and friendships among the colonists including a close relationship with John Winthrop. By the summer of 1637, Williams was back in the middle of Massachusetts Bay affairs after Governor Vane requested him to negotiate with Canonicus for the return of two Englishmen who had been taken captive while traveling with the murdered English captain John Oldham.[40] Williams agreed and thus began his long-standing role as envoy between the Bay Colony and the Narragansett. The summer of 1637 was a particularly fraught time for Native leaders in the region because of the ongoing attacks between the English and the Pequot. That winter the Pequot had laid siege to the English fort at Saybrook in retaliation for English attacks on Block Island in which English troops had killed several Pequot. In April, the Pequot had attacked English settlers near the Connecticut River in Wethersfield. In response, the English declared war against the Pequot on May 1, 1637.

On that same day, Miantonomi held talks with Williams to try to determine how the Narragansett would proceed. In the buildup to the war, both English and Pequot leaders had courted the Narragansett in attempts to gain an alliance. Miantonomi and his council eventually decided to side with the English, provided that the English abide by several conditions. In the May 1 letter to Winthrop, Williams lists the requirements necessary for a Narragansett alliance. As stipulated by Miantonomi, the requirements were intended to uphold communal values and promote the growth of the Narragansett confederacy, both in terms of people and trade. Among other things, Miantonomi established rules regarding the duration of the attack, the location of the fighting, and most importantly, the treatment of any potential Pequot captives. Not only was Wequash present at the meeting between Williams and Miantonomi, but he was also tasked with playing a central role in Miantonomi's battle demands.[41] As one of his requirements, Miantonomi requested that the English leaders employ Wequash as a one of two guides that the English take with them in their attack on the Pequot fort at Mystic. As Williams writes, Miantonomi "especially" recommends that the English take "two Pequots, viz., Wequash and Wuttackquiackommin, valiant men . . . who have lived these three or four years with the Narragansett, and know every pass and passage amongst them." He also asks that the men be given "armor to enter [Pequot] houses," because, as Miantonomi explains, "it would be pleasing to all natives, that women and children be spared, &c."[42] The order of Miantonomi's demands makes it clear that the English are to take along the two Pequot guides and allow them to enter Pequot houses as part of a larger Narragansett military strategy focused on recovering Pequot captives.[43]

Gathering Pequot captives was not a peripheral task—rather, the Narragansett confederacy joined with the English against the Pequot in large part because of their desire to obtain Pequot captives. In their negotiations with the English, Miantonomi, Uncas, Wequash, and the other Indigenous leaders repeatedly address the issue of captives before, during, and after the war. The interconnected ties between the Pequot, Narragansett, Niantic, and Mohegan meant that the sachems desired captives as a means to bring their relatives back into their own villages, saving their family members from destruction and rebuilding their communities in the aftermath of colonial epidemics and warfare. Further, sachems such as Miantonomi, Uncas, and Ninigret were interested in integrating Pequot survivors into their communities in order to obtain rights to Pequot lands, Pequot resources, and Pequot trade relationships. As Michael Oberg writes, some sachems "hoped to supplant the Pequots by adding the strength of the survivors to their own network of village communities. They each hoped to place themselves at the center of the Pequots' network of intercultural trade, to dominate the wampum economy as the Pequots had done."[44] Commissioned directly by Miantonomi with the gathering and care of captives, Wequash is placed in a position not only to grow the Narragansett confederacy but to rebuild his own Pequot community as well.[45]

Our knowledge of Wequash's kinship ties tell us that Wequash's was present at the May 1 meeting because of his Narragansett relatives, but Williams's letter also helps us piece together the larger ebb and flow of the network of relations that motivated Wequash's participation in the Pequot War. In writing that Wequash had lived among the Narragansett for three or four years, Williams's letter indicates that Wequash had relocated among the Narragansett sometime around 1633 or 1634. This time period coincides with a series of communal conflicts among the Pequot exacerbated by colonial encroachment. In 1634 Dutch traders captured and murdered the Pequot sachem Tatobem after a conflict over trade. Tatobem's death initiated an internal struggle within the Pequot confederacy as the remaining Pequot attempted to choose a new leader.[46] Because of his existing leadership role, Wequash may have been one of several people contending for a leadership role.[47] Though we have limited details about Wequash's leadership aims, we do know that he was not appointed sachem and that Tatobem's son, Sassacus, was chosen sachem in his father's stead.[48]

Indigenous kinship ties were powerful and long-lasting in part because of their reciprocal nature. Being a good relative was an active role, not a static one, and it came with specific communal responsibilities. Kinship ties needed to be maintained and cultivated by all parties. New kinship responsibilities were constantly being created through marriages, adoption, or diplomatic alliances. Though the evidence is scant, the appointment of Sassacus may have caused a reordering of Wequash's kinship ties, as it led him and his followers to relocate and live among their Narragansett relatives. Among the Southern New England Algonquian, a sachem's followers could challenge a sachem's rule or even choose to join a new community if they disagreed with their leader or felt that a leader was not adequately caring for the people.[49] In the wake of Sassacus's succession, Wequash and his followers joined a large number of Pequot that were reaffirming their kinship ties with the Narragansett.[50] In the fall and winter of 1634, the Pequot leaders Wuttackquiackkommin and Sassawwaw (or Soso) and the Mohegan sachem Uncas (who was Tatobem's son-in-law) and their families also shifted their alliance from the Pequot to the Narragansett.[51] Today, the story of the split remains a significant part of Pequot and Mohegan history. It is remembered through a wampum collar once owned by Uncas and housed in the Tantaquidgeon Museum in Uncasville, Connecticut.

This inter- and intracommunal conflict following Tatobem's death was part of the larger context that contributed to the outbreak of the Pequot War. As archaeologist Kevin McBride writes, the Pequot War was "the culmination of decades of tension between Native tribes further stressed by the arrival of the Europeans."[52] As a trade war, an intratribal conflict, and a colonial land grab, the war and its aftermath were devastating for Wequash and the other Indigenous leaders who had family members on both sides of the conflict. Moreover, the battles of the war were upon lands where Wequash and his family members had lived, planted, and performed ceremonies for hundreds of years. Intimately familiar as places where communities were sustained, the horrors of the war had turned them into sites of terror. It is within the context of communal and social breakdown where we must locate Wequash's actions both during and after the war.

In the midst of a world that was falling apart, Wequash focused on holding his family together. Even before the fighting began, Wequash worked to keep his relatives safe. In a petition written after the war, the Pequot leader Robin Cassacinamon would recount Wequash's protective actions. In 1647 Cassacinamon explained that he and the other Pequot at Nameag were not present during the Mystic Massacre because they had heeded Wequash's advice. Cassacinamon tells the English that he played no part "in shedding the English blood, but by the advice of Wequash fled from the country being promised by Wequash that the English should not hurt us if wee did not Joyne in warre against them."[53] The 1647 petition includes the names of nearly sixty Pequot who had fled with Cassacinamon. Wequash's warning protected a whole Pequot community. His military alliance with Miantonomi and the English against the Pequot did not stop him from maintaining his obligations to his Pequot relatives.

On May 26, 1637, the morning of the Mystic Massacre, Wequash rose early and joined the rest of the Narragansett, Niantic, and Mohegan who had aligned with the English. The night before they had spent camped out in the woods around the Pequot fort at Mystic. At dawn the English surrounded the fort and prepared to attack while the Indigenous allies formed a second line behind them. The Native soldiers present likely anticipated the attack would follow in line with traditional ways of war, which focused heavily on captive gathering and displays of strength. Following

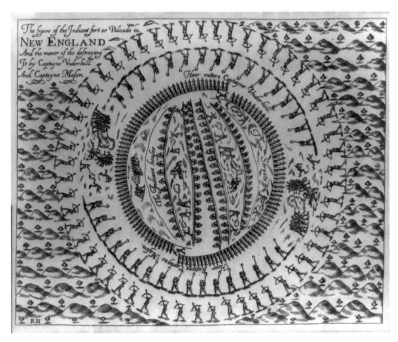

FIGURE 2. John Underhill's 1638 drawing of the Mystic Massacre, "The Figure of the Indians' Fort or Palizado." Courtesy of the Library of Congress.

Miantonomi's orders, Wequash's focus would have been on gathering Pequot captives and bringing them back to the Narragansett and the Niantic. English attempts to catch the Pequot off-guard were unsuccessful. After the initial attack, the Pequot quickly regrouped and retaliated, killing half of John Mason's company of twenty-two men.[54] While Wequash, the Mohegan, and the Narragansett watched, Mason ordered his men to set fire to the fort, crying out, "We should never kill them after that manner.... We must burn them."[55] Their scorched-earth approach trapped and killed several hundred Pequot men, women, and children inside the fort. Many of those who escaped were tracked down and captured, enslaved, or killed. Very few Pequot housed in the fort survived the day.[56]

While watching the burning of the Pequot Fort, Wequash not only witnessed the agonizing deaths of his family members, but he also faced the fact that he would be unable to complete his mission—he couldn't retrieve the Pequot from the burning fort. In 1638 Captain Underhill would write include a justification of the massacre and a woodcut engraving of the battle itself in his tract *Newes from America*. In his account, Underhill recorded the responses of the Native military leaders who had allied with the English against the Pequot. As the fort was going up in flames, Underhill writes, "Our *Indians* came to us, and much rejoyced at our victories, and greatly admired the manner of *English* mens fight." However, they balked at the English violence, crying, "*mach it, mach it*; that is, it is naught, it is naught, because it is too furious, and slaies too many men."[57] Those Indigenous leaders who had aligned with the English had not anticipated the violence that was to follow—in the aftermath of the war, many of them abandoned their ties with the English as they recognized that the English desire to obtain land and build English settlements would take precedence over any alliances they might make with Indigenous people.

The anguish of the Pequot War did not disappear at the war's end. English soldiers and their Indigenous allies tracked down the Pequot who had survived the war. Those who were accused of killing Englishmen in battle were executed. Some of the rest were exiled into slavery in the Caribbean; many were forced into servitude among the English, the Mohegan, and the Narragansett. In the aftermath of the war, the English victors declared the end of the Pequot as a people, writing in the 1638 Treaty of Hartford that the people "shall no more be called Peaquots" and the survivors could not "live in the country that was formerly theirs." Attempting a complete erasure of the Pequot, the Treaty of Hartford stated that "*Pequot* as a name, an identity, a territory, would cease to exist."[58] The repercussions of the Pequot War did not end in the seventeenth century but continues to the present day. Members of the Mashantucket Pequot and the Eastern Pequot nations continue their attempts to regather their relatives and reclaim their lands.

But it was not only the Pequot who suffered in the war's aftermath. The devastating violence of English warfare and the English leaders' failure to uphold Indigenous warfare practices meant that in the aftermath of Pequot War, the Narragansett, Niantic, and Mohegan who had aligned themselves with the English also struggled with a world out of balance. Though they were present at the Mystic Massacre as English allies, Wequash, Miantonomi, and the other Indigenous leaders recognized that the same English warfare that had destroyed many of their Pequot relatives could eventually destroy their own families as well. Northeast Indigenous leaders would continue to struggle with what it meant to rebalance their communities in the days, months, and years after the war's end.

The Origins of the Indigenous Conversion Narrative

It is the picture of Wequash in crisis that first makes its way into the English print record. In *New Englands First Fruits*, Weld and Peter introduce Wequash to their English readers by locating him in the immediate aftermath of the Mystic Massacre. As Weld and Peter write, after "feeling and beholding the might power of God in our English Forces, how they fell upon the *Pegans*, where divers hundreds of them were slaine in an houre: The Lord, as a God of glory in great terror did appeare unto the Soule and Conscience of this poor Wretch."[59] Focused on telling the story of Wequash's soul in ways that relate to their English readers, the Bay Colony authors interpret Wequash's anguish over the violence of the war as evidence that the Pequot man was taking the first step of Christian salvation—in conversion narrative terms, it was a moment of contrition. For the Puritans salvation was wholly an act of God. Contrition, or the recognition of one's failing, was one of the first steps indicating that God was preparing a soul for salvation. As Puritan minister Richard Mather explains, "a soul must go through a wilderness-like condition, that is, he must be afflicted with sight and sense of spiritual misery & sin, before he can attain to any state of saving rest & grace in Christ Jesus."[60]

The Bay Colony authors note that the terror of the massacre served as the means by which Wequash was brought to knowledge of the Christian God. As they write, "before that time [Wequash] had low apprehensions of our God, having conceived him to be (as he said) but a Musketto God, or a God like unto a flye; and as meane thoughts of the English that served this God, that they were silly weake men; yet from that time he was convinced and perswaded that our God was a most dreadfull God; and that one English man by the help of his God was able to slay and put to flight an hundred Indians."[61] Not only does the violence bring Wequash to see the power of a Christian God, but conveniently, it also brings him closer to the English. By intertwining English military power with divine favor, Weld and Peter remind metropolitan readers of the divine "good" that their military actions produced.

Although we can see evidence of the Bay Colony authors' narrative interpretation in their description of Wequash's response to the war, given the conditions of the Mystic Massacre, it is not surprising that Wequash's experience during the fighting may have produced a changed spiritual outlook.[62] Watching friends and relatives attempt to escape a burning fort while English soldiers stood by to push them back in was a traumatizing experience for Wequash and the other Indigenous people present. In the aftermath of the battle, Wequash seems to have taken it upon himself to perform a series of ceremonies intended to restore balance to his community in the face of spiritual disorder. Among the southern New England Algonquian, the sachem was responsible for maintaining social and political stability. In order to protect and sustain their followers, sachems cultivated a complicated network of relationships that included relationships with other human beings as well as with land, animals, and spiritual, nonphysical beings as well. These beings were imbued with powerful forces often termed *manitou*. Manitou could reside in people, animals, nature, or function on their own. As an imbued force, rather, "manitou was part of life, not above it."[63] Neither good nor evil, manitou was "an ambivalent power, which could be turned to creation or destruction."[64] Indigenous communities like the Pequot kept manitou in balance through proper performance of prayers, rituals, fasts, and other ceremonies that allowed them to gain manitou or the favor of beings imbued with manitou. A world out of balance, as evidenced by wars, suffering, and diseases, was an indication that the proper ceremonies had not been performed.[65] The destruction of the Mystic Massacre marked a clear instance of imbalance for Wequash and his relatives. Upon leaving the battlefield, Wequash began his search for new ceremonies as part of his responsibility to restore balance to his Pequot community. One of the ceremonies Wequash eventually chose to enact may have been that of Christian conversion.[66]

Contrition and Captive Gathering

While the colonial authors interpret the violence of the war as the initial call of Christ upon the Pequot man's soul, they read Wequash's actions in the war's aftermath as further evidence that he is making his way along the path to Christian salvation. After the massacre, Wequash seems to have been restless and wandering. As the authors of *New Englands First Fruits* write, Wequash "could have no rest or quiet because hee was ignorant of the Englishmans God: he went up and down bemoaning his condition, and filling every place where he came with sighes and groanes."[67] For the English narrators, Wequash's grief signals that he has reached the second step in the conversion process—humiliation—or the acknowledgment that one cannot attain salvation on one's own. In 1645 Thomas Shepard would explain humiliation as a process in which one is "exhorted . . . to lie down in the dust before the Lord, and under the Lord," in order to "intreat the Lord that he would put thee upon his wheel, and mould thy heart to his will."[68]

Though the English interpreted Wequash's response to the Mystic Massacre as evidence of his movement toward Christian salvation, his actions were also in line with long-standing Pequot practice. For the Pequot and their relatives, grief was displayed publicly. Women who had lost loved ones cut their hair. Both men and women in mourning might paint their faces black using ashes. When children died, relatives gathered to mourn and lament for several days.[69] Items might be given away in honor of the deceased. In the face of grief, communities came together to mourn and to provide care for those who were so consumed with loss that they could not perform daily tasks. In facing the mass destruction of his community, Wequash was paralyzed by loss, imbalance, and pain.

For the English authors interpreting Wequash's tale, the Pequot man's grief led him to take the next step toward Christian salvation—acceptance of the Lord's call or vocation. Within a Puritan typology of salvation, "only after being lowered could a convert rise."[70] While wandering up and down in grief, the Bay Colony authors tell us that Wequash encountered "some English (well acquainted with his Language)." It was from these "English" that Wequash "enquired after God with such incessant diligence that they were constrained constantly for his satisfaction to spend more than halfe the night in conversing with him."[71] Though Weld and Peter do not note the context of Wequash's conversations with the English, it is assumed that they are of a religious nature. Drawn first to the Christian God and then to the English, Wequash is well on his way to becoming a model convert.

Despite Weld and Peter's seamless narration, the nature of Wequash's conversations with "some English" are likely just as focused on diplomacy as they are on the state of Wequash's soul. In *A Key into the Language of America*, Roger Williams would make it clear that he was the "some English" with whom Wequash had met. In 1643, when *New Englands First Fruits* was printed, Williams and the Bay Colony leaders were once again at odds with one another. This time the dispute was over colonial land claims. While living among the Narragansett, Williams had treated with the Narragansett sachems Canonicus and Miantonomi for several tracts of Narragansett lands to use for his growing Providence Plantations. In directly negotiating with the Narragansett, Williams circumvented the authority of the Bay Colony, which had long claimed that the lands should be distributed by colonial officials according to charter rights. Williams was in London at the same time as Weld and Peter. Both parties were attempting to convince English officials of their authority to make land claims in the colonies. As J. Patrick Cesarini and Jeffrey Glover point out, both Williams and the Bay Colony officials turned to print as part of their attempts to justify their own actions and vilify those of the other. More specifically, both of their accounts contained their own interpretation of the state of Wequash's soul. In their battles with one another, Wequash's tale and its interpretation became a central point of contestation.[72]

In *A Key into the Language of America*, Williams points out that he did not have only one meeting with Wequash, but rather had "several discourses with him in his Life." In the preface to *A Key*, Williams focuses on one specific meeting he had with Wequash "two or three years before" Wequash's death. In this meeting, Williams explains that the conversation was focused on "the *Condition* of all *mankind*, & his Own in particular, how *God* created *Man* and *Allthings*: How *Man* fell from God, and of his present *Enmity* against God."[73] For both Williams and the Bay Colony authors, this specific meeting marks the moment when Wequash was exposed to Christian salvation—the next step in the Christian conversion process. Yet, while Williams and Wequash seem to have talked about spiritual concerns, a look at Wequash's actions at the time suggest that his meetings with Williams began as part of a larger discussion about Wequash's Pequot relatives, specifically those taken captive by the English.[74] As translator and negotiator between the Narragansett sachems and the Bay Colony, Williams was in constant talks with Governor Winthrop about the state of the Pequot captives after the Pequot War. Not only was he a go-between, but Williams was also negotiating for his own captives. As he writes to Winthrop in the month after the Mystic Massacre: "I am bold (if I may not offend in it) to request the keeping and bringing up of one of the Children. I have fixed mine eye on this litle one with the red about his neck, but I will not be peremptory in my choice but will rest in your loving pleasure for him or any etc."[75] Importantly, Williams was not the only English leader with whom Wequash met in the aftermath of the Pequot War. Wequash also befriended the English commander of Saybrook Fort, Lion Gardiner, formed an alliance with the Massachusetts Commander Israel Stoughton, and had at least one meeting with Governor Winthrop, possibly more.[76] Significantly, all of the English leaders with whom Wequash met after the war were deeply involved in the distribution of Pequot captives and Pequot lands.[77] While the authors of *New Englands First Fruits* read Wequash's postwar performance as evidence of his movement toward Christian salvation, his actions are also explainable within the context of kinship. Though the war had been a profound spiritual crisis which may have led him to show interest in English Christianity, Wequash's alliance with the English had not deterred him from his role as a captive gatherer. Rather, it seems to have deepened his resolve to bring his community back together.[78]

Further evidence that Wequash was regathering his relatives can be found in Williams's letters. A few months after the Mystic Massacre, Roger Williams wrote to Winthrop, warning him that Wequash and Uncas, the

Mohegan sachem, were regathering captives. As he writes, "there are many of the scattered Pequot rendezvoused with Uncas the Mohegan Sachem and Wequash the Pequot, who being employed as one of the guides to the English in their late wars, is grown rich, and a Sachem with the Pequots: and hath five or six runaways."[79] Some estimate that the number of captives Wequash had with him at the time was much higher, closer to thirty.[80] Significantly, Wequash's gathering of the captives coincides with the period during which Weld and Peter describe him going "up and down bemoaning his condition and filling every place he came with sighes and groanes."[81] Wequash's "sighes and groanes" were an indication of his distress, but his movements "up and down" were evidence of his action.

"To Dwell among the English at Connecticut"

Both *New Englands First Fruits* and *A Key into the Language of America* carefully document Wequash's movements and make note of the places where he chose to settle. For the English observers, Wequash's physical movements were spiritually significant because they served as evidence that could potentially reveal the true state of the Pequot man's soul. To reinforce their claims of God's stirrings upon Wequash's soul, the authors of *New Englands First Fruits* couple the movements of Wequash's heart with those of his body. As they write, after "enquir[ing] after God with such incessant diligence" Wequash eventually decided to "to dwell amongst the English at *Connecticut*."[82] The Puritans believed in the necessity of "fixing Indians in a geographically bounded place on which cultural negotiations would occur."[83] Being "fixed" in place allowed the English to observe Indigenous movements and ostensibly "teach" them how to farm and build like the English. Conversion and Indigenous performances of English culture, or as the English termed it, "civility," went hand in hand. An Indigenous person's ability to build an English house served as evidence that they were intellectually capable of comprehending Christian salvation. As Thomas Shepard writes, because Indigenous people stood at a "vast distance . . . from common civility, almost humanity itself," they had to be taught English ways before they could fully grasp the depth of Christian belief.[84] Yet "fixing" Indigenous people in specific places not only allowed for English instruction; it also allowed colonists to exert further control over Indigenous lands by limiting Indigenous movement and narrowing Indigenous land claims. In locating himself near the English, Wequash's actions provide evidence for English readers that he is ready to establish ties with the English and be part of their community.

Once Wequash began to "dwell among the English," the Bay Colony leaders report that he "grew greatly in the knowledge of Christ, and in the Principles of Religion, and became thorowly reformed according to his light."[85] In Puritan terms, Wequash's settling at Connecticut is evidence that the Pequot leader had achieved the fourth stage of conversion, the call to salvation, also termed "justification." In responding to the call of God upon the soul, the penitent becomes part of the elect—those chosen by God for salvation. By mapping out Wequash's physical relocation to dwell near the English, the colonial authors clearly intended to provide evidence for their readers of Wequash's rapidly increasing spiritual acumen. And yet, consistent with his subsequent actions, Wequash's move to Connecticut was also motivated by the bonds of kinship.[86]

For Wequash and the Pequot, the lands around Saybrook Fort were not English lands but Indigenous ones—lands they had cared for, cultivated, and claimed for centuries. The lands around Saybrook Fort or around the Connecticut River, better known to Wequash as Kwinitekw or Quinetuck, had long been home to Wequash's relatives. Many communities along the coast would locate their summer houses, or wigwams, near the river and its banks. As Brooks explains, the valleys around the river were home to a number of "horticultural hamlets, long inhabited by 'mobile farmers' who cultivated some of the most fertile fields in the world, enhanced by spring freshets and deep alluvial soils, and who utilized the surrounding floodplains and upland forests for seasonal hunting, fishing and gathering."[87] When the temperatures dropped, the communities would move inland toward their winter wigwams. Usually the two locations were not far apart. This agricultural abundance and community history made the lands around the Connecticut River valley an apt place to rebuild the Pequot community. In an April 1638 letter to Governor Winthrop, Williams provides evidence that Wequash had indeed relocated to the river valley. However, Wequash's move was not solely driven beyond a desire to be near the English. As Williams explains to Winthrop, "The Pequots are gathered into one, and plant their old fields, Wequash and

Uncas [are] carrying away the people and their treasure, which belong to yourselves."[88] In preparation for summer planting and fishing, Wequash and Uncas moved their relatives back to their traditional summer homes around the river valley. More than just regathering the people, Wequash was preparing for their continued survival.

While Wequash's decision to relocate himself to the lands around the Connecticut River valley were made with his community in mind, he had a personal connection to the place as well. In *A Key into the Language of America*, Roger Williams notes that the specific location of Wequash's Connecticut dwelling was two miles away from the home of the English land speculator and later Parliamentarian George Fenwick—"in *Say-Brook* Fort at the mouth of that River."[89] Though Fenwick would eventually treat with Uncas for use of the lands around Saybrook Fort, when Wequash moved to the Connecticut River Valley after the Pequot War in 1638 or 1639, the English settlers did not have any recognized rights to the land.[90] Rather, at the time, Indigenous people and settlers alike recognized the lands as under the jurisdiction Wequash's aunt, the powerful Narragansett-Niantic saunkskwa Quaiapin. It was through her that Wequash and Uncas had been granted access to the lands around the neck of the river. It seems that Quaiapin had granted Wequash's the land for the use of his child, her nephew. In a 1640 or 1641 treaty with the missionary Henry Whitfield, Wequash provided Whitfield access to the "land called the Neck lying beyond the East river in Menunkatuck which reacheth unto Tuckshishoagg."[91] Whitfield was a prominent minister in the region and also a leader in founding the town of Guilford, Connecticut, at the mouth of the river. By treating with Whitfield, Wequash formalized a relationship with those moving upon his lands. Additionally, establishing formal relations with Whitfield and the other settlers allowed Wequash to monitor the English settlers' movements through the Connecticut River Valley and model to the English how to be good neighbors to the Indigenous communities.[92]

Crafting a Conversion Narrative

In *The Name of War* historian Jill Lepore reminds us that war is not merely a series of events but is also a story. As she writes, "War cultivates language: it requires justification, it demands description."[93] Likewise, for the Puritan settlers in New England, the occurrence of Indigenous conversion was not nearly as important as the story of it told. Like war, conversion demanded description and interpretation. As one of the stated "principle end[s]" of the Massachusetts Bay Colony, conversion stories had high stakes. Since narratives of conversion were the sole form of evidence proving to English readers that a conversion event had taken place, believable narratives not only provided legitimacy for the colony but also helped to ensure its continued survival. It was a demanding task to tell the story of the Indigenous soul in ways that both captured what Puritans believed to be the workings of God and would convince English readers of an authentic spiritual transformation.

Although Wequash's conversion narrative in *New Englands First Fruits* can be read a type of historical archive that, when located alongside other historical accounts and interpreted in light of Indigenous studies methodologies, can yield a new depiction of the life of a Pequot sachem, *New Englands First Fruits* is not only a historical or cultural document—it is a literary one as well, and the way the story is told is important. The tract's form tells us just as much about the authors writing it and as it does about the subjects they chronicle. More than a window into the life of the Bay Colony's first claimed Indigenous convert, *New Englands First Fruits* also helps us glimpse the ways in which the English chroniclers and their texts were changed by their encounters with Native people.

The lands around the mouth of the Connecticut River were the location where Wequash gathered together his Pequot relatives, but they were also the site where the New England Indigenous conversion narrative genre was born. A site of multiple relational exchanges, the shores of the Connecticut River are central to both Wequash's Pequot story and to the colonial narrative that would develop out of his life and death. While Wequash was living near the riverbanks, he met the Puritan minister Thomas Shepard, whose account would eventually form the basis of Wequash's tale in *New Englands First Fruit*. After his meeting with Wequash, Shepard would write to his friend Thomas Weld and describe the profound influence that Wequash's words and actions had on his understanding of Christian salvation in New England.

Though Thomas Shepard and Wequash had vastly different connections to the lands around the Connecticut River, on some level they were both drawn to its banks through the ties of kinship. In June of 1642, Shepard was serving as a minister at the First Church in Newtown (Cambridge), Massachusetts, when he left his home and made the five-day, hundred-mile journey to Hartford, Connecticut. For Shepard, his second wife, Johanna, and his two sons, Thomas Jr. and Samuel, the trip was an opportunity to catch up with old friends and family members. It may also have been the first time that the young Samuel met his maternal grandparents, the minister Thomas Hooker and his wife, Susanna, who had moved to the region to found Connecticut Colony. Though Shepard and Hooker were connected through marriage, the two ministers also had a long-standing friendship, as the elder Hooker had been a mentor to Shepard in England. While on the banks of the Connecticut River Shepard also visited another old friend from England, George Fenwick, the English politician who had treated with Uncas for the lands around Saybrook Fort. In 1632, when both Fenwick and Shepard were living in England, Fenwick had housed Shepard and his first wife, Margaret, in his Newcastle home. Fenwick had given the young preacher shelter after Archbishop William Laud had forced Shepard out of London for his dissenting views.[94]

While visiting Fenwick at Saybrook, Shepard found himself in the middle of another family gathering—albeit a more somber one. In early July, Shepard and Fenwick made the trek to the mouth of the Connecticut River to pay their respects to Wequash, who was now on his deathbed. As the colonial governor of Saybrook and a longtime land speculator, Fenwick knew many Pequot and Mohegan leaders. He seems to have had special ties with Wequash, as the two men often met together. After Fenwick visited Wequash on his deathbed, Wequash seems to have arranged for his son, Wenamoag, to be left in Fenwick's care.[95] As Williams writes, Wequash "freely bequeathed his son to Mr. Fenwick."[96] While the English interpret Wequash's giving of his son to Fenwick as evidence of both Wequash's religious conviction and loyalty to the English, Wequash may have had another purpose in mind. As Brooks explains, "it had long been a tradition in eastern Indigenous networks for neighboring nations to engage in an 'exchange of sons' to build and 'seal' the alliances among them. These men were educated in another community's ways to become effective and 'knowledgeable interpreters and mediators,' enabling communication and conflict resolution in regional space." As they grew older, the men who had been exchanged "sustain[ed] loyalties to both communities" and "became careful and reliable mediators in intertribal councils."[97] Mirroring his own upbringing, in which he moved between the Pequot, the Niantic, and the Narragansett, Wequash may have arranged for his son to be cared for by Fenwick in order to build up alliances with the English. Even in his final days, the Pequot leader continued to act as a diplomat, hoping to facilitate good relationship with his neighbors and secure a better future of his people.

Shepard's ties to Wequash are less clear. However, as an active participant in both the Pequot War and in New England's colonial mission to Indigenous people, Shepard may have worked with Wequash before the sachem was confined to his deathbed. Or he may have attended Wequash's death at the urging of their mutual friend, George Fenwick. In either case, when Shepard and Fenwick made their way to Wequash's bedside, they were part of a constant stream of friends and family members gathering to help the dying man transition to the next world. Among the visitors likely included Wequash's relatives from the Mohegan, Pequot, Niantic, and Narragansett. Other English leaders also came to pay their respects, including Roger Williams and Governor John Winthrop. For Wequash's Pequot community, death was a time of remembering, a time of gathering, and a time to perform ceremonies to guide the dying relative through to the next life. As he neared the end of his life, Wequash remembered the past and prepared for his future. He reminisced about old times, participated in religious ceremonies, and arranged for the care of his young son. In gathering together at the death of community leader, Wequash and his relatives did as they had always done.[98]

Yet while Wequash's death followed traditional ceremonies, it was also different. The upheaval of the Pequot War and the continuing settlement of the English colonists marked Wequash's death just as it had marked his life. Wequash's alliance with the English and his performance of English religious practices meant that some of the old ceremonies were replaced with new English ones. In his last days, *New Englands First Fruits* records, Wequash refused the administrations of the Indigenous powwow in favor of Christian prayer. Whether this was actually the case or not is hard to tell. If Wequash did refuse the powwow, it is even more difficult to decipher his reasoning—was it in honor of his English visitors, the result of a changed belief, or something else? In any case, the ceremonies looked different in a settler-colonial world. In *New Englands First Fruits*, which we must remember is largely drawn from Shepard's account, the authors make it explicit that Wequash's rejection of the *"Powow"* is the result of his true faith. They record his final words as evidence: *"If Jesus Christ say that Wequash shall live, then Wequash must live; if Jesus Christ say that Wequash shall dye, then Wequash is willing to dye, and will not lengthen out his life by any such meanes."*[99]

The matter of Wequash's dying was of particular concern to the English who had gathered. Each sought to capture Wequash's final words in order to make a particular claim about not only the state of Wequash's soul but the success or failure of their own colonial mission. For Winthrop, Shepard, and the other English visitors, Wequash's words served as confirmation that Wequash was both a religious and political ally. Yet, for Williams, the matter was more complicated. Like Winthrop, Shepard, and Fenwick, Williams was also present at Wequash's deathbed. In *A Key into the Language of America*, Williams writes the dying Wequash was less confident about Christian practice. Instead, Williams writes that Wequash "in broken English" anxiously exclaimed, "Me so big naughty Heart, me heart all one stone!" With these words, Williams claimed that Wequash spoke "savory expressions using to breath from compute and broken Hearts, and a sence of inward hardnesse and unbrokennesse."[100] Lacking the clear assurance of salvation, Wequash remained between two worlds. As Kristina Bross suggests, Williams includes this scene both to illustrate his role in Indigenous missions and also because Williams is "competing with Bay Colony authorities for discursive control of Wequash's deathbed scene."[101]

Beyond their differing claims regarding the state of Wequash's soul, the two accounts also differ regarding the cause of Wequash's death. In his account, Williams makes no mention of Wequash's cause of death merely reporting that Wequash "lay very sick."[102] Yet the authors of *New Englands First Fruits* cite his death as the result of deliberate action. As they write, "some of the Indians, whose hearts Satan had filled did secretly give him poyson."[103] In his journal, John Winthrop affirms their claims, writing that the Pequot leader's death was "not without suspicion of poison" from "other Indians [whom he had] labored much to convert."[104] While the differing accounts of Wequash's last words are hard to interpret outside the context of the colonial mission, the accounts regarding his cause of death can be located within the larger context of Indigenous-colonial relations in the aftermath of the Pequot War.

Though tragic, Wequash's death was not unique among the Indigenous allies who had sided with the English during the Pequot War. In the 1640s, tensions were high among many of the Narragansett, Niantic, and Mohegan leaders who had aided the English during the Pequot War. In the war's aftermath, many former English allies felt they were being unfairly treated, especially in regard to the distribution of Pequot captives and Pequot lands. The brutal system of human enslavement and captivity set up by the English after the war and the fact that the English ended up claiming the majority of the Pequot lands and captives led to increasing frustrations among the former allies both with the English and with one another. Wequash, his brother Wequashcook, his uncle Ninigret, and Uncas had all repeatedly come into conflict with the Narragansett sachems Miantonomi and Canonicus over captives and land. The Narragansett sachems Miantonomi and Canonicus rebuffed their claims and instead accused Wequash and Uncas of taking captives that had been promised to the Narragansett.

Tensions were so high among the Indigenous communities that in the early 1640s a number of the sachems faced death threats or were killed by other leaders. In 1643 John Winthrop reported that Uncas encountered "a Pequot Indian" who "shot him with an arrow through the arm, and presently fled to the Narrowgansets." After surviving this first attack, Winthrop writes that other attempts were made to "take away Uncas life by poison and by sorcery."[105] Uncas also faced an attack from Miantonomi's ally Sequaseen, a Wangunk sachem of the River Indians at Suckiog.[106] In retaliation, Uncas "burned to the ground the wigwams in Sequassen's village"—an attack that provoked Miantonomi to defend his ally. The fight between Uncas and Miantonomi eventually resulted in a war between the Narragansett and the Mohegan that ended with Uncas clubbing Miantonomi to death under the sanction of English authorities.[107] In this light, Wequash's poisoning may have been the consequence of his actions and identity in the aftermath of the Pequot War—either his work gathering Pequot or his status as an ally and relative of sachems like Uncas, Ninigret, and Wequashcook, who were increasingly antagonistic to Narragansett leaders. After the war, Wequash had acquired not only powerful allies but powerful enemies as well. Wequash's political actions in the aftermath of the war are not separate from his spiritual or communal ones. In both following Christian ceremonies and gathering together the captives, Wequash was working to better his people.

The Changing Story of Conversion

Wequash's death and the circumstances surrounding it seemed to have had a profound and lasting influence on Thomas Shepard. More than merely evidence of a successful Indigenous conversion, by Shepard's interpretation, Wequash's death was a moment when the workings of God were made visible on earth. After returning to his Newtown pulpit, Shepard wrote in his journal that his trip to the Connecticut River had provided him with "a glorious glimpse of Christ" that allowed him to "see ... afresh God's great plot."[108] Michael McGiffert writes that for Shepard, "God's plot was the great plan of human salvation." As he explains, "Shepard and his people envisioned a divine scenario governing the living of their lives and the saving of their souls. They became actors with parts to play in a cosmic drama of redemption."[109] In the chaos of the colonial world, clear glimpses of a divine plan were few and far between. For Shepard, true salvation was difficult to observe and even more difficult to obtain. In a tract written a year before Wequash's death at the river's edge, Shepard warned that "Jesus Christ is not got with a wet finger." Rather, "it is a tough work, a wonderfull hard matter to be saved." While God has offered salvation to all, "he hath elected but few."[110]

For Shepard, the difficulty of assurance lay in the fact that being convinced of one's own election is evidence that one is not actually part of the elect. In a somewhat paradoxical line of thinking, Shepard and his fellow ministers believed that the pride necessary to lay claim to assurance of salvation is, in itself, evidence that one is not relying on God's provision. Rather, one must continually pass through humiliation, self-abdication, and acknowledgment of one's own abject poverty of both self and spirit in the quest for salvation. If a convert does not properly acknowledge dependence on God during trials, the convert faces the possibility of self-deception—a practice Shepard saw as "particularly impedimental to a congregant's elective process."[111] Thus, in writing that he saw evidence of God's plot during his time in visiting the Connecticut River valley, Shepard makes a somewhat bold statement. Reflecting further upon the visit, Shepard recounts, "My heart was exceedingly refreshed, enlarged, and lifted up in some sweet assurance, though mixed with some scruples, and in special that the Lord would be with me in my place."[112] It seems possible that in observing Wequash's life and death, Shepard had found the evidence of assurance he rarely found elsewhere.

The enthusiasm Shepard describes in his journal is mirrored in the letter he wrote to Weld that would eventually form the basis of the story of Wequash as recounted in *New Englands First Fruits*. In the letter, Shepard not only describes Wequash's dying words, but he also makes clear the profound impact that Wequash's death had on him. As Shepard writes, "Wequash, the famous Indian at the Rivers mouth is dead, and *certainly in heaven*; gloriously did the Grace of Christ shine forth in his conversation" (emphasis added). He continues, Wequash "knew Christ, he loved Christ, he preached Christ up and down, and then suffered *Martyrdom for Christ*; and when he dyed, he gave his soule to Christ, and his only child to the English, rejoicing in this hope, that the child should know more of Christ then its poore Father ever did." To emphasize that they are recording Shepard's response and not their own, Weld and Peter preface Shepard's description by writing that it come from "Mr. Sh a godly Minister in the Bay" whose "lines are full plain and pithy."[113] After being profoundly moved by Wequash's death, Shepard hopes to in turn, move Weld, who then includes Shepard's description in his tract as part of his attempts to sway subsequent readers.

While *New Englands First Fruits* is a deliberately crafted fundraising account, Shepard's acclaim for Wequash seems to extend beyond mere propaganda. Like many Puritan ministers, Shepard reserved the category of martyr for those who exemplified the highest form of Christian faith—those who, through their death, made Christ visible on earth. For Shepard, the suspicious circumstances surrounding Wequash's death alongside the Pequot leader's dying words and his performance of English Christian religious practices meant that Wequash's performance of death paralleled a number of historic Christian practices associated with Christian martyrdom. As Adrian Chastain Weimer explains, "Early English Protestants shared a historical imagination filled with stories of martyrs and persecutors, stories that encompassed the sweep of Christian history from the early church to the English Reformation."[114] In New England, the practices associated with martyrdom became a central means by which colonists articulated their colonial mission. For the New England Puritans, martyrdom was the means by which God was made visible on earth. As Weimer writes, "the shared ideal of holy suffering . . . allowed visible piety to break through social and theological boundaries."[115] Yet, more than making God visible, Shepard also believed Wequash's death had implications for the colonial project. Shepard identified Wequash's dying ceremonies as those confirming the Pequot leader's entry into the English, Christian community—Wequash's death as martyr marked him as Shepard's new brother in Christ. In witnessing the death of a martyr, Shepard believed that he had caught a glimpse of God's movements on earth, and in witnessing the death of a Pequot martyr, Shepard believed that he was able to see God's plan for the colonies playing out before his eyes.

Wequash's death comes at the beginning of a long-standing debate among the Puritans about the implications of Indigenous performances of conversion for Indigenous political rights. What did it mean to be a "brother" in Christ, and what rights did that status afford? At the heart of the debate was the question of kinship—did conversion indicate a new kinship status among the Indigenous convert and the English congregation, or was it merely a performance that could be dismissed? Eventually, as we see in chapter 4, the English make a clear decision to ignore the possibility of kinship between English settlers and Indigenous people. In ignoring the possibility of kinship, the English withhold the rights of citizenship to Indigenous people and excuse themselves from adhering to the kinship obligations they agreed to in signing Indigenous treaties. Though kinship is dismissed by the colonists on the whole, Shepard incorporates it into his narrative interpretation of Wequash's life and death.

Wequash's conversion came a time when the rules for what was deemed an authentic performance of conversion were changing. For much of the Christian church's history, penitent Christians had been telling their stories of salvation. In a practice first recognized in the teachings of Origen, the third-century Greek theologian, Christian leaders had long encouraged congregants to give public testimonies about their private spiritual journeys.[116] Public testimony had its roots in early church confessional practices. Eventually, this practice was adapted by church leaders and became the sacrament of penance, which would become a central part of Christian religious practice. However, in the seventeenth century, the newly developing Puritan religious sect began to employ variations of public conversion narratives as a means of verifying that God had truly called those who claimed membership in their ranks.

Though Puritan congregations in both New England and Old employed conversion narratives, the form took on new meaning in the colonies because in New England "conversion was the bedrock on which the church and state rested."[117] This new emphasis on merging the church and the state started early. In 1633 Winthrop began to informally request potential church members to give a testimony of faith. In 1634 the First Church at Boston adapted a more formal version of the procedure, and by 1640 a testimony of faith had become a requirement for membership in many New England churches. Though the practice was prevalent throughout the colonies, the specific requirements for conversion varied widely. These testimonies served a number of functions, but eventually membership in the church became a necessary prerequisite for landownership, voting, and political office. One's ability to recite an authentic conversion narrative was directly tied to one's ability to participate in daily communal life in the colonies.

The changed function of the conversion narrative concurrently produced new generic conventions. Namely, conversion narratives in New England became laced with anxiety. Potential church members' narratives of salvation were twined with crippling pangs of doubt. As Patricia Caldwell writes, in New England "conversion took place directly through affliction — affliction that was terrible but also comprehensible and expressible. . . . In many stories the outward suffering seems absolutely necessary in order to *make* sin and salvation comprehensible and expressible."[118] While Caldwell locates the impetus for anxiety as the experience of being located within the unknown American landscape, other scholars have pointed to anxiety's theological roots. In late 1630s and early 1640s, after the trials of the Antinomian Controversy and the challenges of the Pequot War, Puritans in New England were preoccupied with rooting out spiritual dissimulation. As Andy Dorsey writes, after the Antinomian Controversy, "the question guiding [the New England Puritans] on the path to regeneration was not 'how do I know [I] am saved?' but 'how do I know I'm not a hypocrite?'"[119]

While the changed function of the conversion narrative was the product of a number of political, religious, and social factors, one man had a large role in facilitating the change through his own records of conversion narratives—Puritan minister Thomas Shepard. As the most prolific recorder of conversion narratives in New England and a prominent minister who spent years explicating the nuances of doubt and assurance, Shepard forwarded a new theological and political understanding of salvation in the early years of the colony. Shepard's own recitation of conversion was shaded with doubt. In his *Autobiography*, which served as one of the earliest and most detailed spiritual biographies penned in the colonies, Shepard explains how "the most striking feature of his life ... was its unsettledness."[120] When Shepard first landed in New England 1635, he was weary from an arduous journey across the ocean and years spent trying to evade authorities back in England. Once in New England, Shepard's troubles continued, and he soon found himself faced with both the Antinomian Controversy and the Pequot War—events that Shepard saw as linked events intended to test the faithful.[121] For Shepard, trials were a necessary part of the salvation process because they serve to remind the convert that one was unable to achieve salvation on merit. Humility, or more specifically the recognition that original sin "cannot be paid in wages or good works," was a necessary first step toward salvation. And while trials could draw one to salvation, they could also draw one away. The challenge was determining whether one's actions were performed out of dependence or hypocrisy—the former serving as evidence of true salvation and the latter as evidence of potential damnation.

In 1638, after Hutchinson and her followers had been banished from New England, Shepard began to set up his own system of checks and balances intended to root out hypocrisy. Along with his preaching, Shepard started to monitor the salvation accounts of his potential congregants by recording their narratives of conversion—a practice he would continue until his death. Between 1638 and 1649, Shepard recorded at least sixty-six conversion narratives, and it is these recorded narratives that provide the bulk of our knowledge about the conversion narrative genre in the early colonial period. All the narratives in Shepard's notebooks are those of English settlers. And, in line with Shepard's own *Autobiography*, almost all of the narratives are marked by a sense of uncertainty. As Caldwell writes,

"The Englishman ends his conversion narrative with one foot in heaven; his brother starts out for heaven but gets side-tracked in New England, where he continues his seeking but somehow needs to postpone his final salvation."[122]

Wequash's narrative is not counted as one of the conversion narratives recorded by Shepard, but it should be. In addition to being recorded by Shepard, Wequash's account has all the other hallmarks of a Shepard-style conversion narrative, including a detailed description of the movement of a soul through the phases of conversion; verification of the account and the authenticity of its teller by established church members, namely Shepard himself and George Fenwick; Wequash's narrative is necessary for his inclusion in a Christian community. Furthermore, the form of Wequash's narrative also mirrors those of Shepard's other conversion narratives in that it is told with a mix of description and narration. In the context of Shepard's other conversion narratives, Wequash's stands out as one of the most assured narratives that Shepard recorded. Not only was Wequash's narrative the only one to end with a claim of martyrdom, but it was also the only narrative in which Shepard makes an unequivocal claim of assurance regarding the state of a convert's soul.

Why does Shepard read Wequash's conversion with such unequivocal confidence? Given the larger context of the tract's publication, it is possible that Shepard's account was propagandistic—an attempt to provide evidence to English readers the mission was on the right track. Shepard almost certainly knew that Weld was in England on a fundraising track when he penned the letter to his friend, and he may have wanted to "help" out the mission by providing the Bay Colony agents with useful with "evidence" of religious success. Shepard clearly wrote with an audience in mind. Yet to claim that the Puritan minister would completely fabricate an account of martyrdom is to misread Shepard's spiritual convictions and dismiss evidence from his lifetime of teaching and preaching. As McGiffert writes, "any notion that [Shepard] was soft or pliable or complicit in sanctified fakery is disproved by the spiritual discipline he imposed on himself." Shepard "knew how easy it was to deceive oneself and others in matters of the spirit." As a result, "he took great pains to ensure . . . that the wrong people would not get as far as the public confession."[123] Shepard's reputation, and that of the larger Puritan mission, depended on evidential accounts of religious progress.

If we believe that Shepard was convinced he saw something remarkable in Wequash's performance of conversion, we may then turn to Wequash himself. Experienced in English ceremonies and aware of the desires of his English observers, Wequash potentially adapted his performance of conversion to meet the expectations of the attendant ministers. In the ever-changing landscape of the settler-colonial world, Indigenous people and settlers modified their individual and communal practices in reaction to each other. As the colony developed, Indigenous converts "guided by conversion sermons and by watching exemplary models . . . learned to discipline the senses and frame their experience within appropriate testimonial templates in order to interpret and intuit signs of grace correctly."[124] The suggestion that Wequash adapted his performance of conversion is further supported by the differing accounts of Wequash's final days produced by Shepard and Williams. Whereas Shepard interprets Wequash's performance as proof of salvation, Williams sees it as evidence of equivocation. Yet, to say that Wequash was merely showing the colonists what they wanted to see or that he was practiced in the art of deception ignores Wequash's ability to act upon his own agency in ways that would support and sustain his people. Though the time after the Pequot War was a time of great distress for Wequash and his community, he remained an active leader—choosing to locate himself in particular place and create specific alliances in line with his communal and personal aims. In his other public performances, the Pequot leader made decisions and engaged in diplomatic relationships with the English in ways that were not solely intended to manipulate or confuse. Rather, Wequash's actions throughout his life were consistent and driven by his kinship ties. It is in light of kinship that we should read Wequash's performance of conversion.

The significance of Wequash's conversion narrative lies in an understanding of the many relationships that facilitated the tale's creation and production. In contrast to the other narratives Shepard recorded, Wequash was not a stranger in a strange land. As such, his narrative was not beset by anxiety, nor was it laced with uncertainty. Rather, it was confident and assured. After the Pequot War Wequash leveraged his relationships with various English leaders in order to regather his scattered people. This is not to say that the conversion accounts are merely diplomacy disguised as religious literature. Rather, for the Pequot as for the English, religion, diplomacy, and community were all intertwined. Wequash's alliance with the English did not preclude him from maintaining his ties with his Algonquian kin in the same way that his alliance with the Narragansett did not mean he had abandoned his ties to the Pequot. Kinship functioned as a web, not a wall. Thus, in performing a conversion narrative, Wequash was signaling his desire to extend his kinship ties to the English community, or to use Brooks's well-known phrase, Wequash was working to bring the English settlers into the common pot—the intricate web of relationships that governed and sustained native space.[125] Well versed in the implications and protocols of communal and spiritual ceremonies, Wequash was comfortable in his status as both a convert and a diplomat and his actions were those intended to create new forms of community.

While kinship is broad and encompassing, not all kinship ties are equal. The differences in Wequash's relationships with Shepard and Williams can in part account for the differences within the two conversion narratives. In the political world after the Pequot War, the Bay Colony leaders were a much more powerful party than Williams and his followers. For example, Wequash knew it was the Bay Colony leaders, and Governor Winthrop in particular, who were responsible for distributing Pequot captives after the war. This fact may have made Wequash more receptive to the particular version of salvation the Bay Colony offered—an enthusiasm evident in the conversion narrative that he performed for Bay Colony observers. Likewise, Wequash's relationship with Williams filtered the way in which Wequash performed conversion in the presence of the Separatist minister. In his letters, Williams records several meetings with Wequash. Over the course of their relationship, the two leaders seemed to view one another with varying degrees of trust and suspicion. At times, Wequash approached Williams as a useful ally. At other times, he worked against Williams and the Narragansett to further the aims of his Pequot kin. These conflicting exchanges not only influenced Wequash's approach to Williams; it also affected how Williams understood their relationship and represented Wequash to his English readers—a tension that extended to Williams' spiritual interpretation of Wequash's soul. What these relationships indicate is that for both Wequash and the colonists, the conversion narrative genre functioned on multiple levels: as a means of articulating a religious experience, as a method for establishing diplomatic relationships, and as a narrative that created new forms of community. Wequash's understanding of the many functions of the conversion narrative genre alongside his desire to employ the genre for its multiple functions led Shepard to interpret the Pequot leader's conversion account as authentic.

Though the ability to directly trace Wequash's influence on subsequent narratives of conversion is difficult, we can compare his account in *New Englands First Fruits* to those that followed. The steps Wequash used to enact his performance of conversion became standard steps that subsequent missionaries and English observers looked for in conversion narratives of other Indigenous converts—among these steps included the convert's showing a firm commitment to an English community, a willingness to put aside "Indigenous ways" in favor of English ones, and a desire to proselytize one's kin. If we think about Wequash's conversion narrative as the first Indigenous conversion narrative circulated among readers in both New England and Old, we can arguably position his account as a precursor to later, more popular conversion narrative accounts like those contained in John Eliot and Thomas Mayhew's 1653 tract *Tears of Repentance*—a tract intended to prove that the Indian mission had progressed to the point that the converts were finally ready to form their own church. Despite attracting popularity among English readers, the Indigenous conversion narratives recorded in *Tears of Repentance* were not convincing enough for the gathered church members to approve the formation of an Indigenous church.[126] The reason for the failure of the initial testimonies seems to have been that they lacked the intense assurance of faith found in Wequash's own narrative—or, as Rivett writes, the testimonies "failed to produce the 'curiosity' that [the missionaries] claimed to be observing among the native population."[127] While there are several reasons that the Natick converts performed conversion differently, one reason may have been the changing colonial and communal conditions. After the Pequot War, the Bay Colony continued to consolidate control in the region, meaning that the possibility for reciprocal relationships was not as readily available to later converts as it had been for Wequash.

Yet Wequash's significance extends beyond his generic contributions to New England literary conventions. As I have shown, he was more than just a discursive figure whose narrative made its way into missionary texts. He was an important Pequot leader. Wequash's actions, and those of his fellow sachems, facilitated the regrowth of the Pequot nation. When Wequash died in 1642, his brother Wequashcook took over his task. In 1664 Wequashcook convinced New England commissioners Daniel Gookin and George Denison to officially to restore the lands claimed by Wequash and Uncas to the Pequot.[128] In his 1677 will, Wequashcook passed that land down to his "wife and children," attempting to ensure that Pequot land would continue to remain in the hands of Pequot people for succeeding generations.[129] Today, Wequash's Pequot descendants continue to live in the lands that Wequash and his family helped to protect. When Wequash engaged with the English leaders, it was in light of his role as a diplomat. When he gathered his fellow Pequot as captives, it was in accordance with his responsibility to restore balance. When he performed Christian practices, it was with a mind to sustain and restore his people. Despite the variation in the textual records referring to Wequash, Wequash himself was consistent. A guide, a leader, and a convert—Wequash was first and foremost a Pequot.

CHAPTER TWO

Questions, Answers, and Treaty-Making

Cutshamekin's Influence on John Eliot's Political Imagination

—ɷ—

Three years after the transatlantic debates between the Bay Colony and Roger Williams over the state of Indigenous conversion in the New England colonies, the Bay Colony made its first sustained efforts to actively develop their meager "first fruits" into a full-fledged harvest. In 1646 Massachusetts Bay leaders officially tasked local ministers to make "knowne ye heavenly counsell of God among ye Indians."[1] One of the first to go was Roxbury minister John Eliot. Despite Eliot's later fame as the "Apostle to the Indians," his initial attempts at proselytization were disastrous. In his missionary tract *The Day-Breaking If Not the Sun-Rising of the Gospel with the Indians in New-England* (1647) and its follow-up, *The Clear Sun-Shine of the Gospel Breaking Forth upon the Indians in New-England* (1648), Eliot provides some brief details about his maiden missionary journey. His journey began on an early September morning in 1646 as the summer heat was slowly giving way to the cool breezes of fall. Together with a few other Puritan ministers and a Montauket interpreter, Cockenoe, Eliot walked about four miles from Roxbury to Neponset, the headquarters of the Massachusett sachem Cutshamekin.[2] Upon his arrival, Eliot and his party greeted the gathering Massachusett and then walked directly to the "principall *Wigwam*," where Cutshamekin resided.[3] Once there, they proceeded to pray and preach to the sachem and his followers. As the missionary later explained, Cutshamekin and his followers were not impressed but instead were "weary, and rather despised what I said."[4] Frustrated by this sound dismissal, Eliot shifted his missionary focus to the less prominent Massachusett leader Waban and his followers, whom Eliot reports were receptive to the Christian message.[5]

When recounting the details of his visit for his English readers, Eliot draws upon a Puritan theology of saving grace to insist that the failure was

60

no fault of his own but rather the consequence of Cutshamekin's lack of preparation. He provides evidence of the sachem's hard-heartedness by comparing the questions asked by both groups of Massachusett after the missionaries' sermon. Whereas Waban and his followers asked, "How might wee come to know Jesus Christ," Cutshamekin and the Massachusett at Neponset pestered the missionaries with demands seemingly unrelated to the content of the sermon. These included inquiries such as "What was the cause of Thunder," the "Ebbing and Flowing of the Sea" and "the wind?" Clarifying the distinction for his readers, Eliot explains that Waban's questions show "cleare understanding" and reflect evidence of the "special wisedom of God"—a response that was "far different from what some other *Indians* under *Kitshomakin* ... had done."[6] Though Cutshamekin eventually joined Eliot's Praying Indian community and even served as the first appointed sachem of the praying town at Natick, Eliot's writings continually portray the Massachusett sachem with suspicion. In an account written as the sachem was nearing death, Eliot reiterates his skepticism about Cutshamekin's religious motives, explaining that though the sachem is "constant in his profession," he was "doubtfull in respect of the throughnesse of his heart."[7]

Contemporary scholars continue to rely heavily on Eliot's portrayal of Cutshamekin as an unrepentant convert when characterizing the role of the Massachusett sachem within the New England missionary project. Yet, whereas Eliot saw Cutshamekin's defiance as evidence of sin, observers today often cite it as an indication of Indigenous resistance. Cutshamekin's rejection of Eliot's conversion attempts serve as evidence that the sachem remained committed to his Massachusett beliefs and community. Pointing to the palpable tension between the Puritan missionary and the Massachusett sachem, they argue that Cutshamekin's eventual partnership with Eliot was one born out of necessity rather than desire. By the 1640s, the Massachusett were reeling from the mass devastation wrought by European diseases at the same time as they were isolated from many of their former allies in the aftermath of the Pequot War. Scholars have posited that Cutshamekin joined the Praying Indian community at Natick out of desperation because it was the sole means of unifying his fragmented community and maintaining some modicum of power in the face of colonial chaos.[8] In contemporary analysis, Eliot's hard-hearted convert has been transformed into a resistant or rebellious sachem-hero working to subvert a developing colonial system in order to promote the interests of his people.

While characterizations of Cutshamekin as either rebellious or resistant aptly reflect the coerced position into which the sachem was placed by colonial powers, they remain, on some level, within Eliot's original binary. Transformed from "bad Indian" to "good," Cutshamekin continues to be defined by Eliot's favor or lack thereof. In this chapter, I forward a more expansive reading of Cutshamekin and the role he played in colonial literary formation by analyzing references to him in terms of his responsibilities as a cross-cultural diplomat—responsibilities that were intricately connected to his status as a Massachusett sachem. A historical analysis of the many pre-1646 references to Cutshamekin and the Massachusett makes it clear that Cutshamekin was an important political leader, well-known among Indigenous and English leaders alike long before Eliot began his missionary work. Cutshamekin was the brother of Chickatawbut, a powerful Massachusett sachem who established diplomatic ties with the Bay Colony authorities. When Cutshamekin was appointed sachem of the Massachusett in 1633, he continued to grow the diplomatic networks his brother had created. During the Pequot War, Cutshamekin served as a guide and diplomatic liaison for the English. By the time of Eliot's 1646 visit to Neponset, Cutshamekin had already spent more than twenty-five years instructing English leaders in the ways of Indigenous diplomacy.

Approaching Cutshamekin as a diplomat not only provides us with a new perspective on an overlooked seventeenth-century Massachusett sachem, but it also allows us to reexamine the role that the Cutshamekin's Indigenous diplomacy played in forming Eliot conceptualization and articulation of his Indigenous mission. Cutshamekin's influence on Eliot comes to the fore when we closely analyze the conditions and content of Eliot's writings. Like the descriptions of Wequash circulated by Roger Williams, Thomas Shepard, and the Bay Colony officials in 1643, Eliot penned his portrayals of Cutshamekin in order to emphasize the conversion potential among the Massachusett and illuminate the success of New England missionary efforts. Adding to Eliot's tendency to characterize Cutshamekin primarily in terms of his conversion potential is the fact that many of Eliot's descriptions of the sachem were composed in retrospect as Eliot and his fellow missionaries attempted to construct a coherent and comprehensive narrative of missionary growth.

However, by reevaluating the rapport between Eliot and Cutshamekin as one of mutual dependence rather than that of proselytizer and potential convert, I show that Cutshamekin's extensive experience and guidance shaped the ways in which Eliot understood and articulated the aims of his Indian mission. Cutshamekin's influence over Eliot is evident from the two men's first recorded meeting in 1646, when the sachem guided Eliot through a series of diplomatic procedures and treaty protocols familiar to New England and Indigenous political leaders. Later, Cutshamekin's guidance helped determine the governing practices that Eliot adapted for the Praying Indian towns. When Eliot began his attempts to form Praying Indian towns, he had extremely little practical experience in political organization. By contrast, Cutshamekin had extensive governing experience, and his status as a sachem meant that he held significant sway over Eliot's potential Massachusett converts. A reading of the textual encounters between the two men over time reveals the growing rapport and mutual dependency that developed between the untested missionary and the experienced sachem.

Eliot prolifically recorded his missionary efforts in letters and tracts. He was responsible for a large portion of the mission tracts published in the wake of *New Englands First Fruits*. Today, the eleven mission tracts published by the Corporation for the Propagation of the Gospel are collective referred to as "The Eliot Tracts"—a lasting reminder of Eliot's influence. It is within Eliot's writings that we can see the beginning formations of many of the genres that missionaries would develop to articulate and facilitate their missionary project. Eliot's account of his first meeting with Cutshamekin in his 1647 tract not only captures the start of the New England missionary project but also inaugurates a distinct genre of missionary writing—the spiritual question genre. In subsequent writings, Eliot and his fellow missionaries continued to transcribe the questions asked and answered by potential converts as a means of illustrating the development of their mission for English readers. Over time, the question-and-answer session became a staple of Bay Colony missionary writings. As Kristina Bross notes, the mission tracts published between 1647 and 1671 contain "nearly two hundred questions" asked and answered by Indigenous people.

64   CHAPTER TWO

More than merely evidence of Indian preparation or the lack thereof, the question-and-answer sessions eventually became "the generic predecessors of the conversion narratives, sermons, dialogues, and dying speeches that later appear in the tracts as evidence of the converts' salvation."[9] The questions first put forward by Cutshamekin eventually developed into a standard means by which English missionaries and readers alike measured the progress of the Puritans' mission to the Indians.

When we analyze the conditions within which the Bay Colony's practice of exchanging questions and answers with potential Indigenous converts developed, we can see that the sessions bear several hallmarks of seventeenth-century Native diplomatic practices. Specifically, they reflect the discursive practices that Cutshamekin himself employed in the years before the missionaries arrived. By placing the question-and-answer sessions in terms of their import to Native, specifically Massachusett, diplomatic practices, the sessions take on a new resonance. The process of exchanging questions and answers was not merely a means by which potential converts showcased their ecclesiastical knowledge for English observers but was also reflective of Indigenous treaty-making practices in the Northeast. Because it was a familiar genre, Indigenous participants approached the question-and-answer sessions as a forum for negotiating and renegotiating the terms of their prior agreements with the English.

Scholars who have addressed the post-sermon question-and-answer sessions have primarily positioned the practice in terms of its relationship to Protestant New England literary practices—an analysis fueled by Eliot himself.[10] When describing his sessions, Eliot terms them "Catechisme[s]," effectively locating his actions within a long line of Christian proselytizers who interrogated potential or newly converted practitioners to verify the penitent's comprehension of spiritual matters.[11] Yet sole focus on the English context of the missionary texts ignores the conditions within which the texts themselves were created. While the question-and-answer sessions are unmistakably shaped by the aims of the Puritan missionaries—or as Bross writes, the questions "exist . . . because Eliot took the ongoing encounter of Indians and missionaries and constructed a narrative for English consumption"—as a genre of discourse that facilitated an exchange between the missionaries and their potential converts, the question-and-answer session also "exists because it works."[12] Cutshamekin participated in the question-and-answer sessions as part of his larger attempts to instruct Eliot and the English in the discursive practices that governed Native space. Although Eliot would later include Cutshamekin's questions in his tracts for English readers, the context out of which they developed was Indigenous.

Cutshamekin's influence on Eliot was not limited to the question-and-answer sessions. The Massachusett sachem also helped form the English missionary's conceptions of political governance. Following their 1646 meetings, Cutshamekin continued to guide Eliot as he went about the process of forming the first Praying Indian community at Natick—a community that is significantly governed by what Jean O'Brien terms a "hybrid government," incorporating "elements from three kinds of polities: English, Indian, and scriptural."[13] Around the same time as he and Cutshamekin were working to establish the governing system at Natick, Eliot was also concerned about England's political system which was in the midst of the English Civil War. In late 1651 or early 1652, Eliot penned his political treatise *The Christian Commonwealth*, addressed to Oliver Cromwell and his followers. Noted as "the first book of political theory written by an American," Eliot's tract proposed a new governing system for England based on the practices instituted at Natick.[14] While the tract has been cited as the product of Eliot's utopic vision rendered through the lens of Puritan millennial theology, I contend that a close reading of the tract in light of Eliot's relationship with Cutshamekin reveals evidence that Eliot's utopic imagination was shaped in part by Cutshamekin's deft political instruction. Derived from the governing structure established at Natick, the foundational principles of the system that Eliot proscribes for England relied on existing Massachusett practices. Deliberately or not, *The Christian Commonwealth* endorses kinship units as a means of organizing society at the same time as it promotes a judicial system parallel to the one practiced by Cutshamekin and the Massachusett. *The Christian Commonwealth* provides evidence that Cutshamekin's influence was not limited to Eliot's missionary practices, but rather that the sachem's instruction became embedded into Eliot's political imagination. Irrevocably changed through his relationship with the sachem, Eliot textually adapts Cutshamekin's instructions and sends them back across the Atlantic in a guide he hoped would shape the political future of the English nation.

Setting the Stage

Because Eliot's writings have so thoroughly embedded Cutshamekin within the New England missionary narrative, his status as a political leader is often overlooked, or when mentioned, is seen as tangential to his interactions with the Puritan missionaries. However, Cutshamekin's actions within the New England mission are inseparable from his responsibilities as a sachem. In both roles, Cutshamekin was guided by his attempts to facilitate common pot diplomacy—to teach the English that "the actions of the newcomers would affect the whole."[15] Contextualizing Cutshamekin's actions within this framework allows us to map the sachem's actions with consistency. While Eliot's September 1646 visit to Cutshamekin marks the start of the New England missionary project, Eliot's trek to Neponset was by no means the first time the sachem had received English visitors. Members of his Massachusett nation were some of the first to engage with the arriving English settlers. In 1622 Cutshamekin's brother, the sachem Chickatawbut, confronted Myles Standish and the starving Plymouth colonists after they had destroyed the grave of his mother in their attempts to find corn.[16] Chickatawbut later established ties with the Bay Colony settlers and eventually became a well-known figure at Governor Winthrop's dinner table.[17] At Chickatawbut's death from small pox in 1633, Cutshamekin was appointed sachem in his stead.[18] Continuing to build upon the diplomatic ties established by his brother, Cutshamekin served as a key intermediary and translator facilitating negotiations among the Massachusett, the Narragansett, the Pequot, and the Bay Colony. In this role, he advised colonial leaders on how to properly treat with the local Indigenous nations. Neal Salisbury cites Cutshamekin as "the most effective single agent in dissuading the Narragansett from neutrality" in the Pequot War.[19]

Cutshamekin's diplomatic sagacity not only gives us a glimpse into the long history of exchange between the Bay Colony and the Massachusett but also provides an important social context for the question-and-answer sessions that would later come to define New England missionary writing. Though the nature of the colonial records makes it challenging to recover Cutshamekin's early conversations with the Bay Colony, descriptions of the sachem's actions and the cultural patterns they reflect can be a key to uncovering both the manner and meaning of the sachem's cross-cultural discourse. Evidence of Cutshamekin's long history of diplomatic negotiation can be glimpsed in Governor Winthrop's account of the sachem's actions during the Pequot War. Like Wequash, Cutshamekin allied with the English and Narragansett out of his kinship obligations to protect his community. In 1636 Winthrop appointed the sachem to serve as an interpreter for an English punitive expedition to Block Island to find the Pequot whom the Bay Colony leaders held responsible for the death of English trader John Oldham.[20]

Though Winthrop had appointed Cutshamekin as an aid the English, Cutshamekin performed his role out of his responsibilities as a sachem. One task of the sachem was to "mediate . . . contact between the world outside of the community" by entertaining visitors, managing diplomatic affairs, and liaising with other sachems.[21] Before colonial settlement, northeastern leaders had long negotiated among themselves using treaties, an established multitribal diplomatic genre. As Lumbee legal scholar Robert Williams Jr. writes, the treaty genre was a "remarkably adaptive language [that] could be used to conclude wars and make peace, cement military alliances, or secure a valued trade partner among groups with diverse languages, customs, and traditions." More than merely a legal arrangement, treaties bound communities together. For Indigenous participants, "treaties were seen . . . as divinely mandated covenants of law and peace between peoples." They "required treaty partners to acknowledge their shared humanity and to act upon a set of constitutional values reflection the unity of interests generated by their agreement."[22] In his role as mediator, Cutshamekin facilitated agreements between the Massachusett and their neighbors that recognized the potential ties of kinship and negotiated the ways in which those kinship obligations would be upheld and maintained.

Cutshamekin's diplomatics can be glimpsed in an incident Winthrop recounts from the 1636 expedition. As the English neared Narragansett territory, Winthrop writes that Cutshamekin, "being armed with a corslet and a piece," silently "crept into a swamp and killed a Pequot." The sachem subsequently "flayed off the skin of his head [and] sent it to Canonicus."[23] Cutshamekin's actions serve as a message to Canonicus and the Narragansett, assuring them that the Massachusett and Massachusett Bay were willing to aid them in their fight against the Pequot—a message to which Canonicus responded.[24] After receiving the scalp, Winthrop writes that the Narragansett sachem "presently sent it to all the sachems about him. & returned manye thankes to the Englishe" at the same time as he "sent [a] fath: of wampom to Cutshamkin."[25] Invoking the web of kinship ties and alliances that existed among the nations of the Indigenous Northeast, Canonicus's actions signal that the Narragansett would align with the Massachusett and the English against the Pequot.[26] His decision to send wampum to Cutshamekin directly, rather than to the English, illustrates the use of another tool of northeastern Indigenous diplomacy, wampum. Made of white beads from whelk shells and purple-black beads from quahog shells, wampum and wampum belts "bound people together, and bound words to deeds."[27] In sending the wampum directly to Cutshamekin, Canonicus simultaneously recognizes the ties of kinship between the Narragansett and the Massachusett and acknowledges that the role that the Massachusett sachem played in facilitating diplomacy.[28] In October 1636 the Narragansett sachems Canonicus and Miantonomi met with Cutshamekin and the Bay Colony leaders and formalized their alliance against the Pequot.[29]

Throughout the Pequot War, Cutshamekin continued his attempts to maintain alliances between the Narragansett, the Massachusett, and the English. However, after the 1638 Treaty of Hartford formally ended the Pequot War, tensions between the Bay Colony and the Narragansett escalated. The two former allies now continually attacked one another as the Bay Colony attempted to set itself up as the established power in the region and obtain ownership over Pequot lands and captives. Cutshamekin and his fellow sachems strove to maneuver between both parties with limited success. On June 22, 1643, two of Cutshamekin's allies, the Pawtuxet sachem Soconoco and the Shawomet sachem Pumham, approached Governor Winthrop with a request that they be accorded protection from the Narragansett in return for their allegiance. Winthrop readily agreed to their request.[30] The sachems' request was even more appealing to Winthrop because it was a direct challenge to the Bay Colony's former ally turned rival, the Narragansett, as both Soconoco and Pumham were Narragansett tributaries.

In the midst of their attempts to create alliances that would weaken the Narragansett after the Pequot War, the Bay Colony turned once more

Questions, Answers, and Treaty-Making   69

to Cutshamekin. Manipulating both Cutshamekin's alliance with the Bay Colony and his knowledge of Northeast Indigenous kinship connections, Massachusetts Bay leaders forced the sachem to publicly testify against Miantonomi in a land dispute between the Bay Colony, the Narragansett, and Samuel Gorton—an English settler who, like Roger Williams, continually challenged the Bay Colony's land rights in the region.[31] In 1642 Miantonomi had treated with Gorton for access to a large tract of land claimed by Soconoco and Pumham south of Pawtuxet. Miantonomi based his right to make the treaty as a result of the tributary status that the two sachems had earlier established with the Narragansett. The Bay Colony required Cutshamekin to serve as their expert witness and explain the nature of tributary claims among the local Indigenous nations. Backed into a corner, Cutshamekin testified that the Pawtuxet and Shawomet sachems were "free sachems as himself." He explained that even though Soconoco and Pumham sometimes sent Miantonomi gifts in honor of his status, they retained the rights to their own land.[32] The Bay Colony then used Cutshamekin's testimony as justification to nullify Gorton's land claims and place Soconoco and Pumham (and their land) under Bay Colony jurisdiction. Cutshamekin's testimony effectively severed his connections to his former Narragansett allies.

Following his testimony against Miantonomi, Cutshamekin moved to shore up his ties with the Bay Colony.[33] In December of 1643, a few months after the treaty between Soconoco, Pumham, and the Bay Colony, Cutshamekin, his nephew and eventual successor, Josias Wompatuck, and the Agawam sachem Masconomet privately met with Winthrop to initiate a similar treaty with the Bay Colony. Though the treaty would require a significant curtailing of Massachusett power, Cutshamekin likely decided it would be in the best interests of the Massachusett to initiate a treaty with the Bay Colony on his own terms in order to retain some negotiation rights rather than be forced into English subjection or overtaken by the now-angered Narragansett.[34] In March of 1644, four sachems and one saunkskwa formally signed an agreement with the Bay Colony officials at the courthouse in Boston. In addition to Cutshamekin and Masconomet, signatories included Nipmuc sachems Nashowanon and Wossamegon and the Pawtucket saunkskwa "Squa Sachem." The terms of the treaty stated that Cutshamekin and the others "put orselues, or subjects, lands,

& estates under the government & jurisdiction of the Massachusets, to bee governed & ptected by them."[35]

Negotiating Submission

The signing of these treaties marked a turning point in the relationship between the Bay Colony and its Indigenous allies.[36] As Salisbury explains, the treaties created "a new legal status" for Cutshamekin and the Massachusett in which they "were neither independent nor assimilated into white society"[37] Yet despite the clear shift in power dynamics, Cutshamekin remained a powerful leader in his own right. At the time of the 1644 treaty, he retained several followers and tributaries. He was also caretaker for large tracts of land. When Cutshamekin treated with the Bay Colony, he did not just speak for himself and his fellow Massachusett. Rather, he sought protection from Massachusetts Bay in "his own name and the names of all the sachems of Watchusett, and all the Indians from Merrimack to Tecticutt."[38] Regardless of his agreement with the Bay Colony, Cutshamekin's status as a sachem could not be revoked at the hands of the English. It was as a sachem with his community in mind that Cutshamekin entered into talks with the English.

While the 1644 treaty marks a change in political power between the Bay Colony and the Massachusett, it also provides the generic background for the question-and-answer sessions that would later permeate Bay Colony missionary writings. These 1644 negotiations between the Bay Colony, Cutshamekin, and his fellow sachems took place nearly two years before Eliot started his missionary work and serve as the first recorded instance of Cutshamekin's participation in a question-and-answer session. In both the 1644 treaties and his later exchanges with Eliot, Cutshamekin's words cannot be separated from the larger actions surrounding them. Among the Indigenous tribes of the Northeast, diplomacy was performed through a number of linguistic and physical practices. As Cree literary scholar Stephanie Fitzgerald writes, Indigenous legal performance of the time was a "ritualized act" that was intended to "transmit . . . 'social knowledge, memory, and identity.'"[39] Bay Colony court records indicate that the treaty between Cutshamekin, his fellow sachems, and the Bay Colony consisted of two parts: First, the sachems assented to a formal prepared statement. Second, they participated in a question-and-answer session in which English officials asked "Certaine Questions" of the sachems intended to ensure that they "understand the articles"—the two ceremonies went hand in hand.[40]

While we cannot be sure, it seems likely that Winthrop's inclusion of the question-and-answer session was a direct result of Cutshamekin's presence. Both the 1643 treaty with Soconoco and Pumham and the 1644 treaty with Cutshamekin employ identical written statements; however, Bay Colony officials include the question-and-answer session only in the account of their meeting with Cutshamekin. Their decision to include the question-and-answer session would have been both practical and political. In the records of his proceedings with Soconoco and Pumham, Winthrop explains that the treaty was conducted through the actions of an interpreter, Benedict Arnold, indicating that the sachems did not have a strong command of the English language.[41] Arnold is not mentioned at the 1644 meetings with Cutshamekin—an omission that was presumably the result of the sachem's English fluency.[42] Furthermore, as less powerful sachems, Soconoco and Pumham did not have the same established relationships with Bay Colony leaders as Cutshamekin, who, by the time of the 1644 treaty, had already participated in numerous diplomatic dealings with Winthrop and the Bay Colony. Because of their established relationship, Winthrop either felt comfortable asking Cutshamekin additional questions or felt that the questions were a necessary means of clarifying the sachem's intentions.

Regardless of Winthrop's intentions, Cutshamekin's experience in diplomatic exchange led the sachem to use the formal, public nature of the post-treaty question-and-answer session as a means of protecting his right to continue Massachusett practices.[43] Relying on the language and conventions of treaty literature, the sachem reacts to Winthrop's questions as an invitation for negotiation rather than a means of providing consent. His responses amend and adapt the language of the questions in order to explicitly spell out additional rights for the Indigenous signers. For example, in the first question, the Bay Colony officials ask if the sachems are willing to "worship ye onely true God, wch made heaven & earth, & not to blaspheme him." When replying, Cutshamekin and his fellow sachems change the wording of the question. They explain that they are willing to "*reverence* ye God . . . and to *speake well* of him" because they see that the English God "doth better to ye English than othr gods do to others."[44]

This slight but significant rewording means that the sachems agree only to respect the English God, not to worship him—an important distinction that corresponds to Algonquian cosmological understandings. Like Wequash and the Pequot discussed in the previous chapter, the Massachusett also believed the world was full of manitou, or "the spirit that flows through all beings."[45] In agreeing to revere the Christian God because of the favor that he has bestowed upon the English, Cutshamekin and the sachems consent to include the Christian God as one source of manitou among the many other sources already present in their belief system. Through their slight turn of phrase, the sachems avoid acquiescing to the Puritans' request that they accept monotheism. Rather, they carefully craft their response to situate Christianity with their existing practices.

During the post-treaty question-and-answer session, Cutshamekin and his fellow sachems also added stipulations for English signers. When Winthrop and the Bay Colony authorities asked if the sachems would be willing "to suffer their children to learn to reade Gods word, yt they may learn to know God aright, & worship him in his owne way," the sachems responded by placing limits on English authority. Their children could be instructed in Christianity only "as opportunity will serve" and only as long as the "English live among ym." Rather than providing the Bay Colony authorities with carte blanche authorization to instruct their children, the sachems retain the right to determine the length and extent of English education. Further, the sachems only grant the English educational access as long as the English are living among them. This means that the English can only provide instruction to Indigenous children when they reside within a specific location—a location determined by the sachems themselves. In this deft linguistic manipulation, the sachems use the question-and-answer process to further negotiate with the English in a public performance of sovereignty.

In line with Indigenous treaty-making conventions, Cutshamekin and his fellow signatories likely saw the 1644 treaty as a starting point for continued negotiations between themselves and the Bay Colony that would be worked out through reciprocal relationships. Within the ever-shifting web that bound together the Indigenous communities along the northeastern Atlantic coast, treaty-making was both a political and spiritual act requiring leaders to repeatedly come together and define the terms of their communal relationship.[46] Cutshamekin's willingness to respect English power and acknowledge Christian beliefs in exchange for protection was illustrative of his sustained desire to work with the English using the conventions of common pot diplomacy.

However, Governor Winthrop interpreted the treaty as evidence that the sachem and his followers were eager to participate in both the political and spiritual life of the Bay Colony.[47] Following his initial February 1644 meeting with Cutshamekin, an optimistic Governor Winthrop wrote in his journal, "We now began to conceive hope that the Lord's time was at hand for opening a door of light and grace to those Indians."[48] Cutshamekin's performance of diplomacy and his understanding of English practice had a reflective effect. Though grounded in Indigenous history, the sachem adapted his diplomatic practices to fit an English context—the result being that the sachem's adeptness at diplomacy confirmed existing English assumptions that they were the ones bringing "civility" and Christianity to the "wilderness."

Diplomacy and Conversion

Nearly two years after the 1644 treaty was signed, Eliot and his fellow ministers embarked upon their missionary journey to Neponset with confidence and zeal, "having sought God" rather than an invitation from Cutshamekin.[49] Using their interpretation of the 1644 treaty as a practical guide for enacting their mission, Eliot and his fellow Bay Colony missionaries chose Cutshamekin as their first missionary target because of his command of the English language and because "his preeminence among the sachems of 1644 probably led [them] to assume that he was the one most eager to receive Christian instruction."[50] As Eliot recounts, upon arrival the missionary and his party approached Neponset with salutations and then proceeded directly to Cutshamekin's "principall *Wigwam*." The ministers then began to pray and preach to the Massachusett who gathered outside Cutshamekin's door.[51]

Following the conventions of Protestant missions, the missionaries' opening sermon was intended to transmit "all the principall matter of religion" to the gathered attendees. This included a description of the Ten Commandments, the wrath of God, and the salvation offered by Jesus Christ, who was, Eliot told his listeners, "the only meanes of recovery from sinne and wrath and eternall death." In closing, the ministers detailed a Christian cosmology of creation and proclaimed that God was "the maker of all things." They then offered a call for salvation, presenting their listeners with a choice—to accept Christian teachings or reject them. The call for salvation took the form of a question-and-answer session. The Puritan ministers first asked Cutshamekin and the gathered Massachusett clarifying questions and then solicited additional questions. As Eliot explains, the questions were intended as a means by which the missionaries "might skrue by variety of meanes something or other of God into them."[52]

The missionaries' attempts did not go as planned, and a discouraged Eliot lists only three partial questions that resulted from the encounter. The questions, which seem to have been asked by Cutshamekin, included, "1. What was the cause of Thunder. 2. Of the Ebbing and Flowing of the Sea. 3. Of the Wind."[53] Yet, while Eliot dismissed Cutshamekin's questions because they "did not signal a desire to enter into Christian dialogue," the questions do not seem to represent the complete rejection that Eliot ascribes to them.[54] If we consider Cutshamekin's status as a diplomat and his past usage of question-and-answer sessions, we can read the sachem's post-sermon questions as an attempt to negotiate the terms of Eliot's proselytization request. More specifically, the sachem's questions gesture to his desire to interrogate the complicated ties between politics and religion that lay at the heart of the Puritan missionary project.

In his analysis of Cutshamekin's questions, Craig White points out that the sachem's focus on natural phenomena may have been a response to Puritan descriptions of God as the creator. White suggests that Massachusetts' questions "may have been urging Eliot to relate origin stories such as might have been exchanged if their guests had been visiting Indians."[55] However, Cutshamekin's past performance indicates that the sachem's questions are more than just a general attempt at discussion; rather, they point to a specific method of diplomatic negotiation. All three of the natural phenomena Cutshamekin mentions—thunder, the sea, and the wind—were natural elements known among the Massachusett as sites of particularly powerful manitou. The occurrence of thunder was a sign of a thunderbird's visit.[56] Providing rain for the earth and substance for the people, the thunderbirds generally signaled renewal, and the birds often left a stone as a sign of their visit. As powerful protectors, the thunderbirds helped shield the people from their counterpart, "the giant horned or antlered, under(water) world serpent." The serpent rendered the sea a liminal place. A source of life and death, the serpent was both feared and treated with great respect. As "halves of the same unity," the two beings (one in the sky and one in the sea) represented a central means by which the Algonquian spiritual and physical worlds remained balanced.[57] The presence of the underwater serpent is invoked by Cutshamekin's second question, which asks Eliot the source of "the Ebbing and Flowing of the Sea."

Cutshamekin's decision to evoke these two powerful beings is in line with his status as a diplomat attempting to retain balance within his community. Fitzgerald explains that the thunderbird and the serpent were significant figures in diplomatic exchanges and their images "have been found on pre-contact amulets and pictographs."[58] For the Massachusett, the delicate power balance represented by the two creatures was clearly threatened by the arrival of the European settlers—a threat Cutshamekin may be alluding to with his reference to wind. In his 1634 *New England's Prospect* English colonist William Wood recounted a story he heard from the local people about an early encounter with an arriving European ship. As Wood writes, his Indigenous source had described the ship as a "walking Island," taking "the Mast to be a Tree, the Saile white Clouds, and the discharging of Ordinance for Lightning and Thunder."[59] In locating the English alongside the symbols of manitou like the thunderbird and the underwater serpent, Native people along the coast presciently "recognized the Europeans as dangerous and powerful."[60] Invoking the political and spiritual threat represented by the colonists, Cutshamekin employs the conventions of diplomacy to transform the English question-and-answer session into a discussion with Eliot that asks the missionary to articulate the role the colonists intended to play within the existing governing system.[61]

Eliot was stymied by Cutshamekin's response, and he left the exchange frustrated at his failed proselytization attempts. The missionary's response indicates that the question-and-answer genre failed to achieve its desired ends—or to use Kenneth Burke's well-known phrase, it failed to facilitate the "acting together" of the Bay Colony and the Massachusett at Neponset. One reason for this failure was political. The emergence of the 1644 treaty and its concurrent redefinition of Massachusett-English relations as well as the emergence of the Puritan mission constituted a new social situation for question-and-answer session. Whereas Winthrop had deployed the question-and-answer sessions in 1644 as a means of facilitating cross-cultural diplomacy, Eliot had little experience in Indigenous diplomacy and instead attempted to enact the genre to garner spiritual consent.

The missionary's use of the question-and-answer session was also shaped by the scientific and theological discourses taking place within the English world during the mid-seventeenth century. As Rivett indicates, the publication of Eliot's missionary tracts coincided with the rise of British empiricism, and as such, Eliot's questions attempted to "conjoin . . . the enigma of grace and Baconian procedures of natural science such that a holy empiricism of sorts became a hallmark of Puritan practices of faith."[62] The questions and answers recorded in the mission tracts drew in English readers who hoped to peer into the souls of an exoticized other whose subjectivities seemed to be made accessible through text.

Before his missionary ventures, one of Eliot's most prominent roles outside the pulpit was as a juror in Anne Hutchinson's church trial. The recorded transcripts of the Hutchinson trial consist of a series of interrogations that the Bay Colony leaders hoped would bring hidden things to light—or, as Eliot states during the trial, would force Hutchinson to "express her selfe playnly."[63] While the interrogators hoped Hutchinson would publicly confess her heterodoxy and then face the necessary punishment required to bring her back into society, Hutchinson responded with questions of her own, questions that often challenged the authority of the Bay Colony establishment by appealing to scriptural passages.[64] Angered at Hutchinson's unwillingness to confess and repent, Eliot and the other authorities became increasingly accusatory in their questioning.[65] For English readers already skeptical of the New England colonial project, the transcripts of the Hutchinson trial continued to portray Eliot and the colonial Puritan orthodoxy in an unfavorable light. In recording the questions and answers of potential Indigenous converts, Bross suggests that Eliot hoped to redeem the Bay Colony's image by foregrounding the success of their earlier forays into Indian missions.[66]

Yet despite the failings of his first missionary attempt, Eliot did not abandon the question-and-answer session altogether. The missionary's later accounts prolifically employ the practice as a means of detailing the progress of the Indian mission. In fact, Eliot's assiduous use of the question-and-answer session eventually renders it a central genre of the missionary project—one that combined elements of both Algonquian diplomacy and Puritan spiritual practice. In terms of genre theory, the "new conditions" of the Puritan mission produced a "new genre—and a new recurrent situation."[67] The creation of this new genre was partly the result of the changing social conditions of Massachusett-English relations that occurred with the development of the Puritan mission. The increasing consolidation of English authority in the region meant that missionaries had an amplified ability to determine the generic aims of Indigenous proselytes.

At the same time, the missionaries themselves were also becoming more aware of Indigenous social practices. Anxious to advance his mission-ary aims, Eliot began to study the Massachusett language and over time became familiar with its linguistic conventions. As Steffi Dippold points out, Eliot and his fellow missionaries closely studied Wôpanâak, because "colonial semiotics relied on the keen comprehension, incorporation, and appreciation of native practices."[68] As part of his missionary aims, Eliot also sought to strengthen his ties with leaders like Cutshamekin, whom he termed "the Sachems of greatest note," because "that doth greatly animate and encourage such as are well-affected, and is a dampening to those that are scoffers and opposers."[69]

The emergence of this new genre is evident in Eliot's 1647 tract *The Clear Sun-Shine of the Gospel Breaking Forth upon the Indians in New-England*. A year after his first failed attempt at missions, Eliot records another set of post-sermon questions asked and answered by potential Indigenous converts. Once again, Eliot's record prioritizes the interro-gations of the newly converted Cutshamekin. Attempting to showcase the sachem's burgeoning knowledge of Christian salvation, Eliot focuses on the sachem's fluent use of Christian dialogue.[70] Rather than referenc-ing Massachusett cosmology, Cutshamekin now repeats the language of Christianity, and of sin in particular. Eliot's recollection begins with Cutshamekin's description of how he is plagued by his sinful heart, which the sachem explains is now "more sinful than ever it was before." Bemoaning the fact that following his conversion he has not become less sinful but more, Cutshamekin asks Eliot "whether is this a sin or not?"[71]

For English readers, the sachem's question invokes a key tenant of Protestantism—Cutshamekin's conversion has produced within him an awareness of sin that he previously lacked. The sachem's question acknowledges the fact that his conversion had made him realize how sinful he was and still remains. He essentially asks: "Is it sinful to still be as sinful as I was now that I know how sinful I was?" Eager to claim Cutshamekin's growing command of Protestant discourse as evidence of the sachem's heartfelt desire to participate in the English Christian community, Eliot glosses the question: "This question could not be learned from the English, nor did it seem a coyned feigned thing, but a reall matter gathered from the experience of his own heart, and from an inward observation of himself."[72]

Despite Eliot's assurances that the questions are evidence that the sachem's spiritual transformation has resulted in a seemingly divine knowledge of English generic conventions, if we contextualize the exchange in terms of Cutshamekin's past history, the question serves as evidence that even after his performance of conversion, Cutshamekin continues to employ Massachusett linguistic and diplomatic practices. Though he uses the language of Protestant conversion, Cutshamekin's question continues his earlier dialogue with Eliot about the relationship between Indigenous and English systems. When located within a Massachusett cosmology, which prioritized the close ties between manitou and humanity, we can in part see Cutshamekin's question as a means of asking why the manitou present in the Christian God is not working for himself and his people. With almost palpable desperation, Cutshamekin seems to demand of Eliot, "Why are things not getting better now that I am diligently performing Christian rituals?" The first part of the question evokes the time before he committed to joining Eliot's community: "Before I knew God . . . I thought I was well." Yet, instead of gaining manitou after his conversion, Cutshamekin feels he is losing strength. He exclaims, "my heart is but very little better then it was, and I am afraid it will be as bad againe as it was before."[73] Though cloaked in the language of Christian conversion, the sachem's question continues to interrogate the effectiveness of Christianity in relationship to Algonquian cosmology. "Why," the sachem seems to be asking the missionary, "is it not working?"

Though Eliot's writings attempt to portray Cutshamekin as subject to Bay Colony political and religious authority, the sachem continued to hold significant sway among his Massachusett followers. In November of 1648 Eliot writes, "Our *Cutshamoquin* hath some subjects in *Marthas Vineyard*, and they hearing of his praying to God, some of them doe the like there."[74] The influential sachem also maintained his standing among the other regional Indigenous leaders. In 1651 Eliot reports an incident in which Cutshamekin "was in the Countrey neere *Narragansett*, about appeasing some strife among some *Sachems*."[75] Still serving as a central figure in negotiations between the settlers and the local Indigenous nations, Cutshamekin's performance of conversion does not dampen his status as a leader or change his influence as a cross-cultural diplomat. Cloaked in the language of Christian practice, the question-and-answer sessions continued to be a forum within which the sachem defined and negotiated the terms of his relationship with the English.

Sachem Diplomacy and the Founding of Natick

In 1650, as Eliot was making plans to formalize the establishment of the Praying Indian town of Natick, we can see evidence that the sachem continued to instruct the missionary in the language of diplomacy. Eliot viewed the formation of praying towns as a vehicle for "fixing Indians in a geographically bounded place on which cultural negotiations would occur." Gathering potential converts together would allow Eliot to provide them with the focused instruction he believed necessary for an intellectual understanding of Christian doctrine. Yet before doctrine came cultural accommodation. As O'Brien notes, "Eliot's ideas about missionization envisioned the transformation of Indian land use, social institutions, and cultural forms as precursors to actual religious conversion."[76] For English observers, the Praying Indian towns continued the colonial work performed by Indigenous conversion narratives. Both signaled a change of allegiance. An Indigenous person's decision to relocate to a Praying Indian town, much like their performance of conversion, indicated to the English their willingness to abandon their kinship ties with an Indigenous community in favor of kinship with the English.

Yet, in reality, many of the Indigenous people who moved to Natick made their decision to move as a result of their Indigenous kinship ties. Communally relocating to Natick provided them with a chance to gather with relatives from whom they had been separated as a result of war, disease, or encroaching English land claims.[77] Those who came to Natick were promised English protection and land security—something they lacked elsewhere. As O'Brien writes, some of those who moved to Natick were not moving at all, but returning to ancestral lands they hoped they could secure by "having them bounded within the English system."[78] Cutshamekin was among those who moved to Natick out of his obligation to his Massachusett kin, and a number of his Massachusett and Nipmuc relatives from Nonantum and Neponset moved as well. As their sachem, Cutshamekin continued his leadership role by instructing Eliot in Indigenous ways and, when necessary, by standing against Eliot in defense of his people.

When the missionary made his initial public call among the Massachusett to form a Praying Indian community, Cutshamekin strongly warned him against it. In the 1650 tract *The Light Appearing More and More*, Eliot explains that Cutshamekin "openly contested with me against our proceeding to make a Town." According to Eliot, Cutshamekin's opposition to the formation of a praying town stemmed from his fear that "religion will make a great change" to existing social structures, in part because it would curtail the sachem's powers, or in Eliot's words, it would "cut . . . off [the sachems] from their former tyranny." In writing to his English audience, Eliot belittles Cutshamekin's concerns regarding social upheaval by explaining that sachem rule was akin to dictatorship in which the sachems "hold their people in absolute servitude" and extract "tribute" according to their whims. The result of the servitude for Eliot was that the Massachusett were "*in great awe of their Sachem.*" Eliot argues that Christianity, by contrast, would give the Praying Indians increased autonomy in that it allowed them a framework within which to "admonish" the sachem to follow God's laws and at the same time, it also diminished their need to pay tribute to the sachem.[79]

Despite Eliot's heavyhanded narration, Cutshamekin's history provides a more probable reason why he was opposed to the establishment of a praying town at Natick—his past experience with Massachusett Bay politics and his concurrent concern for Algonquian sovereignty. Eliot and his fellow missionaries intended Natick to serve as the start of a larger project—one for which the sachems had not given their consent. As Eliot writes, the praying town structure was to be "a general way" for the Bay Colony "to instruct all the Indians in all parts." No longer limiting their efforts to the Massachusett, the English hoped to create Praying Indian towns among "the

Monohegans, Narragansett, &c."[80] More than just the occasional religious instruction that the sachems agreed to in the 1644 treaty, the establishment of multiple Indian polities controlled by the English would provide additional means for English regulation of Indigenous bodies and spaces.

Cutshamekin's challenge to Eliot's proposal is once again performed within the structures of Algonquian diplomatic conventions. As Eliot writes, Cutshamekin drew upon his existing status as regional leader to mount his opposition to the praying towns in consensus with his fellow sachems. In his public challenge, Cutshamekin tells Eliot that "all the Sachems in the Countrey were against it." His reference to communal consensus alongside his public interrogation of Eliot signals to the attendant Massachusett that Cutshamekin was invoking his status as a powerful leader. As Eliot explains, "when [Cutshamekin] did so carry himself, all the Indians were filled with fear, their countenances grew pale, and most of them slunk away." Eliot's response to the sachem's challenge unwittingly plays out within the same system of signification. Responding with "bold resolution," Eliot tells Cutshamekin, "it was Gods work I was about, and he was with me, and I feared not him, nor all the sachems in the country." According to Eliot's account, his invocation of divine power and his ties to the Bay Colony were enough to convince the Massachusett that he was the more powerful leader. In response, Eliot writes, Cutshamekin's "spirit shrunk before me." As Eliot later claims, Cutshamekin's response stemmed from the sachem's loss of public puissance, in which "[the Massachusett] account him that shrinks to be conquered, and the other to conquer; which alas, I knew not."[81] In recounting this story to his English supporters, Eliot frames this episode as proof that he has "conquered" the sachem by diminishing his status among his Massachusett followers.

While this episode is interesting for its invocation of Algonquian diplomatic rituals, what is more striking in terms of the development of a communal discourse are Cutshamekin's actions afterward. Despite his clear public humiliation, Cutshamekin continues to advance the interests of the larger community over his own. Eliot writes that the sachem "went a little way with me" and further explained the reasons for his opposition to Eliot's plan. Appealing to Eliot's own interests, Cutshamekin explains that Eliot's plan would not only upset the Algonquian social order but, if implemented, would also hinder Eliot's own efforts at proselytization. As Cutshamekin explains, the proposal for the praying town resulted in "all the Sachems" deciding to "set themselves against praying to God."[82] The discussion between Eliot and the sachem provides yet more evidence that Cutshamekin continued to try to facilitate the working together of the English and the Algonquian by bringing the English into the common pot—attempts that were recognized and received by his fellow Massachusett.

Eliot includes his public confrontation with Cutshamekin to celebrate what he sees as the increasing authority and success of the Puritan mission. Yet Eliot's subsequent actions in relation to Cutshamekin reinforce the fact that Eliot himself continued to be aware of, and potentially threatened by, the sachem's sustained influence over Eliot's potential Massachusett converts. In a calculated move, Eliot waited to hold elections for Natick leadership until Cutshamekin was out of town. In 1651, while Cutshamekin was "appeasing some strife among some *Sachems,*" Eliot held the elections to which Cutshamekin was opposed.[83] Intended to determine a new "civill order and Government," the elections served as the necessary first step in Eliot's plan to transform the Praying Indians from a "scattered course of life" into English "civility." In August of 1651 Eliot gathered together representatives from both Nonantum and Neponset so that he might "forme them . . . into a visible Church-state." For guidance in this new commonwealth, Eliot instructs those gathered "that they should looke onlely into the Scriptures, and out of the word of God fetch all their Wisedome, Lawes, and Government."[84]

Though Eliot waited until Cutshamekin was absent to hold the initial elections for governance at Natick, Cutshamekin's presence was still prominently felt. As Eliot writes, "Before that day came, even then when it was appointed for *Cutshamoquin,* the chiefe *Sachem,* and therefore chosen the chiefe (for hee is constant in profession, though doubtfull in respect of the throughnesse of his heart)."[85] In this convoluted phrasing, Eliot acknowledges that despite his attempt to curtail the sachem's influence, Cutshamekin's followers still chose their sachem to serve as their leader. Though Eliot is attempting to establish a "new" system of governance, he cannot evade the influence of Cutshamekin and the staying power of the established system. By continuing to instruct Eliot and the English in the ways of Indigenous governance, Cutshamekin and the Massachusett worked to ensure that Natick was, from its inception, "an Indian place."[86]

The *Christian Commonwealth* and the Transatlantic Cutshamekin

Attention to Eliot's writings about Cutshamekin reveal that the sachem and the missionary had a long history of conflict and cooperation. In fact, it was through conflict that cooperation occurred. Cutshamekin's willingness to challenge, to educate, and to negotiate with Eliot on both spiritual and political matters led the missionary to gradually adopt many of Cutshamekin's practices as his own. Relatedly, Eliot's repeated frustration with the sachem and his influence reveals the status that Cutshamekin retained among his Massachusett followers and the concurrent power he held over Eliot. Though the process of exchange between the two men is often obscured by Eliot's narrative voice, from his first meeting with Eliot until his death, Cutshamekin played a significant role in shaping Eliot's thoughts, actions, and writings.[87]

Importantly, Cutshamekin's influence remains evident in Eliot's writings even after the sachem's death in the winter of 1651–52. In the months after the sachem's death, Eliot continued to develop the governing structures at Natick. At the same time, he was hard at work penning *The Christian Commonwealth*, a tract that proscribed a new governing system for the English nation.[88] The 1649 execution of King Charles I and the rise of the English Commonwealth inspired Eliot's hopes that England could be "first in that blessed work of setting up the Kingdom of the Lord Jesus."[89] Eliot's utopic ideas of a future Christian commonwealth and his work at Natick were linked. In his tract, Eliot pointed to Natick as evidence that he had experience implementing the governing ideas laid out in *The Christian Commonwealth*. Natick, he claimed, was governed using principles that "the Lord hath commanded in the holy Scriptures."[90] According to Eliot, proof of his system's efficacy came from its ability to transform Indigenous coverts from their "wild and scattered manner of life" in one of "Civil Government and Order." Eliot hoped that by using the governing structures he had instituted at Natick as a guide, the English could avoid the pitfalls of the Bay Colony. As Natalie Spar writes, Eliot "imagined Natick's government as an antidote to the problems he saw in English and colonial politics."[91]

Though relatively few scholars have undertaken in-depth studies of Eliot's *The Christian Commonwealth*, the tract has primarily been noted for its significance as a representative sampling of Puritan utopic thought in the wake of the English Civil War. As J. F. Maclear, James Holstun, and Theodore Dwight Bozeman argue, the tract and the governing system it details have strong roots in seventeenth-century English religious and political thought, namely the contemporary strains of millennialism and utopianism promoted by English Puritans like the Fifth Monarchists and New England minister John Cotton.[92] Written as Oliver Cromwell and the Rump Parliament were determining the future of the English Commonwealth after the beheading of King Charles I, the tract details a system of government that attempts to rely on the "Prophecies and Promises of holy Scripture" as the means of ruling "the Government and Administration of all affairs in the Commonwealth."[93] More recently, scholars such as Kathryn Gray and Natalie Spar have noted the relationship between Eliot's location at Natick and the concepts detailed within *The Christian Commonwealth*. As Spar notes, the tract "reveals the traces of Wampanoag life and thought in Eliot's developing political philosophy."[94] Spar cites Eliot's study of the Wampanoag language as the source of Algonquian influence in his tract.

While language study likely played a role in shaping Eliot's thought, it is more probable that his learning about Wampanoag society was derived from Eliot's own relationships with Algonquian people—people like Cutshamekin who had been deliberately instructing Eliot in Wampanoag ways. Though Eliot claims that the governing system he proposes in *The Christian Commonwealth* is one "instituted by God himself in the holy Scriptures," many of the primary tenets bear an unmistakable resemblance to the Massachusett governing systems practiced by Cutshamekin and his followers.[95] Among them are the process by which leaders were elected and the means by which justice was enacted. Advocating a hierarchical governing system, Eliot proposes that society be organized into kinship groups of tens, fifties, hundreds, and thousands. Male members of each group would determine their own leaders, who would then rule for life. Instead of a separate court system, the rulers of all polities, large and small, would adjudicate disputes among their electorate. This meant that judicial decisions were first arbitrated within a family unit. Rulers would rule and judge in both a religious and political capacity. Significantly, the two fundamental principles of governance that most closely echo Wampanoag practice are also those in which Eliot most prominently diverged from existing English and New England systems.

In the first two chapters of *The Christian Commonwealth*, Eliot lays out what he imagines to be the social organization and political structures necessary for a "divine institution of civil Government that may suit the State of England."[96] As he explains, the basic structure for his ideal society was to be the kinship unit. Every member of society would first be part of a smaller, primarily familial unit of ten. These family units would then align themselves into larger units of fifty, one hundred, one thousand, and so on. While the family unit was a central structure of household organization in colonial New England, kinship did not determine social organization or voting rights. As Eliot explains in his 1633 letter to Sir Simonds D'Ewes, the Massachusetts Bay system was one in which the "governor and all the Court are yearly elected by the body of freemen, and changeable, according to their abilities and defects."[97] In the Bay Colony, those allowed to vote, the "freemen," consisted only of "men who were both church members and company stockholders."[98] In other words, religious belief and wealth were the primary factors determining one's place in the social order.

By contrast, in *The Christian Commonwealth*, "publick Free-men" would be "bound personally to act, in the choice of their publick Rulers" resulting in elected leaders of ten, fifty, one hundred, etc. Eliot clarifies that his definition of "publick Free-man" includes all males except male "servants, or Sons living with their parents."[99] Rather than church membership or wealth, Eliot uses a man's inclusion in a kinship unit as the primary qualification for his voting rights. Eliot provides biblical endorsement for his kinship-structured society through marginal references to both Exodus 18: 25 and Deuteronomy 1:15—two verses describing the process by which Moses organized the tribes of Israel. While Eliot's biblical citations reinforce the numerical units promoted by Eliot, they do not provide support for the election of leaders. Rather, both verses describe a top-down system, with Moses at the head. Moses's authority is divinely ordained, and as such it is Moses who determines the rulers of all societal units, both small and large, not the people themselves. In

Eliot's system, each man was individually responsible to vote for leaders and determine a leader's efficacy, regardless of spiritual belief. This gestures toward an inherent (male) political right that transcends both status and the state of one's soul. At the same time, individual autonomy was kept in check through one's communal relationships and commitment to "orderly and seasonable practice of all the Commandments of God."[100] By allowing individuals within a family unit to choose their own leaders, Eliot proposes a system that significantly diverts from both Bay Colony practice and the biblical sources he cites as evidence. Holstun attributes Eliot's divergence from biblical precedence as the result of the minister's "lifelong and seemingly unconscious democratic misreading of Exodus."[101] Yet while Eliot's interpretation may point to the influence of New England congregationalism, it is more than a mere democratic spin on biblical precedent. His changed conception of governance finds its closest parallel in the system that Cutshamekin, the Massachusett, and their relatives had practiced before the formation of Natick.[102]

Despite Eliot's disparaging rhetoric throughout his tracts that either castigates the sachems as dictators or dismisses the Algonquian for their lack of governance, Eliot's conversations with Cutshamekin and his reaction to the elections at Natick indicate that the missionary clearly knew that the Massachusett had a long-standing, kinship-based system for determining their own leaders. Even though Eliot attempted to give his Praying Indians the chance to replace Cutshamekin by holding elections in the sachem's absence, the sachem retained the favor of his people—he was "the chiefe Sachem, and therefore chosen the chiefe." As detailed in chapter 1, among the Indigenous Northeast, society was organized into kinship units that would, at times, join together into larger confederations or alliances. The people determined their own leaders. In many Algonquian communities in the Northeast, women not only voted and held office, but they also initiated the election process. Leadership transitions often began with the clan mothers, who appointed potential future leaders to be approved by the community. Though leadership often followed hereditary lines, leaders were ultimately responsible to the people for their authority to govern.[103] If members of a kinship group were dissatisfied with a new sachem or saunkskwa, or if they lacked confidence in a long-standing ruler, they had recourse. As evidenced by the actions of Wequash and Uncas in the wake of the Pequot War, those unhappy with their leaders could leave the community and join another kinship group or form a new one.[104] Dissatisfied villagers could also take their complaints to a member of the leaders' advisory council who could bring up the matter in council meetings. The sachems and saunkskwas that successfully sustained the support of their followers were those best able to maintain societal balance and as such would retain their position until their deaths.

The parallels between the system Eliot proposes in *The Christian Commonwealth* and the Massachusett social order can also be glimpsed in the way Eliot lays out his judicial system. In his tract, Eliot proposes a system in which elected rulers would also serve as judges. Like his proposed system of election, his proposed judicial system deviates from Mosaic, English, and New England precedent in which judicial positions were determined by a leader, by heredity, or by a governing body. In Eliot's system, the judges are directly elected by the people.[105] For smaller cases, the elected ruler would serve as judge, and each ruler of ten was to set aside a designated time in which he would "solemnly . . . hear and determine Causes, and guide the common Affairs" of his followers. "Higher cases" that required "more time and deliberation" would be adjudicated by a combined court consisting of the elected ruler of fifty and each of the rulers of ten who served under his jurisdiction.[106]

While Eliot's concern with the formation of a new judicial system resonated with the larger English and New England drive for security in the face of a shifting political system, it can also be traced to his concern regarding the treatment of the Massachusett after their 1644 treaty with Massachusetts Bay. As Eliot writes in *Strength Out of Weaknesse*, though the Massachusett had "formerly subjected themselves unto the English," the only benefit they received from this act was "protection." Because of "the difference of language, and paucitie of Interpreters," Eliot was concerned that the English had not established systems for resolving Massachusett disputes. Realizing that the only justice being performed among the Massachusett was that practiced by Cutshamekin and his fellow Indigenous leaders, Eliot advocated for a transfer of judicial authority from Massachusetts Bay to the Praying Indians themselves.[107] In establishing this system, Eliot again worked within existing Massachusett structures.

Among the Massachusett and many other nations in the Indigenous Northeast, a sachem or saunkskwa was also the primary judicial figure within a community.[108] Larger judicial disputes would be determined by the sachem or saunkskwa and their tribal council. Arbitrating in inter- and intratribal disputes, Cutshamekin and his fellow leaders had an already established system of justice based on maintaining reciprocity and balance among kin and allies.

Despite Eliot's intentions, *The Christian Commonwealth* did not reach English readers. Though Eliot wrote his tract in 1651 or 1652, it was not printed until 1659, when the Fifth Monarchist Livewell Chapman published it as part of a larger push by the Fifth Monarchists to "rally the nation to their program" after Cromwell's death.[109] By then, Puritan hope that a Christian utopia could be founded in England was waning. After the Restoration of Charles II, the antimonarchical nature of the tract led New England authorities to view it with increasing concern. In May 1661 Eliot was brought before the General Court, and his work was censored "for being justly offensive, and in special relating to kingly government in England." All copies of the work were ordered destroyed. A few days before the order, Eliot went before the court and humbly proclaimed the English monarchy "an eminent forme of government" to which the people of New England were "subjected unto."[110]

Yet the fact that the tract was not successful in comparison to Eliot's other writings reinforces the fact that Eliot's ideas about political organization were contrary to those of the rest of the Puritan establishment. By implanting Cutshamekin's ideas into his utopic vision, Eliot illustrates the extent to which the sachem's ideas became embedded into his theoretical and political understandings. More than just a means of controlling the Massachusett or a way to convince English readers of colonial success, Eliot employs Indigenous governing systems as a means of imagining a new future for the English nation. This points to a successful transfer of information from one leader to the next, and it is in *The Christian Commonwealth* where we see the completion of Cutshamekin's process of education. Though Eliot would later adapt his ideas about governance as his intentions for the praying towns changed, Cutshamekin's teachings and example not only served as a central bedrock Eliot's missionary writing but also shaped the missionary's vision for a utopic English future.

Cutshamekin's Afterlife

In the 1660 tract *A Further Accompt of the Progress of the Gospel*, the now-established John Eliot transcribes the conversion narrative accounts of several of his Indigenous converts in attempt to "prove" to his readers that the Praying Indians were now ready to form their own church community. The 1660 tract is the third in a series Eliot crafted containing detailed conversion narratives performed by the Praying Indians at Natick.[111] In sending his questions back across the Atlantic, Eliot hoped to shore up ties between the New England missionaries and their metropolitan supporters by providing his readers with "empirical verification that God's 'promise to his plantation' was finally bearing its fruits."[112] Although Cutshamekin has passed away, his memory and influence still lived on among his Massachusett kin.[113] Not only do subsequent Praying Indians refer back to Cutshamekin, but they also follow his linguistic example by shaping the narrative forms of the Bay Colony to publicly negotiate the terms on which they would accept Christian instruction.

Evidence of Cutshamekin's sustained presence is most clearly illustrated in the conversion narrative Eliot records from Nishohkou, one of Cutshamekin's fellow Neponset Indians. Though Nishohkou eventually performs Christian conversion, the penitent Indian uses the form of the Indigenous conversion narrative to register his past frustrations with the Bay Colony. More than merely an account of his own spiritual journey, Nishohkou's conversion narrative also contains a pointed critique of the colony's political actions. He begins by recounting a number of instances in which he was dismissive of Christian religion. He then arrives at a pivotal moment in his narrative—the moment of saving grace. As the Massachusett man explains, the death of his wife and child led him to "almost believe." However, his movement toward belief is thwarted by the actions of the Bay Colony militia. Nishohkou recounts that during their Sunday gathering, he and his fellow Praying Indians were surrounded by English soldiers who "took away our Guns, and caused us to bring them as far as *Roxbury*." For Nishohkou, the soldiers' actions are a hypocritical violation of Puritan teaching about the Sabbath. As he explains, if the soldiers had "desired to keep the Sabbath" they would

90 CHAPTER TWO

"not have then come." Nishohkou's disappointment at Puritan hypocrisy is palpable. "That night," he recounts, "my heart was broken off, my heart said, God is not, the Sabbath is not, it is not the Lords Day, for were it so, the Souldiers would not have then come." In response, a disappointed Nishohkou "casts off praying."[114]

In taking away their arms on the Sabbath, the Bay Colony not only violated their spiritual teachings but also ignored the terms of their 1644 treaty with Cutshamekin and the Massachusett. As Jenny Hale Pulsipher recounts, signatories of the 1644 treaty were regarded as "subjects of Massachusetts colonial government," meaning "these Indians had the right to buy and sell land and other property, to receive equal treatment under law, to carry firearms, and to move freely about the colony, just as their English neighbors did."[115] While Nishohkou's account does not directly criticize the Bay Colony's political actions, he invokes the memory of Cutshamekin to hold the English accountable. Nishohkou explains that after the removal of their weapons, the Praying Indians came "before the Magistrates" where "*Cutshamoquin* asked, Why they came on the Sabbath day." In response, the magistrates justify their actions by claiming only that "it was lawful."[116]

Though Nishohkou eventually performed conversion, his narrative provides evidence that conversion, like treaty-making, was a relational process that was continually being negotiated and renegotiated by Praying Indian converts. Following in the footsteps of Cutshamekin and Wequash, later leaders like Nishohkou continued to shape the genres of the missionary project to ensure that they could interrogate, challenge, and critique the political and spiritual actions of the English settlers. The effect of these genres would not have been lost on transatlantic readers. While both the question-and-answer session and the Indigenous conversion narrative provided English readers with a recognizable means of chronicling the progress of Indigenous salvation, these genres also served to define Indigenous performances of salvation as deeply intertwined with long-standing beliefs about reciprocity, sovereignty, and common pot diplomacy.

CHAPTER THREE

Corn, Community, and Cassacinamon

Indigenous Science in John Winthrop Jr.'s "Of Maiz"

—⁂—

My dear wife, we are here in a paradise. Though we have not beef and
mutton, &c. yet (God be praised) we want them not; *our Indian corn answers for all.*
—Governor John Winthrop Sr., letter to Margaret Winthrop,
November 29, 1630

On a pleasant London afternoon in July of 1662, while the locals
were out enjoying the weather, the governor of Connecticut
Colony, John Winthrop Jr., was inside preparing an envelope, the contents
of which had taken him six months to write.[1] After sealing the envelope
with a dab of red sealing wax, Winthrop Jr. sent it off, addressed to "Mr.
Henry Oldenburg Secretary of the Royal Society at Pallmall In London."[2]
Inside the envelope were two documents: a covering letter and a short
treatise titled "Of Maiz."[3] Winthrop had written the treatise at the request
of Robert Boyle, one of the founding members of the Royal Society, and in
it he described the growing and usage of maize, also known as Indian corn,
a plant that was rapidly becoming the staple crop of the New England
colonies.[4] His anxiety about the report is evident in the covering letter:
after explaining that he has rewritten the document several times, the
Connecticut governor profusely apologizes for the "many impertinencies"
his document contains and warns that the contents of the letter may be
"unsutable" for the perusal of the larger society.[5]

Winthrop Jr.'s hesitancy surrounding his treatise on corn marks a departure from the otherwise eager approach that characterized his exchanges with
the Royal Society. Composed of England's most eminent scientific minds,
the Royal Society functioned to create and arbitrate scientific knowledge at a
time when England's imperial endeavors rapidly increased Britain's exposure
to the world outside of its borders.[6] While visiting London in January 1662,
Winthrop Jr. had been appointed the society's first colonial member. In this

91

role, he had given numerous talks on topics like mining, gold refining, and ship building. Society members eagerly listened to Winthrop Jr.'s reports, hoping to learn all they could about England's colonial holdings in North America. While Winthrop's listeners were men of science, they were also men of empire. Many, including Boyle, were central players in the English colonial project. The scientific information Winthrop Jr. shared was not only empirically important, but it also helped advance the colonial project. As an on-the-ground observer, Winthrop Jr. could provide the Royal Society members and the Crown with intimate knowledge about the people and materials of New England and thus help them better control what had been, up to this point, an unruly colonial enterprise.[7]

Winthrop Jr. was well aware of the ties that bound scientific advancement and colonial rule in post-Restoration England. The primary reason that Winthrop Jr. was in London in 1662 was to negotiate a royal charter for Connecticut Colony after the Restoration of Charles II.[8] Desirous to maintain relations with the British crown and secure royal funding at the same time as he advocated for colonial autonomy, Winthrop Jr. carefully calculated all of his exchanges with the Royal Society. It is these complicated ties between colonization, scientific discovery, and power that prompted Winthrop Jr.'s anxiety about his treatise on corn. In describing the central role that Indian corn, or *Zea mays*, played in his colonial settlement, Winthrop Jr.'s treatise uncovers the fundamental ways in which he and his fellow colonists had been transformed by their time spent in Indigenous spaces. Upon their arrival in North America, the settlers oriented their lives around corn, adapting their bodies and their communities to reflect the Indigenous practices already governing the Northeast region. From the start, colonial settlers in Massachusetts Bay and Connecticut not only depended upon corn for food but also used it as their primary currency, employed it as a central component of diplomatic exchanges, planted it as a means of identifying and staking land claims, and adapted it as an important signifier in religious ceremonies. Corn anchored colonial communities. As their dependence on corn grew, so did their reliance upon Indigenous scientists, many of whom were women. These mothers, grandmothers, aunts, and sisters planted, tended, harvested, and cooked Indian corn and taught the colonists to do the same.

A reading of "Of Maiz" reveals that the "unsutable" details that Winthrop Jr. desired to conceal from the Royal Society are those chronicling the deep dependence the Connecticut colonists had on their Indigenous neighbors.

Winthrop Jr.'s own community at Nameag, later renamed New London, had been formed under the direction and guidance of Pequot leader Robin Cassacinamon. The two communities worked together to establish themselves along the mouth of the Pequot (Thames) River. In the years after the Pequot War, Robin Cassacinamon and the Pequot were rebuilding their community on ancestral homelands while Winthrop Jr. and his English settlers were attempting to form a new communal settlement and create new industries for Connecticut Colony. Though Winthrop Jr. had read about the properties of *Zea mays* before he arrived in New England, it was Cassacinamon and his fellow Pequot who taught the colonial leader the foundational role corn played in forming and sustaining communities.

Writing about Indian corn for the Royal Society not only required Winthrop Jr. to reveal the central role Indigenous science played in colonial knowledge and community formation, but it also forced him to directly challenge established English scientific knowledge. Winthrop Jr. was not the first Englishman to write about New England's staple crop. Both the 1597 and the 1633 edition of John Gerard's *The Herball, or Generall Historie of Plantes* contain identical entries on maize, which Gerard terms "turkie corne." As one of the primary sources for agricultural knowledge at the time, Gerard's *Herball* was an authority when it came to English planting practices. When describing maize, Gerard dismissed it as a plant that "yield[ed] little or no nourishment." According to Gerard, "turkie corn" was suited only for the "barbarous Indians, which know no better" and who "are constrained to make a vertue out of necessitie."[9] Thus, in defending the merits of Indian corn, Winthrop Jr. implicitly aligned himself and the colonists with the "barbarous Indians" Gerard had derided. Rather than bringing "civilization" to the Indigenous people as the dictates of colonization required, Winthrop's tract reveals the ways in which the settlers themselves had been fundamentally changed by Indigenous scientific knowledge.

The story behind Winthrop Jr.'s 1662 scientific treatise "Of Maiz" illuminates the central role Indigenous science played in colonial knowledge formation. Winthrop's story of corn is inseparable from his relationship with Robin Cassacinamon and the Pequot community at Nameag, as the two men had a close working relationship that started shortly after Winthrop's arrival in New England and continued throughout their lives. The exchanges between the English leader and the Pequot sachem mark a departure from those I have examined in the book thus far. Both

Cassacinamon and Winthrop Jr. lived during the second generation of colonial settlement—Cassacinamon was a teenager during the Pequot War and lived most of his life near the English, which gave him extensive knowledge of English systems and colonial aims. Winthrop Jr. also had the benefit of learning from a colonial past as he watched his father, Bay Colony governor John Winthrop, navigate the challenges of forming a colonial settlement. Both Cassacinamon and Winthrop Jr.'s familiarity with colonial and Indigenous governance allowed them to negotiate political and social systems in ways that the earlier generations had not. Analyzing the relationship between these two men gives us an opportunity to see how later generations of colonists and Indigenous people continued to adapt to and shape the aims of the political systems within which they operated.

While the texts I have looked at so far have been empirically informed, writers like Shepard and Eliot were primarily focused on chronicling "the science of the soul" rather than documenting the natural world.[10] Winthrop Jr., on the other hand, was an advanced alchemist, herbalist, and natural philosopher who was in conversation with many leading scientists of his time. By attending to the influence that Indigenous people had in informing Winthrop Jr.'s scientific treatise, we can better understand the role Indigenous science played in shaping early discourses of scientific empiricism. "Of Maiz" was written as the same time as Winthrop and others were attempting to craft "rhetorical strategies to frame their own knowledge or the knowledge of their [nonwhite] informants."[11] Winthrop and his fellow English empiricists strove to appear as detached observers documenting the revealed truths of the natural world. However, when writing his treatise, Winthrop's dependence upon Indigenous scientists coupled with the established knowledge about corn in Gerard's *Herball* made a detached narrative stance difficult. Rather, his defense of corn required him to draw upon his own relationships with Indigenous people and Indigenous objects as evidence—the result being that one of the earliest empirical tracts written for the Royal Society from the New England colonies was deeply shaped, in both tone and content, by Indigenous scientific ways of knowing.

While kinship and Indigenous diplomacy remain central to this chapter, in focusing on corn, I consider another set of kinship relations—those with the nonhuman. Among many Indigenous nations, kinship ties not only connect human relatives but also draw humans together with the nonhuman world: with plants, with animals, with the land, and with other spiritual beings. Objects have life and objects have power, or manitou. As Dakota and Assiniboine scholar Samantha Majhor writes, "Indigenous people have posited a different relationship, indeed a sense of kinship that confers mutual responsibility, between human and nonhuman beings from the beginning."[12] Among northeastern Indigenous nations, and indeed Indigenous nations throughout North America, corn is a prominent object of power. Indigenous people recognized corn's ability to adapt to its environment, to produce a high yield, and to be preserved as a food source for a future time. Corn sustained life. As Winthrop Jr.'s knowledge of corn increased, so did his understanding of the role it played in community. Learning about corn and its uses brought him into relationship with Native people and Native places, specifically Cassacinamon's Pequot followers. While Winthrop Jr. would adapt knowledge of corn to suit the needs of the English settlers, in order to understand the plant, he had to understand the Indigenous people, places, and communities within which the plant most efficiently produced and sustained life.

In telling the story of Winthrop's relationship with corn and with Cassacinamon, I follow the path Winthrop himself maps out in his treatise. On its surface, "Of Maiz" follows the generic conventions of other scientific accounts of its time. Winthrop first summarizes the existing knowledge of the crop, then provides an updated description of it; next he details the planting seasons and best planting practices; and finally he lists the plant's potential uses as food, medicine, or other commodities. However, a look at the story behind Winthrop's engagement with corn reveals that the way his treatise tells the story of corn mirrors his own relational journey with corn as described in his letters and journals. In each section of his treatise, Winthrop invokes a different relational aspect of the plant. He begins his description of corn by laying out existing English knowledge—the same knowledge Winthrop would have had while living and studying in England before he set sail for the colonies. Then he moves on to detail the physical properties of corn, thus paralleling his initial encounters with Indian corn as a trade object. Next, Winthrop describes Indigenous planting practices and usages, echoing his own growth in knowledge as he was taught about corn by Indigenous scientists. Finally, he ends his treatise with a description of corn as it was used by both English and Indigenous planters, capturing the interdependency that developed between Winthrop's Connecticut settlers and Robin Cassacinamon's Pequot community at Nameag. As "Of Maiz" tells the story of New England's staple crop, it also chronicles Winthrop's own movement from a metropolitan observer to a colonist who becomes deeply embedded into the complex and intertwined network that connects the English, colonial, and Indigenous world.

The story I tell of Winthrop's encounter with *Zea mays* has been gleaned from a number of sources. While the treatise itself provides one version of the Connecticut governor's encounter with corn, the letters he exchanges with his father and other English settlers tell another version. Like many colonial authors, Winthrop Jr. adapts the story of colonial life to fit the intended audience. When father and son write to one another, they give detailed anecdotes of individual Indigenous leaders, locations, towns, and cities. They also give frank accounts of the hardships they face—chronicling deaths, diseases, and hunger. Yet when writing back to England in their official capacities, these details are erased. The tone changes. In official documents, individual Indigenous people are replaced by generalities and hardships are omitted. Instead, the colonial leaders paint a rosy picture of a growing colony working together toward a utopic future. Like the maize seed itself, which grows in many different climates and sustains a number of communities, the story of Winthrop's encounter with corn and Indigenous science can be found scattered among the official documents, the personal exchanges of settlers with each other and with Indigenous leaders, the landscapes themselves, and the long-standing Indigenous narratives that continue to shape corn's growth today.

Gérard's "Of Turkie Corn"

As a plant *Zea mays* started traversing the world hundreds of years before Winthrop Jr. made his voyage across the Atlantic. Likely originating as a crop in the Balsas River region of southwestern Mexico, the colorful corn plant traveled through the Americas alongside networks of kinship, diplomacy, and trade. When corn arrived in a new place, it often transformed the community by changing food patterns and altering planting practices. After hundreds of years of cultivation, Indigenous farmers engineered the corn plant to most effectively sustain human life. The seeds of corn, packed together in a single husk, make it an incredibly efficient source of nourishment. Yet, as Citizen Potawatomi scientist Robin Wall Kimmerer explains, the properties of *Zea mays* also make it an inherently relational crop. The corn's husk necessitates the need for human cultivation, as the plant cannot distribute its seeds apart from humans. As Kimmerer writes, "using Indigenous science, the human and the plant are linked as co-creators; humans are midwives to this creation, not masters. The plant innovates and the people nurture and direct that creativity. They are joined in a covenant of reciprocity, of mutual flourishing."[13] In contrast to many of the plants that serve as food, corn cannot survive without human care. Every ripe ear of corn pays homage to hours of human engagement in planting, watering, protecting, and harvesting the nourishing plant. Corn sustains the people as the people sustain the corn.

While corn served as a staple crop for many Indigenous communities in the Americas, when it crossed the Atlantic on board European ships, it no longer held together communities but rather served as a colonial curiosity. The first colonial record of the crop comes in Christopher Columbus's accounts after he encountered the plant among the Taino. In his records, Columbus termed the plant "maize," an adaptation of the Taino word meaning "Bringer of Life."[14] He brought back ears of corn for court officials—a practice many future colonists would continue. It was within the colonial context that Winthrop Jr. first encountered corn. As a young man in England, Winthrop Jr. was a student at Trinity College Dublin. While there, he began a lifelong pursuit to unlock the secrets of the natural world through observation and investigation. The young Puritan scientist was particularly interested in alchemy, or the study of the properties of metals and their philosophical and spiritual value. As Walter Woodward explains, "Winthrop found in alchemical culture an intellectual and Christian natural philosophy to which he could fully commit and through which he could seek knowledge and material gains while fulfilling his Christian duty to improve the world and serve others." As part of his alchemical interest and his desire to advance society, Winthrop devoured scientific accounts and began conversing with many of the leading English empiricists of his day.[15]

In the course of his studies, Winthrop Jr. likely encountered the works of the English mathematician and astronomer Thomas Harriot. A tutor for Sir Walter Raleigh, Harriot was chosen as the scientific adviser on the 1585–86 voyage that Raleigh funded to Powhatan territories in present-day Virginia. In 1588 Harriot printed a report of the voyage entitled *A Briefe and True Report of the New Found Land of Virginia*. When Harriot wrote about corn, he included multiple names for the plant, each illustrating a different relational context in which the plant was observed. As he writes, the Powhatan call the plant "Pagatowr," while "the same in the West Indies is called Mayze." The English "call it Guinney wheate or Turkie wheate, according to the names of the countreys from whence the like has beene brought."[16] Harriot starts his description by locating the plant within an Indigenous network of relations. Yet, in order to make the plant legible within a European system, he reclassifies the plant and locates it within a different set of relations. In *Briefe and True Report*, Harriot places corn alongside other "Commodities as Virginia is Knowne to Yeelde for victual and sustenance of mans life." This is one of three categories that Harriot creates to order his report. The other two are "Merchantable Commodies," and "Thinges as is behoveful for those which shall plant and inhabit to now of." Using these three categories, Harriot reorders all of the plants, animals, and people he encountered on his journey. These categories identify the items of Powhatan life in terms of their usefulness to a colonial empire. Realizing there is little desire for corn in a European context, Harriot lists it not as a source of wealth but as a potential source of food. Harriot aligns Indian corn with a familiar English crop, the "ordinary English peaze," and explains that corn can be used to perpetuate familiar English practices: "it maketh a very good bread" and can also be used to create necessary English beverages—ale and beer. When translated to an English audience by an English observer, corn serves as evidence that English ways of life can be successfully replicated in colonial lands.

Upon return from his voyage, Harriot not only printed his observations of corn in his *Report* but, like Columbus, he also brought back kernels of the plant. While Harriot's description of corn spread to English readers interested in learning about and colonizing lands different from their own, it was Harriot's seeds that eventually worked their way into English scientific discourse.[17] Among those who received seeds from Harriot's voyage were the English barber-surgeon-turned-gardener John Gerard, who would become influential in English agricultural science for his 1597 work *The Herball*, which was revised and expanded in 1633. While it is likely that Winthrop Jr. read Harriot's *Brief and True Report* at Trinity, he certainly read Gerard's *Herball*, as he would later quote it directly in his treatise for the Royal Society. Comprised of more than 1,600 folio pages with nearly 2,000 woodcuts, Gerard's *Herball* was a foundational English text of early modern science, describing most of the known plants of the Western world. Like Harriot, Gerard also had a connection to Sir Walter Raleigh through his patron William Cecil, Lord Burghley, who served as Queen Elizabeth's chief adviser and treasurer. Cecil had hired Gerard to supervise his gardens. Later Gerard would rise to be curator of the Physic Garden of the College of Physicians of London, giving him access to the plants and seeds acquired from the Raleigh voyages.[18]

The small colorful seeds of *Zea mays* that had been transported from the hands of the Powhatan women, across the Atlantic, then through any number of curious English observers, finally made their way to Gerard's "owne garden," where they would eventually "come to ripenesse."[19] Under Gerard's care, the seeds were not only grown in a new climate; they also received yet another backstory. Rather than a highly cultivated crop grown by a network of Indigenous planters using scientific communal knowledge as corn had been in Powhatan hands, or as a potential food source for a colonizing English community as Harriot cites it, Gerard understood Indian corn as a mythical and magical crop detached from any networks of knowledge or human care.

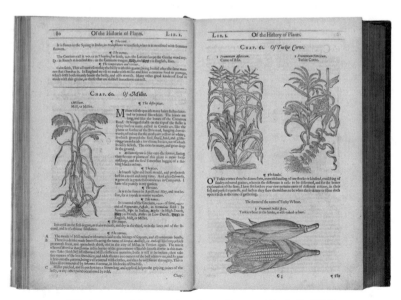

FIGURE 3. "Turkie corn" from John Gerard's 1633 *Herball*. STC 11751 copy 1, pp. 80–81, image 068926. Used be permission of the Folger Shakespeare Library.

As Gerard writes in his *Herball*, "turkey corn" was a plant grown "out of America and the Islands adjoyining, as out of Florida and *Virginia, or Norembega.*" Used to describe the lands on the northeastern coast of North America, "Norumbega" designated an imaginary, utopic city that settlers fantasized would be the perfect place to create a new and better English society.[20] As Richard D'Abate explains, "For the English, 'Norumbega' became the sign that most persuasively and efficiently communicated the attractiveness of settlement in the New World. Its imagined geography and its imagined qualities were reflections of or acceptable displacements for England's own idea of itself."[21] Twice removed from their sustaining networks, the seeds Gerard planted in his garden had moved into the realm of fairy tale—a type of magic bean appearing out of nowhere.

Despite their utopic promises, the displaced seeds of corn produced a dismal yield when Gerard planted them in his English garden. In his *Herball*, Gerard observes that the bread that he made from the ground kernels "is of hard digestion, and yeeldeth to the body little or no nourishment." Finding "no certaine proofe or experience concerning the vertues of this kinde of Corne," Gerard writes off the plant as useful only to "the barbarous Indians, which know no better, are constrained to make a virtue of necessities, and thinke it a good food." Indian corn, he writes "nourisheth but little, and is of hard and evill digestion, a more convenient food for swine than for men."[22] Harriot and Gerard's accounts would be the primary lens through which early modern English readers accessed the staple crop of the Americas. Casual readers would likely have been quick to dismiss Indian corn as an "uncivilized" crop with little value for English markets or English bodies. These accounts provided that basis for John Winthrop Jr.'s knowledge on corn, and with them Winthrop would have to wrestle when he found himself and his English community's survival dependent upon the small, colorful ear of corn.

"Before It Was So Well Knowne"

At age twenty-five John Winthrop Jr. set sail for New England intent on helping his father advance the colonial empire. As he boarded *The Lyon* in London to make the Atlantic voyage, he brought along numerous crates of carefully packed books.[23] Tucked among them was likely a copy of John

Gerard's 1633 *Herball*. For wealthy colonial families like the Winthrops, English texts offered a way to remain connected to England despite their Atlantic separation. "Concerned that they might become 'savage' in the American 'wilderness,' settlers carefully selected books to sustain and direct them—and to foster English culture" in the colonial world.[24] Herbals and other English husbandry manuals were regularly imported into the English colonies and used as guides for recreating the English households they had left behind. For Winthrop Jr., botanical books like the *Herball* also served a medicinal purpose. Well known throughout the New England colonies for his medical remedies, his gardening manuals provided him with advice on the roots and herbs that could be mixed, powdered, or boiled to provide relief for the many maladies that afflicted the arriving settlers. Throughout his years as a colonial scientist and politician, Winthrop would spend countless hours attending to the sick and recommending remedies to both colonists and Indigenous people.[25]

As Winthrop Jr. would soon come to find out, European book-knowledge was not directly transposable onto the lands of the colonial world. Survival required more than gardening manuals. The plants that Columbus, Harriot, and Gerard had taken out of context and turned into colonial commodities had to be repositioned within a different, much older, Indigenous network of relationships in order for them to sustain life. Even before he boarded the passenger ship that would take him across the Atlantic, Winthrop began learning how to relocate corn within an Indigenous network of relations. His first introduction to the networks that governed Indigenous lands was through trade. In the spring of 1631, while he was still in England preparing to embark, Winthrop Jr. received instructions from his father detailing a number of goods that he was to bring on his trip across the Atlantic. The elder Winthrop had arrived in New England a year before his son. Leading a fleet of eleven ships and about seven hundred people, Winthrop Sr. had spent 1630–31 attempting to establish an English settlement on Massachusett, Nipmuc, Pocumtuc, Pequot, and Wampanoag lands. The first few months of settlement were difficult, and a number of colonists died as the settlers struggled to adapt to their new environment. Winthrop Sr. hoped that a new supply of English goods could help restore the flagging English bodies. Among the food goods Winthrop requested from his son included items like "sugar, fruit, figges and pepper." While many of these food items were not native to the British Isles, by the seventeenth century they had become incorporated into the daily patterns of English life. In addition to consumables, Winthrop Sr. also requested items the settlers could use to make English clothing, including "oyled calves skins," "welt leather shoes and stockins for Children; and hats of all syzes," along with "two or three hundred sheepskins and lambs skins with the wooll on, dyed red."[26] In bringing over the items of Englishness, Winthrop Jr. both provided physical necessities like food and clothing to the settlers and allowed them to remain connected to their English homelands through their consumption.

As Winthrop Jr. packed the ship's hull with English goods, he was also being introduced to the goods and relationships that structured and defined the Indigenous Northeast. In an April 30, 1631, letter written from London before his departure, Winthrop Jr. informs his father that he has arranged to have Captain Clayborne from Virginia "deliver 100 tunnes of Indian wheat from Virginia to you."[27] "Indian wheat" was one of the many terms used for *Zea mays*. The process of buying and trading maize was one of the means by which English wealth was transferred to the colonies. After receiving money from Winthrop Jr. in England, Clayborne would buy maize from the Indigenous people near his Virginia settlement in exchange "for trucke," which consisted of trading commodities like "toyes, beads, Copper, tooles, knives, glasses and such like."[28] The corn was then delivered to Massachusetts Bay, where it could be used by Governor Winthrop for food and trade.[29] This brief reference marks the start of Winthrop's personal interaction with corn. No longer the valueless object it had been for Gerard, corn became desirable to the English colonists because of its use within a colonial economy—an economy that depended on Indigenous people and Indigenous goods for trade. Exchanging English goods for Indigenous ones, then using those goods to sustain English life, marks the first shift Winthrop Jr. made from metropolitan to colonist.

For Indigenous tribes in the Northeast, corn had long been an important part of the trade economy. Corn's significance was intertwined with its life-giving properties. An extremely productive plant with high yields, Indigenous people transformed corn into a number of food sources.[30] Corn also helped determine the yearly rhythms and ceremonies of Indigenous Northeast communities, marked communal territories, and cemented treaties. As a life-giving substance, the gift of corn affirmed one's commitment to sustaining the lives of others. As such, corn was also used to maintain relationships within communities and with neighboring communities as it was passed along networks of exchange and diplomacy. Offered as a gift to other leaders, buried with the dead, and used as tribute after warfare, corn sustained life and brought communities together.

"The Beautifull Noble Eare of Corne"

While trade brought John Winthrop Jr. to the periphery of the networks governing Indigenous space, it was not until he disembarked from his twelve-week voyage across the Atlantic that the eager settler would likely have had his first glimpse of an actual kernel of corn or held a tightly packed ear in his hand. After examining an ear of corn, Winthrop was impressed by its beauty. In his 1662 treatise, Winthrop Jr. introduces his readers to corn by means of a visual description. Attempting to counter Gerard's claim that corn was "a more convenient food for swine than for men," Winthrop Jr. waxes poetically about the "beautifull noble eare of Corne." In a section of florid and poetic prose, Winthrop Jr. writes that the ear is "cloathed and armed with strong thick huskes of many doubles, which provident nature hath made usefull to it many wayes." Inside the husk, he found even more splendor: "the composure of the eare is very beautifull being sett in Even Rowes, every Graine in each Row over against the other, at equally distance." The kernels themselves merit their own praise. As Winthrop Jr. tells his readers, "Nature hath delighted it selfe to beautify this Corne with great Variety of Colours, the White, and the Yellow being most common . . . [but] there are also of very many outher Colours, as Red Yellow, Blew, Oliver Colour, and Greenish, and some very black and some of Intermediate degrees of such Colours, also many sorts of mixt Colours and speckled or striped, and these various Coloured Eares often in the same field and some Graines that are of divers Colours in the same Eare." In his over-the-top description, Winthrop signals that he has been taken in by the stunning beauty of the sustaining crop.

The English settlers who arrived before Winthrop Jr. began to incorporate corn into their daily lives almost immediately. Corn was one of the first items the English pilgrims encountered when they landed in 1620 in

Wampanoag territory. As they explored the coast looking for resources, they found a number of in-ground Indigenous storehouses. Indigenous women had hidden the dried corn kernels in preparation for the next planting season. The settlers stole the hidden seeds and interpreted their presence in providential terms. As the Pilgrim leader William Bradford writes in *Of Plymouth Plantation*, "it is to be noted as a special providence of God, and a great mercy to this poor people, that they thus got seed to plant corn the next year, or they might have starved; for they had none, nor any likelihood of getting any, till too late for the planting season."[31] Though Bradford interprets the stolen Wampanoag corn kernels as a gift from the Christian God for his English community, both the English and the Wampanoag recognized the spiritual properties of the plant. As Cherokee literary scholar Betty Donohue writes, from their first arrival in Indigenous space, the newcomers were being instructed in Indigenous ways. One of the first teachers, she notes, was the land itself. The settlers "first had to be initiated and taught to read the Native First Text, the earth. Because the earth is animated by spirits, it can think and act."[32] Though stealing the corn was an act of violence, it also marks a moment of instruction. As Donohue writes, "Bradford's account of the corn discovery attributes a sacred or Providential quality to the event. His ability to connect corn with the sacred creates an unintended narrative that puts Bradford tenuously in line with much American Indian thinking that recognizes the hallowed nature of corn." Through the process of settlement, "all the Englishmen put their hands into the source of Eastern Algonquian culture and were touched by the American Indian ontological and teleological systems operating there."[33]

For his part, Winthrop Jr. likely examined his first ear of Indian corn at his father's house in Boston. By the time Winthrop Jr. arrived, Wampanoag sachems had already started to educate Winthrop Sr. on the value of corn. In his journals, Governor Winthrop details a diplomatic meeting between himself and the Massachusett sachem Chickatawbut in which Chickatawbut presented him with a "hogshead of Indian corn," a sign of well-being for the newly arrived colonial leader. In response, Winthrop provided Chickatawbut with "English clothes" as well as "peas and a mug and some other small things."[34] More than merely a type of currency, corn was exchanged among groups using the concept of reciprocity.

Whether given as a gift or as tribute, corn provided sustenance and life to others. When used to resolve military conflicts or other disputes, corn was a way of restoring balance that had been broken in conflict or strife. When a sachem or saunkskwa received tribute from their people or from other communities, they entered into a social contract. In receiving the corn, the leader agreed to care for the bodies of the individuals or the community from whom the gift had been presented. The movement of corn between Indigenous groups was a part of a larger ethos of care and responsibility.[35] When Europeans exchanged corn, wampum, and other goods with Indigenous nations, they became responsible to uphold good relations with those nations in order to maintain the stability of the whole.

Like Bradford, Winthrop Sr. also attributed a spiritual significance to corn. Two letters the elder Winthrop sent back to his wife, Margaret, during his first year of settlement give us a glimpse into the transformational effect Indian corn had on the colonial leader's early colonial experience. The first was sent on July 23, 1630, a little more than a month after Winthrop arrived in Naumkeag, or Salem. In the letter Winthrop is struggling to adapt to the colonial world as he misses English food and the comforts of home. As he writes, the settlers' diet was "but coarse in respect of what we formerly had," as it consisted primarily of "pease, puddinges, and fish."[36] During their first months, the colonists who had arrived on the Winthrop fleet had little knowledge of the native foods available. Their primary attempts to feed themselves were to replicate a metropolitan diet. Yet they quickly learned to adapt to the foodways of the Indigenous nations among whom they resided. In November of 1630, Winthrop would again write to his wife, but by November, his relationship to food had changed. In the four-month span between the two letters, Winthrop had lived through his first Indigenous harvest. The corn planted in April would have been harvested in August or September. The effect of the harvested corn is evident. In his letter to Margaret, he writes, "my deare wife, we are here in a Paradise, though we have not beef and mutton etc: yet (God be praised) we want them not; *our Indian Corne answers for all*" (emphasis added).[37]

The introduction of corn to the Massachusetts Bay Colony diet transformed the settlers' experience as they adapted their palates to take advantage of the goods available in Indigenous North America. In consuming corn as one of their primary food sources, the English were being instructed in the lifeways of the Indigenous Northeast and were physically changing the composition of their bodies as well. While corn kept settlers alive, they also believed that corn posed a serious risk. Like their early modern English counterparts, the English who landed in the Indigenous Northeast believed that "the human body was ... a complex moral and organic entity composed of fluids and particles, the humors and spirits—in constant flow and flux." Both the physical and emotional elements of a person were determined by "the four elements—earth, air, water, and fire—which in turn provided all raw matter with forms and properties—heat, moisture, cold, and dryness. Because the human body was composed of the same elements and qualities as all other material things, the boundaries between soul, body, and environment were unstable and permeable." As a result of the interconnected ties between "elemental, humoral and spiritual qualities, human physiology and moral character were understood to be continuously and directly influenced and altered by climate, weather, seasonal variations, temperature, air, and food."[38] In arriving in colonial America, settlers were fearful that their location in a new environment and their consumption of Indigenous foods would transform them from English to Indigenous. As such, they worked vigorously to shape their landscape into an English one and retained their use of English goods. Despite their best efforts, the colonists and their bodies were indeed transformed by corn. As Kimmerer writes, "Biochemists confirm that we are indeed people made of corn. Because of its unusual photosynthesis, corn leaves a signature in our tissues written in its particular ratio of carbon isotopes. Corn-eating peoples of the Americas carry a very different ratio of these isotopes in their flesh than the wheat eaters of Europe or the rice eaters of Asia."[39] Trading, eating, and planting *Zea mays* transformed the settlers in mind, body, and spirit.

"Called by the Natives Weachim"

While Winthrop's experience as a colonist led him to a new understanding of corn's role in trade economy and his hunger led him to appreciate corn as a food source, his understanding of corn as "beautiful and noble" came from another set of exchanges—sustained relationships with Indigenous scientists and leaders.[40] By the time Winthrop Jr. wrote "Of Maiz" for the Royal Society, he had been living among Indigenous people for more than thirty years. In 1635, four years after his first arrival in colonial Boston, and after the death of his first wife, Mary Fones, Winthrop Jr. traveled back to England. While he was in London, the Saybrook Company appointed Winthrop governor "of the river Connecticut in New England and of the Harbors and places adjoyninge."[41] In the spring of 1636, Winthrop crossed the Atlantic once again, this time with a second wife, Elizabeth Reade. Upon arrival, he moved south from the Boston region to the mouth of the Connecticut River, where he intended to take up the commission tasked to him by the Saybrook investors.[42] As Winthrop traveled south, he moved from Wampanoag lands in Boston onto Pequot, Western Niantic, and Narragansett land, finally arriving at the mouth of the Connecticut River in the months before the Pequot War began. Among the tasks that Winthrop Jr. was assigned by the Saybrook Company was that of "planting." Not only were he and his followers to "plant themselves either at the harbor or neare the mouth of the river"; they were also to plant fortifications and fields "that these places may be the better strengthened for ther owne saftie."[43]

As Wequash and other Indigenous people of the Northeast knew, the Connecticut River, or Kwinitekw, provided fertile planting grounds. Shortly after Winthrop Jr. arrived in the river valley, he began learning about the region's agricultural practices by observing Indigenous farmers and talking with Indigenous leaders. In 1636 Winthrop Jr. wrote to his father about a day he spent with the Narragansett sachem Canonicus:

> I was up with Canonicus at his great Citty. There be many wigwams but they stand not together as I have heard reported. The ground there seemeth to be farre worse then the ground of the massachusett being light and sandy and Rocky yet they have good Corne without fish; but I understand that they take this course they have every one 2 fields which after the first 2 yeares they let one field rest each yeare, and that kepes their ground continually in hart.[44]

Winthrop Jr. learned about Indigenous crop rotation as he visited the large Narragansett settlement on present-day Conanicut Island, a short distance from Wequash's home at Pasbeshauke, a village at the mouth of the Connecticut River where Winthrop Jr. was working with other English settlers to build Saybrook Fort.

Winthrop's description of the Narragansett fields was written in early April, which meant that he arrived as the women were placing the corn seeds into the ground. Details about the planting season would later make their way into "Of Maiz," where Winthrop Jr. explains, "the time of planting this Corne in that Countrey is any time between the middle of March and the beginning of June, but the most usuall time is from the middle of Aprill to the middle of May."[45] After his discussion on planting season in his tract, Winthrop Jr. then explains how Indigenous scientists knew when it was time to plant: "The Indians observe in some parts of that Countrey a Rule from the comeing up of a Fish called Aloofes into the River and Brookes for the time to being their planting, in other parts they observe the Leaves of some trees beginning to put forth." What Winthrop Jr. terms "aloofes" likely refers to alewives, an anadromous fish that lives in the waters around the Connecticut River. Some farmers used the alewives in their fields for nutrients, but in the description of Narragansett fields that he sent to his father, Winthrop Jr. notes that the Narragansett fields produced "good Corne without fish." Whether they used it as fertilizer or not, Indigenous scientists would observe the alewives as they moved from the ocean waters back to their home rivers in the spring to spawn. Canonicus or other Indigenous scientists might have pointed them out to Winthrop Jr. as they walked along the fields. The Narragansett leader may have explained that when the small, resilient fish moved back home to start a new life cycle, it signaled to the Narragansett it was time to create the necessary ingredients to sustain their communal life as well.

Winthrop Jr.'s description of his visit to Canonicus's fields illustrates some of the differences between Winthrop Jr.'s letters to his father and his letters to the Royal Society. While his letters to his father are filled with details such as the names of Indigenous people, tribes, and places, in "Of Maiz" Winthrop's descriptions of specific Indigenous people and places are largely absent. When writing for the members of the Royal Society, he transforms his personal exchanges into passive ones, taking the stance of an empirical observer translating facts back to the English readers. He references Indigenous people as a whole—using terms like "the Natives," "the Indians," or more simply, "they" or "them." While Winthrop's stance may be the result of his writing with a specific readership in mind, in choosing

Corn, Community, and Cassacinamon 109

to generalize Native people and places, Winthrop effectively transforms them from agents to subjects—moving them from the foreground to the background. In their place, he brings his own actions, and those of the English, to the fore.

Yet despite his empirical tone, Winthrop cannot minimize the role that one particular Indigenous group played in the planting of corn—"the Indian women." As he explains in his tract, it is "the Indian Women" who make "basketts" with corn stalks and also "the Indian women" who make cornmeal cakes (also known as johnnycakes) for the English to consume "as a novelty." Winthrop's mentions of "Indian women" in relation to *Zea mays* are more than just a passing observation. In the Northeast, corn was planted, tended to, and harvested by the community's women scientists, whose life-giving abilities were not limited to childbirth but also extended to growing life from the earth. The women planters knew the best location for the seeds, often placing them near river valleys and other sources of water to ensure the crops were sustained. Creation narratives like those of the Pequot's northern neighbors, the Haudenosaunee, understood their life forces as derived from the actions of Corn Woman—the first to bring forth life on earth. Wampanoag, Pequot, and Narragansett stories also center women and their life-giving abilities. Creation stories were intertwined with planting practices: both sustained the community's life force and were passed down from generation to generation. Corn also brought neighboring communities together. Among the Haudenosaunee, the rise of corn agriculture paralleled the rise of their confederacy. Women were and continue to be "the cultivators of peace" whose actions sustained not only family ties but political ones as well.[46] In this way, Indigenous women combined experience, religion, and science to ensure the best environment for the growth of the corn and the continuance of their people.[47] Though Winthrop doesn't mention specific women in his treatise for the Royal Society, the planters he watched drop corn into the ground, tend to the stalks, and harvest the ears were Indigenous mothers, sisters, and daughters. It was, in fact, a Pequot woman who seems to have brought together Winthrop Jr. and the future Pequot leader Robin Cassacinamon, who would serve to be one of Winthrop Jr.'s most influential teachers.

"The English Have Learned This Good Husbandry of the Indians"

Robin Cassacinamon is best known as the founder of the Mashantucket Pequot tribal nation, and his ligature is included on the nation's tribal seal, which is prominently displayed throughout the Mashantucket Pequot nation today. Cassacinamon and John Winthrop Jr. likely met in the aftermath of the Pequot War, while Cassacinamon was still a teenager. The fact that he survived the war and had not been killed or sold into slavery may have indicated "that [Cassacinamon] was neither a sachem nor a combatant during the fighting."[48] As participants in the Pequot War, both Cassacinamon and Winthrop Jr. would have known the central role that Indian corn played in determining the war's events. The planting, gathering, and distribution of corn is repeatedly mentioned by Indigenous and English participants alike as the events of the war take place.

Before going to war, the Mohegan, Narragansett, Niantic, and Pequot participants would have carefully considered the season of the year, the location of the community's fields, and the time of the harvest. As Winthrop Jr. would explain in his 1662 treatise, Indigenous soldiers would not "goe out against their Enemyes" until the "Corne beginneth to be thus fill in the Eare," as then "they have sufficient supply of Food."[49] For northeastern communities, corn was necessary to sustain all life—whether it was the life of one's neighbors, one's kin, or those with whom one was at war. Warfare was not a contest to eliminate the enemy but to settle disputes. For this reason Winthrop Jr. observes in his tract that Indigenous soldiers would not "Cutt downe, or spoile their Enemies Corne more than they gather to Eat." Winthrop Jr. likely observed these practices at the battles of the Pequot War began. Because the initial battles began in May, during planting time, the Pequot women quickly worked to expand their traditional fields. As Roger Williams wrote to Governor Winthrop in the spring of 1637, the Pequot planters "in some numbers" had "come downe to the sea side . . . to take sturgeon and other fish as also to make new fields of Corne in case the English sould destroy their fields at home."[50] The Narragansett who had reluctantly sided with the English were also thinking of Pequot fields throughout the battles of the Pequot War and its aftermath. Rather than destroying the fields after their victory, the Narragansett wanted to continue to plant and harvest them. They petitioned Governor Winthrop that "the Pequt corne might be enjoyed by the English and themselves."[51]

The English also considered corn and its availability during the events of the Pequot War. While many hungry English soldiers hastily crammed Pequot corn cobs into their bags to take back to the families, some English were concerned about corn's impact on the war as a whole. Puritan minister and coauthor of *New Englands First Fruits* Hugh Peter feared that Indian corn would tempt English soldiers. He wrote to Winthrop Sr., "wee wish [the Corne at Pequoit] were all cut downe, or left to the Narragansicks rather than for us to take it, for we feare it will prove a snare thus to hunt after their goods, whilst wee come forth pretending only the doing of Justice, and wee believe it would strike more terror into the Indians so to doe; It will never quit cost for us to keepe it."[52] Peter recognized that the high-value Pequot corn might lead the English soldiers to abandon their duties and focus on gathering corn for themselves rather than following the orders of their commanders. Yet, at the same time, Peter's words also point to his awareness that corn could be used as a tool of war. He advocates for its destruction in order to "strike . . . terror" into the hearts of the Pequot soldiers.

Another English commander in the Pequot War, Israel Stoughton, wanted to destroy Pequot corn for a different reason. During a march, Stoughton had come across a group of Indigenous people in a Pequot cornfield. Upon his arrival, they fled. However, later, when Stoughton was able to talk with one of the women who were in the field, she told him that the gatherers were relatives: "they were a mixt, Pequids and Narragansetts together." Stoughton recognized the ties of kinship and realized they posed a threat to the English alliance with the Narragansett. Rather than risk the corn being shared with the Pequot by their Narragansett relatives, Stoughton set to work destroying the fields. As he writes, "Near to us it falls much by the weeds, and far from us it will do us little good." In this same letter, he warns the governor, "The Narragansett do gather beans in abundance, and we are silent at it; yet, if they should turn enemy, it would be to our great damage."[53]

In the midst of these larger discussions on corn and its role in the war Cassacinamon first made his way into the English colonial records. In 1637 the Mohegan-Pequot sachem Uncas sent a young Cassacinamon to the home of Roger Williams to "secure the freedom of a Pequot woman residing in Winthrop's household at Nameag." Williams negotiated with Governor Winthrop, who was primarily responsible for distributing Pequot captives in the aftermath of the Pequot War. As described in chapter 1, after the war, many Pequot warriors were executed, other Pequot men, women, and children were placed in English servitude or sold into slavery in the Caribbean, and still others were distributed among the Indigenous leaders who had aligned with the English in the war. Cassacinamon and his community had been placed under Uncas's jurisdiction. The woman captive that Cassacinamon was freeing was an important member of the Pequot tribe—not only was she wanted as a bride for Uncas, who was working to establish his power base in the aftermath of the war, but she was also wanted for her skills as a corn planter and community sustainer. Instructed to remain with the woman in the case that Uncas could not buy her, Cassacinamon stayed in the elder Winthrop's household for a time. Eventually, the young Pequot was successful in his aim, and the captive woman came to live among the Mohegan.[54]

In the aftermath of the war, as the English moved to consolidate their power in the region and the Pequot struggled to regather their relatives, both Robin Cassacinamon and John Winthrop Jr. temporarily left the mouth of the Connecticut River, though they would often journey back to its banks. In 1638 Winthrop Jr. moved back near the Boston region, setting up a salt house at the convergence of the Bass and Danvers Rivers. The colonial scientist hoped to develop a "fishinge businesse" in New England in which the salt would be used to cure the fish before they were shipped.[55] During this time, Robin Cassacinamon was living at Winthrop Sr.'s house and moving back and forth between Boston and Pequot lands at the mouth of the Connecticut River. There is little information available on the future Pequot leader from between 1638 and 1645. Colonial records claim that Cassacinamon was a servant in the Winthrop household during this time, though his exact status is unknown.[56] However, as a leader in preparation, Cassacinamon continued to hone his diplomatic skills. During this time, he "learned English well enough to spend the rest of his life as an interpreter and intermediary between the Algonquians and the English." It was also during this time that Cassacinamon and Winthrop Jr. developed a mutual reliance on one another.[57]

In 1644 both Cassacinamon and Winthrop Jr. started to make plans to move back to Pequot territory, where they each intended to plant corn

FIGURE 4. Native American Sachem (1681). Unknown artist. Gift of Mr. Robert Winthrop. Courtesy of the RISD Museum, Providence, Rhode Island. Subject is now believed to be Robin Cassacinamon.

and plant their communities. In the aftermath of the war, Pequot lands between the Connecticut and the Pawtucket River were contested by a number of groups—both English and Indigenous. Aiming to get out from Mohegan control, Cassacinamon moved himself and his followers back to Nameag, near the mouth of the Pequot (Thames) River, where he hoped John Winthrop Jr.'s political alliance would provide him with English protection. For his part, Winthrop Jr. planned to move to Pequot lands to continue his scientific projects and start a new colonial settlement.[58]

As Shawn Wiemann writes, "The younger Winthrop intended this plantation to be a shining example to other settlements in the region, a haven of economic and intellectual developments." Winthrop Jr. also hoped to use his alliance with Cassacinamon to build up his political power in the contest between the English and their former allies after the Pequot War.[59] Between 1644 and 1646, the two men took several scouting trips throughout the region. During these trips, Cassacinamon met with his relatives and community members. At the same time, he guided Winthrop Jr. through the region and helped the colonial governor determine the best place to settle with his English followers.

Winthrop Jr. records one of their trips in his diary. In November of 1645, Cassacinamon took Winthrop to his home around Nameag. The lands around Nameag were where Cassacinamon had grown up under the care of his relatives. "Nameaug, or Nameag, comes from the Wampanoag word *nameauk*, meaning 'fishing place' or 'where fish are taken.'"[60] As Cassacinamon and Winthrop Jr. crossed through Cassacinamon's homelands, the Pequot leader identified plants, trees, and shrubs and instructed Winthrop Jr. on how to best use the land's resources. In his diary, Winthrop Jr. writes, "I crossed the river and the stream Poquanuc, where Robin told me there were fruit-bearing land without rocks, arable with a goodly number of planting-fields."[61] During their November journey, Cassacinamon introduced Winthrop Jr. to other Indigenous leaders, including the Massachusett sachem Cutshamekin, whom Winthrop Jr. notes was "a relative of Robin."[62] Winthrop, Cassacinamon, and Cutshamekin shared a meal. As a part of the leadership community that maintained balance in the Indigenous Northeast, Cassacinamon knew the importance of bringing outsiders in, and teaching them the proper way to care for Indigenous lands and Indigenous people.

"The Way of Planting Used by the Natives, and English Also"

In 1646 Winthrop Jr. and Cassacinamon moved themselves, their families, and their followers to Nameag permanently. Upon their arrival, the English joined around 300–500 Nameag Pequot under Cassacinamon's leadership.[63] As he was working to build up a new community, Winthrop Jr.

learned the role corn played in sustaining communal life. Winthrop Jr. likely acquired many of the details that he would later include in "Of Maiz" between 1646 and 1660 as the English and Pequot at Nameag planted fields, grew crops, built houses, and shared meals. At Nameag, Winthrop Jr. learned not only to plant and grow corn but also how to harvest and store the crop. It was also at Nameag that Winthrop Jr. learned many of the Indigenous recipes for corn that the Nameag settlers would adapt to survive during their early years, and at Nameag where he came to understand the medicinal value of the corn plant. The process of community building not only changed Winthrop's relationship to corn but changed the ways in which he understood his place in relationship to northeastern Indigenous lands and people. During this time Winthrop Jr. came to think of the plant no longer as a foreign object or a form of currency but as *weachim*, or *wiwáhcum*, the Pequot/Mohegan name for the plant. In his treatise to the Royal Society, he begins by renaming the plant—it is not "Indian corn" or "turkey corn" but weachim, a gift from the creator.[64]

During their first winter, the English settlers lived in longhouses built for them by the Nameag Pequot. They survived the long, cold days by eating the corn the Pequot women had stored. As Winthrop Jr. and the settlers watched the women work, they likely learned how to store corn in underground barns so that there would be seeds for spring. Winthrop Jr. would later describe the process in "Of Maiz": "the Natives commonly thresh [the corn] out as they gather it, and dry it well upon Matts in the Sun, and then bestow in holes in the Ground (which are their Barnes) well lined with Withered Grass, and with Matts, and then covered with the like and over that covered with Earth, so it keeps very well till they use it."[65]

In the spring the English settlers watched as the Nameag Pequot women began planting their fields around the river. Among other techniques, the Indigenous planters taught the settlers to hill the corn, which Winthrop describes in his 1662 treatise as "making a little hill like hopp hills" in order to protect the growing stalks. The small hills protected the seeds but also reinforced the life-giving properties of corn. As Wampanoag researcher and teacher Darius Coombs explains, the mounds into which the seeds were placed echoed the pregnant belly before birth—as both bring forth life.[66] With the hills of corn, the Pequot women also added beans and squash, using the three sisters method in which all three plants support one another's growth, resulting in a greater yield. As Winthrop would write in "Of Maiz," "at every hill of corne, . . . the Indians and some English also," "will plant a kind of Beans with the Corne (they are like those here called French Beans or turkey Beans) and in the Vacant places and between the Hills, they will plant Squashes & pumpions, loading the ground with as much as it will beare."[67] Like the small mounds into which the corn is planted, the three sisters planting method is also spiritually significant as it reminds the people of their independence on one another and on the plants for survival. In using Indigenous methods, the English were taught Indigenous ways.

In learning to plant, harvest, and store corn, Winthrop and the other English settlers at Nameag also entered into the communal rhythms that organized northeastern Algonquian life. Planting season marked the start of a new year and provided hope for a continued future. During fall harvest, the settlers and Pequot alike would have gathered their corn and stored it away for the next year. At harvest, the community came together to feast and celebrate. Joining with their neighbors, the Nameag residents celebrated the Green Corn festival when extended families and tribes would come together to mark the harvest and bury past grievances. It is important to note that English attendance at Indigenous ceremonies did not necessarily mean that the English changed their ways. In 1669 an older John Winthrop Jr. would take advantage of the festivities surrounding the Green Corn festival to obtain further lands for the English. As part of the land-holding Atherton company, John Winthrop Jr. would manipulate his knowledge of the Green Corn dance and its attendant treaty-making to force lands from the Narragansett in the years before King Philip's War.[68]

After harvest, the women stored their seeds in baskets hidden under the earth so that they could return and replant next season. Eventually, the English would bring English-style plows to their fields, but in their early years, they mimicked Indigenous techniques to much avail. In his 1662 treatise, Winthrop would allude to their shared days of planting with a short phrase: "this was the way of planting used by the Natives, and English also." Incorporating three sisters planting into their own practices both provided a better yield for the English and in turn taught them about the dependent relationship between North American crops and communities. As Kimmerer writes, "Our different ways of planting reflect not only the different scales and goals of our work, but also our fundamental relationships with the plant."[69] In teaching the settlers how to plant, Cassacinamon and the Pequot planters were bringing the settlers into a new way of knowing.

In addition to planting and storing corn, the Nameag women also taught the English how to prepare it. The Pequot transformed the harvested corn into a variety of dishes, including succotash and hominy. From the Pequot, the English learned to boil corn, to parch it, and to grind it into flour. Though the English adapted the foods to suit their English tastes— even learning to make beer from malted corn—they also incorporated Indigenous dishes into their daily diets. As Winthrop explains in "On Maiz," "the best sort of Food which the English make of this Corne is that they call Sampe." Sampe is made from corn kernels that are softened, ground, and then stewed and combined with milk, butter, or sugar—akin to grits today. Winthrop explains that the food is not only an English favorite; it is also "a food very pleasant and wholesome, being easy of Digestion, and is of a nature Diurectical and Clensing and hath no Quality of binding the body, as the Herball supposeth, but rather to keepe it in a fit tempera-ture." Furthermore, sampe has healing qualities: it "may be taken as well in Sickness as in health, even in Feavers and other acute Diseases."

As a scientist and herbalist, Winthrop was well known for his medic-inal skills throughout the colonies. In his medicinal practice, he treated the ailments of both English and Indigenous bodies. According to medical understandings of the time, the composition of bodies varied depending on their location in the world. Indigenous bodies required medicines and treatments that would be found in the area where their bodies had grown and developed. Winthrop's knowledge of local flora and fauna, undoubtedly gained from his interactions with Cassacinamon and other Pequot, gave Winthrop knowledge of local herbal treatments. As Woodward writes, "Winthrop's reputation for healing spread among natives as well as the English. Soon the English in other towns such as Roger Williams's were requesting him to send medicines 'fit for Indian Bodies.'" [70]

In the 1633 *Herball* Gerard had not only derided corn as "barbarous" but had claimed that it was "of hard and evill digestion, a more convenient food for swine than for men."[71] As a medical practitioner, Winthrop Jr. had carefully observed the ways in which both Indigenous and English bodies responded to particular foods. In the early years of settlement, Winthrop Jr. noticed that the English were suffering and even dying from their poor diet. By contrast, the Indigenous people were not. Winthrop pinpointed Indigenous consumption of corn as one reason for their healthy bodies. In his treatise he explains, among "the Indians that Eate no other sorte of Corne," "the disease of the Stone is very seldome knowne." *Zea mays*, Winthrop Jr. concludes, "is accounted a good meanes against the Scurvie." In prescribing Indian corn for an English disease, Winthrop Jr. recognized the medicinal value of corn was not only for Indigenous people but for the English as well.

In addition to sharing their corn, the Pequot also helped the English settlers by hunting game and assisting them with labor. As the more established leader in the region, Cassacinamon guided the English in setting up food and shelter and instructed them on their strategic relations with neighboring Indigenous communities.[72] Through their shared resources, the two leaders and their communities learned to depend on one another. Though Winthrop Jr. never doubted the superiority of English ways, the relationship between Cassacinamon and Winthrop Jr. went beyond strategy. The two men continued to work with one another despite the pressures from both of their communities. The Pequot leader helped Winthrop Jr. and the other English settlers in the formation of their village at Nameag and the Connecticut leader recognized Cassacinamon's power—titling him "Governour and Chief Councelor among the Pequots."[73] For Winthrop, the presence of Cassacinamon and the Nameag Pequot provided both food and resources and an opportunity to build up English strongholds and protect them from other Indigenous tribes. As Winthrop Jr. would write to his fellow Nameag settler Thomas Peters in September of 1646, "I looke at the quiet of our plantation principally, and conceive a greater security to have a party of the Indians there, to have their chiefe dependence upon the English. They will easily discover any Indian plots, etc." Later in that same letter, Winthrop Jr. requests that Peters also procure "seede corne" alongside "Rye and winter wheat" to plant at Pequot Plantation for himself and his family.[74]

While "Of Maiz" captures the processes by which English settlers adapted to Pequot practices, it does not paint an entirely rosy picture. Winthrop's treatise also captures English planters' actively changing the

Indigenous landscapes, primarily through keeping cattle. Cattle would later become a key point of conflict between settlers and Indigenous people. As Winthrop Jr. writes in "Of Maiz," the stalks of corn serve as "good Winter Fodder for Cattle." And rather than codfish or alewives for fertilizer, the English begin to use "the Dung of their Cattle well Rotted" to increase their yields. The arrival of English cattle, swine, and other livestock necessitated the building of fences as the English attempted to mark out territories, which disrupted Indigenous fields and challenged existing land-use practices. Though minor to start, these changes would later provide the English with justification to forcibly acquire, carve up, and fence Indigenous lands, hastening the process of dispossession. As cattle farming and English populations increased, so too did the ferocity by which the English would claim and obtain Indigenous lands.

Despite the changes that the English made to Indigenous landscapes and the authority the English settlers imposed, at the start of their relationship Cassacinamon saw his ties with Winthrop Jr. as a means to secure valuable alliances with the English—alliances that would help better the Pequot situation. As a leader in his own right, Cassacinamon yearned to regain Pequot lands for the Pequot and secure their independence from Mohegan oversight.[75] Winthrop Jr. provided this opportunity. Several times outsiders derided and dismissed the relationship between Cassacinamon and Winthrop. The settlements at Pequot Plantation were viewed with suspicion by Connecticut officials, who saw Winthrop as an interloper attempting to secretly take Connecticut colonial territory for the Bay Colony. Uncas meanwhile viewed Winthrop's arrival at Nameag as an attempt to drive away his Pequot tributaries. Uncas's English ally John Mason was continually irritated with Winthrop Jr.'s presence on the Thames River.

Among those frustrated with Winthrop Jr. included Winthrop Sr. His finals words to his son concerned the latter's relationship with Cassacinamon. In 1649, as the elder Winthrop was on his deathbed, his son Adam recorded a final message from Winthrop Sr. to Winthrop Jr. As Adam writes, "[Father] wold requst you as if it wear his last requst, that you wold striue no more about the pequod Indians but leaue theme to the commissioners order."[76] While the elder Winthrop was sympathetic to his son's attempts to form a colonial community at Nameag, he grew increasingly frustrated as the younger Winthrop failed to heed to rulings of the English courts and instead followed the urging of Cassacinamon. The naissance of the dispute was food gathering. In 1646, at the request of Winthrop's fellow settler Thomas Peters, Cassacinamon conducted a hunt to procure meat for the arriving English. Cassacinamon gathered around twenty Nameag Pequot hunters and other relatives.[77] He led them through Pequot territories and then moved them to "the East side of [the] Pequat [River]."[78] Their hunt took them through lands claimed by Uncas, who had not given them permission to hunt in the region and viewed their incursion as an affront to his authority. In retaliation, the Mohegan sachem took around three hundred warriors and attacked the settlements at Pequot Plantation. After Uncas and his warriors physically abused and humiliated the Pequot warriors, they turned to the English by driving away English cattle and ransacking English corn.[79] Cassacinamon and Winthrop Jr. complained about Uncas's actions to the colonial authorities. Winthrop Jr. appealed directly to his father as well, prompting the elder Winthrop's admonition to "leaue [the Nameag Pequot] to the commissioners order." Winthrop Jr. refused to heed his father's dying request. The two communities were becoming increasingly intertwined. Not only did the Pequot provide the English with food, shelter, and protection, Winthrop Jr. and the English also proved to be valuable allies to the Pequot.

Despite his alliance with Cassacinamon, John Winthrop Jr. was an Englishman first, and his primary desire was always to advance the English community. Yet the teachings of Cassacinamon and the Nameag Pequot did not go unheeded. In learning about Indigenous farming practices and land use from Cassacinamon and the Nameag Pequot, Winthrop Jr. developed a new understanding of Indigenous land claims, which led him to support the Nameag people in the quest for land rights. In 1650, after continued disputes between the Mohegan and the Nameag Pequot, Winthrop Jr. worked with Cassacinamon to place the Nameag Pequot under English jurisdiction rather than Mohegan authority. Under this arrangement, Cassacinamon and the Nameag Pequot were granted "the land at Newayunck Neck [Noank]," where they "may Live and plant and fish at said Newayunck [Noank]." Despite the irony of receiving legal jurisdiction for their own land, the English land grant was a victory for the Nameag people. Winthrop Jr. had helped them in their quest—but he had also benefited. He was given the fee simple title of the land.[80] In 1658 Robin Cassacinamon and the Nameag Pequot were allotted even more land. And in 1666 they obtained legal jurisdiction from the English for their ancestral lands around Mashantucket, where they still reside today.[81] Cassacinamon's ability to secure additional land for his followers represents one of the few instances of land gains within a larger story of land loss and dispossession.[82]

"It Is Found by Experience"

Not only did Cassacinamon's teachings on corn prove to have an effect on Winthrop's relationship to the land, but his teaching also changed the way Winthrop thought and wrote about corn. In 1657 Winthrop Jr. was elected governor of Connecticut Colony. He was reelected in 1659 and remained in that position until his death in 1676. Over the years, his settlement at Nameag had grown, as had his influence within the colony. In 1661 Winthrop Jr. was sent back to England to petition for Connecticut Colony. After the Restoration of Charles II, the New England colonies found themselves in a difficult situation. Having clearly sided with Oliver Cromwell's forces during the Civil War, the colonists were now anxious to gain to favor of a king that they had opposed. It was during his time in England as a petitioner that Winthrop was approached by the Royal Society and appointed to serve as their first colonial member. It was also during this trip that Robert Boyle requested Winthrop write a treatise on New England's staple crop.

Woodward suggests that Boyle's request for a treatise on Indian corn may have been the first step in Boyle's larger goal to have Winthrop write a natural history of the New England colonies. Like Richard Ligon's 1657 *A True and Exact History of the Island of Barbados*, a natural history would provide a colonization manual for potential investors. It would also aid English overseers in consolidating control because it would mean they would not be entirely dependent on the words of their colonial counterparts when it came to land distribution and resource allocation. Winthrop resisted Boyle's requests for a natural history. As Winthrop Jr. knew, "By providing intelligence through the natural histories that the society requested, he would increase and rationalize understanding about New

England and enhance incentives for exploiting or taxing New England's resources."[83] Having worked hard to learn about those resources from his Indigenous neighbors, Winthrop Jr. wanted to retain intellectual control of New England's resources for himself and his fellow colonists.

Yet, as a scientist and member of the Royal Society, Winthrop Jr. also desired to provide society members with useful information. "Of Maiz" marks his attempts at a compromise. In writing about corn, Winthrop Jr. is describing a known commodity—one that is not limited to a single region or territory. Yet in touting the virtues of corn to the members of the Royal Society, Winthrop walked a fine line. Not only is he *contradicting* Gerard's claims that corn is "a more convenient food for swine than for men," but he is also exposing the close ties between colonial settlers and Indigenous people. Humoral medical theory meant that the early modern colonists and their English funders were concerned that humors of English bodies might degenerate and degrade in the colonial environment. Consuming Indigenous foods would hasten that degeneration. As Kelly Wisecup writes, "For colonists who travelled to or were born in the Americas, this physical and mental altercation meant that they were likely to process information and produce knowledge in the same ways that Natives and Africans did. From the perspective of Europeans in the Old World, such transformations stood as a sign of colonists' degeneration and of the untrustworthy nature" of colonial texts.[84] Not only did Winthrop Jr.'s physical location within the colonies make his writing suspect, but his personal history with the Nameag Pequot and the criticism he had faced from other colonial leaders over his ties to the Pequot might have led leaders like Robert Boyle to further question his reliability.

In an attempt to mask his reliance on Indigenous sources, Winthrop relays his knowledge of corn to the Royal Society using the language of "experience." As he writes, his knowledge of corn did not come from books or hearsay but had rather been derived from "much Experience," whereas Gerard had written about corn "in those times before it was so well knowne." As Winthrop implies, Gerard's limited experience with the plant resulted in him finding the plant "barbarous," "hard of digestion [with] little or no Nourishment." By contrast, through "much Experience" Winthrop had determined that the plant is "wholesome and pleasant for Food of which great variety may be made out of it."[85] To further authorize his account,

Winthrop includes a second English source. He tells the story of Doctor Wilson, "A learned Physitian that not long since lived in London" who "had every yeare some Quantity [of corn] brought over ready beaten, and fit to be boyled, and did order it to such Patients, as he saw cause for it."[86] Bringing in a second English voice, however distant, reminds readers that Winthrop Jr. is not along in his adoration of Indian corn.

Despite Winthrop's claims of *empirical* experience, the tract itself is anchored in the knowledge that Winthrop derived from his *personal* experience learning from the land, the corn plant, and Indigenous people like Cassacinamon and the Nameag Pequot. Winthrop's continued references to Indigenous terms, practices, and people clearly reveals that Winthrop's scientific knowledge was obtained through relationship and those relationships shaped the ways in which he understands corn and its usage. In looking at the tract and tracing its past and future histories, we can see some of the ways that Cassacinamon and the other Indigenous scientists set the stage for future scientific writing. By teaching Winthrop Jr. not only to focus on the relationship that *Zea mays* had with the natural world but also to attend to the relationships it had with its human cultivators, the Indigenous scientists ensured that Winthrop's scientific writing paid tribute to the long line of cultivators who cared for corn over the centuries. In writing about the planting practices of the Nameag Pequot, Winthrop also posits a posture of scientific discovery that attends to the experience and knowledge of those who are often left out. As one of the first scientific treatises from the New England colonies, "Of Maiz" reminds us how essential Indigenous science was to any successful habitation in North American lands. Though Winthrop Jr. and his fellow colonists would go on to dispossess large number of Native tribes through land dealings, manipulations, and violence, "Of Maiz" stands as a testament to the fact that the original caretakers of the land continued to care, and teach others how to care, for the land—a practice that continues to the present day.

CHAPTER FOUR

Treaties, Reciprocity, and Providence

The Role of Indigenous Justice in Daniel Gookin's
Doings and Sufferings

—〰—

More than thirty years after Roger Williams challenged the Bay Colony's claims of missionary success in *New Englands First Fruits*, the Puritan mission was once again a target for public criticism. However, this time the challenge came from within. In 1677 the prominent Ipswich minister William Hubbard cast doubt on the veracity of the Praying Indians' conversion. As he writes, though "many [English] have endeavoured by kindess to convert [the Indians]," they have "found nothing from them, but *derision* and *Ridiculous Answers*." While Hubbard applauds the valiant efforts of the Bay Colony missionaries, in his view, their energies were misplaced. After nearly thirty years of proselytization attempts, Hubbard believes that the Indigenous people in colonial New England have retained a "natural barbarousness and perfidiousness." Until they are "reduced to more *Civility*," Hubbard suggests, "some wise men are ready to fear Religion will not take much place amongst the body of them."[1] In Hubbard's logic, any efforts at conversion among Indigenous people is a waste of time. Praying or not, for Hubbard all Indigenous people were still too "savage" for any conversion attempts to truly succeed.

Hubbard's claim that Indigenous people had not successfully adapted to English "civility" not only dismissed the Bay Colony's missionary efforts but had a more practical application as well. His critique came at the end of his 1677 tract *The Present State of New England, Being a Narrative of the Troubles with the Indians in New England*. The tract was written to justify English actions during King Philip's War, the 1675–76 war that allied the Wampanoag, Nipmuc, Podunk, Narragansett, Nasaway, and Wabanaki against the English.[2] In claiming that Indigenous people were "natural[ly] barbarous . . . and perfidious," Hubbard provides justification for the English

124

to break their former agreements with the Praying Indians. During King Philip's War, also known as Metacom's Rebellion, many long-standing prejudices against Praying Indians came to the fore.[3] English settlers who had always been suspicious about the authenticity of Indigenous performances of conversion saw the converts' participation in the war, or lack thereof, as inherently duplicitous. As Hilary Wyss writes, during the war the Praying Indians were "valuable to both sides as translators and scribes, yet [their] liminal identity left them mistrusted by both."[4] Fearful that the Praying Indians would choose kinship over conversion, many English settlers treated them with open contempt. In October of 1675 the English authorities rounded up many of the Praying Indians and sent them to an internment-like camp on Deer Island. Lacking food and resources in the middle of winter, many died from hunger and cold. Others were killed, captured, or enslaved during the war.

Sanctioned by the Bay Colony authorities as the official narrative of the war, Hubbard's *A Narrative of the Troubles* shows the extent to which animosity toward Native people—and Praying Indians in particular— permeated the colony. However, *A Narrative of the Troubles* was just one of many documents that New Englanders produced to justify their treatment of Indigenous people during the war. As historian Jill Lepore writes, King Philip's War "was remarkable for how much the colonists wrote about it: more than four hundred letters written during the war survive in New England archives alone, along with more than thirty editions of twenty different printed accounts." Lepore points out that the majority of the colonists who wrote about the war positioned the conflict as one in which "their lives, their land, and their sense of themselves" was at stake.[5] Literary scholar J. Patrick Cesarini notes that like *A Narrative of the Troubles*, many of these colonial war accounts "understood the war in providential terms, primarily as a drama of God's restoration of his favor to the English, and secondarily, of his disfavor to the Indians."[6] In making sense of the war, these accounts collectively took an us-versus-them approach in which the English defined Indigenous people (converted or not) as inherently "savage" and heathen and Europeans as naturally "civilized" and saved. This marks a change in the official rhetoric of the colony. No longer as dependent on Indigenous people for land or resources, colonists moved away from their earlier attempts to justify settlement in the name of religious conversion and instead focused on deliberately dismissing the rights of Indigenous people as a whole.

In the midst of these proliferating anti-Indigenous narratives, one account stands out—Daniel Gookin's 1677 *An Historical Account of the Doings and Sufferings of the Christian Indians in New England, in the Years 1675, 1676, 1677*. Gookin was John Eliot's friend and fellow missionary. In 1661 he was appointed superintendent of the Praying Indian towns—a position in which he was responsible for overseeing the Praying Indian judicial courts. Deeply vested in the Bay Colony's mission, Gookin used his experience as superintendent to try to tell the story of King Philip's War from the Praying Indian perspective. As Lepore writes, "in noticing the war narratives' neglect of Indians (albeit only Christian Indians), Gookin was not only more perceptive than most of his contemporaries, he was also more perceptive than most of the historians who succeeded him, many of whom failed to consider even the possibility of an Indian perspective."[7]

While *Doings and Sufferings* is often cited by historians of King Philip's War for the details it provides about the experience of Indigenous people residing in the mission towns, scholars have largely ignored the narrative elements of Gookin's text. As Cesarini points out, this lack of analysis is in part the result of the text's hybrid form. Gookin employs a combination of genres within *Doings and Sufferings*, including historical narrative, providential interpretation, petition, diplomatic relation, and personal narrative. As a result, the text is "difficult to 'place' or categorize."[8] Another reason Gookin's text has been largely overlooked is because it has not been fully contextualized in relation to the other colonial war accounts of the time. By unpacking both the content and the form of Gookin's narrative, we can locate *Doings and Sufferings* within the longer history of engagement between Indigenous converts, or Indigenous people who perform conversion, and the Puritan colonists I have traced up to this point.

Part of the confusion surrounding *Doings and Sufferings* lies in the fact that Gookin's arguments illustrating the mistreatment of Praying Indians are derived from his many years spent living among Indigenous communities, while the narrative's form and its intended audience are English. As Gookin's epistle dedicatory indicates, his account was written for the English supporters of the Puritan mission, specifically Robert Boyle, head of the Royal Society and overseer of the Corporation for the Propagation of the Gospel in New England. In writing to the mission's supporters, Gookin was attempting to counteract the effects of Hubbard's official narrative of events. Gookin's preoccupation with countering Hubbard's account is found not only in the content of the text but in its form as well. *Doings and Sufferings* is an almost point-by-point rebuttal of *Narrative of the Troubles*. Using alternative legal documents, theological interpretations, and personal narratives, Gookin writes a counternarrative that seeks to directly challenge Hubbard's claims that the Praying Indians are "naturally barbarous" and thus untrustworthy.

As part of his strategy, Gookin uses *Doings and Sufferings* to forward a new definition of "civility." For the English civility was not only a type of social and linguistic performance but also marked one's ability to govern oneself, to own and manage land, and to enter into political contracts. As the events of King Philip's War began, authors such as Hubbard began to use the language of "savagery" to justify their taking Indigenous lands and enslaving Indigenous bodies. In contrast, *Doings and Sufferings* points to the Praying Indians' willingness to keep their treaties with the English as evidence that they were not "savage" but "civil." Relying on the biblical language of covenants, Gookin employs personal narratives, stories, and legal documents from Praying Indian life to convince English readers that throughout the war the Praying Indians had continued to maintain their treaties and agreements with the English. Though mired in the language of religion, Gookin's tract defines "civility" and its concurrent rights as a condition derived from one's actions, performances, and ability to maintain political relationships—not a category accorded as a result of birth, national identity, or ethnicity.

Gookin's claims that the Praying Indians are "civilized" challenges Hubbard's account and is also distinct from the descriptions of Indigenous converts found in previous missionary literature, where the focus was on the potential for "civility" rather than its acquisition.[9] Yet, while Gookin's text eschews English precedent, it echoes the spiritual and social beliefs of the Bay Colony's Indigenous converts. Indigenous diplomatic philosophy in the Northeast defined relationships and alliances using treaties and agreements. For the northeastern Indigenous nations, making and honoring one's treaties was a central tenet of an organized, politically stable, "civilized" society. Not only important for diplomacy, treaties also had a spiritual role. A treaty marked a means by which Indigenous nations in the Northeast maintained social and spiritual balance; the breaking of a treaty was a spiritual breech that yielded disorder, violence, and warfare.

Though Gookin's aim as a missionary was to convert and "civilize," his position as superintendent in charge of approving Indigenous judges and enacting judicial rulings meant that Gookin was necessarily well versed in Algonquian philosophies of war, spirituality, and justice. His education on these matters was performed by the Indigenous community members with whom Gookin adjudicated legal decisions. Most prominent among them was Waban, the Massachusett leader who took over as ruler at Natick after Cutshamekin's death. While the Bay Colony placed Gookin at the head of the judicial system, within the missionary towns, effective governing within the communities depended on Gookin's working within the existing cultural practices of the Indigenous residents, who were themselves rooted in a cultural system in which legal rights were defined through treaties and reciprocity.

Thus, as I argue, *Doings and Sufferings* is not merely the articulation of Gookin's personal opposition to prevalent colonial perspectives. Rather, it is a natural result of almost thirty years of Indigenous diplomatic influence upon the structures and practices of the New England missionary project. Importantly, in *Doings and Sufferings*, Gookin not only uses the concept of treaties and treaty-making to illustrate the "civility" of the Praying Indians, but he also uses this same framework to assess the English as well. In Gookin's estimation, the failure of English leaders to keep their own treaties with the Praying Indians should lead the English authorities to implicitly question the "civility" of the English magistrates. For Gookin, good Christians, be they English or Indigenous, are those who keep their promises.

Judges, Rulers, and Conversion

Gookin is most often referenced by scholars in association with his participation in King Philip's War, but by the time the war began Gookin had already spent several years working in both English and Indigenous legal systems. His location at the intersection of colonial politics is key to understanding his narrative perspective in *Doings and Sufferings*. Throughout his account, Gookin repeatedly invokes legal precedents and court decisions to defend Praying Indians' actions. Gookin's knowledge of legal procedures and colonial law came in large part from his position as a political insider.

The first member of the Gookin family to arrive in New England was Daniel's father, Daniel Sr., who arrived in 1621 as part of his business trading cattle with the Virginia settlers.[10] In 1631 the younger Gookin made his first trip to Virginia to manage his father's Newport News plantation. In 1641, at the age of thirty, Daniel Gookin began his long career in colonial politics when he was elected as a member of Virginia's House of Burgesses. A year later, in one of the earliest recorded actions of Gookin's political career, Gookin legislated a dispute between his brother, John Gookin and the local Nansemond tribe. The Gookin family's plantation in present-day Newport News, Virginia, was located at the confluence of the James and Nansemond Rivers, which placed it "in close proximity to the Nansemond's ceremonial center of Dumpling Island."[11] From the start of his political career, Gookin found himself negotiating between the people whose lands he was upon and the people whose lands he was from.

While some of those negotiations were peaceful, others were not. In 1643 Gookin left Virginia and headed for Maryland after the Virginia colonial governor William Berkeley expelled dissenters. Staying in Maryland for only a short while, Gookin then arrived in Massachusetts Bay in 1644.[12] In 1649 Gookin again became part of the colonial government when he was elected to serve as a Cambridge representative to the General Court. He was also head of the Cambridge militia. He was reelected in 1651. From 1652 until his death in 1687 Gookin was elected almost continually as an assistant to the court. The exception to this was in 1676, when Gookin was voted out of office for a year because of his support for the Praying Indians in King Philip's War.[13] However, his ousting lasted only a short time. Reinstated in 1677, Gookin was immediately tapped to lead a military expedition against the Wabanaki in Maine.[14]

Gookin's political career and his spiritual beliefs eventually led him to participate in John Eliot's Indian mission. When Gookin moved to the Bay Colony in 1644, he lived next to Eliot in Roxbury. The two became friends, and in 1666 Gookin's daughter married Eliot's son. Gookin also began to accompany Eliot on his trips to the Praying Indian towns. Though we don't have clear evidence of when Gookin first started working with Eliot, it is possible that he was part of the missionary project from the beginning.[15] Gookin is first formally mentioned in the missionary literature in 1651 when he joined other church leaders in questioning Indigenous converts to determine their spiritual readiness to form the Praying Indian church at Natick.[16] In the 1650s, Gookin utilized his political expertise to help establish English judicial practices among the Wampanoag when he was appointed Indian superintendent, a position created at Eliot's behest. In 1656 Eliot requested the General Court to appoint "some agents . . . in Massachusetts [Bay] to promote and forward the work among the Indians, both in respect of their government and encouraging some meet instruments for their further help and instruction." In 1657 Eliot again made his request, this time proposing Gookin serve in the role of superintendent.[17] When the role was finally approved in 1658, Gookin was in England, where he had been recruited to work on behalf of the English Protectorate. Between 1655 and 1660, Gookin was back and forth between England and the colonies after being commissioned by Oliver Cromwell to recruit English settlers to colonize the newly obtained island of Jamaica.[18] After the Restoration of Charles II in 1660, Gookin settled back into colonial life and in 1661 he finally took up the role of Indian superintendent. He remained superintendent until his death in 1687. By the time of King Philip's War, Gookin was an established leader in both colonial and Praying Indian governance.

It is important to note that during the time Gookin was active in both the colonial government and the Puritan mission, he was also an avid land speculator. As historian Christine Delucia notes, "Gookin amassed a sizeable checkerboard of claims to Native places, in or nearby traditional homelands of Massachusetts, Pennacooks, Nipmucs, Pequots, and Narragansetts." He acquired his lands by various means: "Sometimes the Massachusetts General Court granted him hundreds of acres as recompense for service; sometimes he tapped into his Algonquian networks to purchase other hundreds of acres."[19] By the time Gookin died, "more than three-quarters of his estate lay in real property." Though was not "fabulously rich," he did die "a wealthy man, thanks to his lands."[20] Clearly, Gookin used his position as superintendent and colonial official to accumulate wealth from dispossessed Indigenous people, sometimes actively doing the dispossessing himself.[21]

While his land speculation allowed him to amass wealth for himself, Gookin's position as superintendent of the missionary towns required him to work with others. As superintendent, Gookin negotiated with Indigenous leaders to establish a judicial system. The Praying Indian judicial system, like the larger missionary project, was derived from a combination of Indigenous law, English law, and Puritan religious concepts of Christian civility.[22] As seen in *The Christian Commonwealth*, Eliot believed that establishing a judicial system within the Praying Indian towns was a necessary first step toward enacting a larger missionary vision. The court served as a means for the missionaries to deploy and enforce English-style rules intended to promote "civilization" among Indigenous people who had come into mission towns. In regulating Indigenous clothing, sexual relationships, and religious practices, the courts gave the missionaries a means to enforce a particular performance of Englishness among their potential converts—a performance they hoped would transform Indigenous participants from their "wild and scattered manner of life" to one of "Civil Government and Order."

Yet, despite the court's imperial aims, many Indigenous people who relocated to praying towns also desired the establishment of colonial courts. Within the increasingly constrained power dynamics of colonial New England, the court system provided one of the only avenues for Indigenous people to participate in colonial governing processes, protect their home-lands from colonial land claims, and obtain military protection from the Bay Colony. The Praying Indian court system developed out of the 1644 treaty between Cutshamekin and the Bay Colony, in which Cutshamekin and his fellow sachems agreed to be "under the government & *jurisdiction*" of the Bay Colony in return for protection.[23] As O'Brien points out, Indigenous leaders who treated with the Bay Colony like Cutshamekin and Waban agreed to be part of the English missionary project in part because "they sought a course of peaceful coexistence holding the promise that an Indian future could be negotiated within the context of English expansion."[24] The establishment of the judicial system offered a means for the allied leaders to strengthen and regulate their communities within a colonial system and provided them with strong diplomatic ties to the English colonists.

While Gookin was appointed to the role of superintendent for his political experience, his ability to govern was dependent on the Indigenous residents themselves as it was the Praying Indian leader Waban, who both created and served as the primary representative of the judicial system in the mission communities. Though Waban is most known for his association with Eliot (it was to Waban that Eliot turned after being rejected by Cutshamekin), the Massachusett leader remained con-nected to his Massachusett relatives. Long before he aligned with Eliot,

Waban was related to leading Massachusett families through his marriage to Tasunsquam, or Tassansquaw, the daughter of Tahattawan, the Massachusett sachem of the Musketaquid.[25] His father-in-law, Tahattawan, had established an alliance with Squa Sachem, a Massachusett saunkskwa. Squa Sachem had taken over leadership duties among the Northern Massachusetts after the death of her husband, Nanepashement.[26] After the devastating epidemics of smallpox had killed many in their communities, some Northern Massachusett tribal members moved with Waban to mission communities. Among them was Waban's father-in-law, Tahattawan, whose village of Nashobah become the location of one of Eliot's praying towns.[27] After her husband's death Squa Sachem made an alliance with John Winthrop, and eventually she moved to Natick.

Waban, Tahattawan, Squa Sachem, and others joined with Eliot out of a desire to protect their communities. Their settlement at Nonantum was near their traditional homelands, and it provided them close proximity to their friends and relatives.[28] However, being part of Eliot's community also meant that they had protection from attacks and the opportunity to build up a new community. Not long after Eliot's first visit with Waban at Nonantum in October 1646, the two men set about adapting Indigenous legal practices to conform to English Christian conventions. In November of 1646, Waban helped Eliot draft the Nonantum Code, a detailed series of laws and proscriptions that Eliot hoped would guide Indigenous people toward English "civility." The codes included rules for domestic relationships, work habits, sexuality, and hygiene.[29] While the codes were approved by Eliot, they still retained some elements of autonomy for Indigenous residents. Waban shaped the codes to avoid many of the most drastic cultural changes Eliot was attempting. As David Ress writes, "the only law dealing with violence concerned beating a wife; the only law on sexual relations sanctioned premarital relations, which were tolerated in Massachusett society, while ignoring adultery, which was not—a significant shift in emphasis. Three of the laws addressed gender differences; two requiring adaptation of English ways (covered breasts and short hair) one banning women from dressing their hair as men had two. Two of the laws required industrious behavior." In short, Waban attempted to create a "kind of synthesis of English and Massachusett ways."[30]

For Eliot, however, the Nonantum Code was an essential first step on the path to Christianization and it was written almost five years before the town of Natick was formed. Following the Nonantum Code, Waban helped draw up another set of laws in 1647. This time he wrote the laws for his father-in-law Tahattawan and the other Massachusett at Nashobah.[31] In writing the judicial codes, Waban worked to create a new start for his beleaguered community. And, on one level, Waban's plan was successful. By bringing his family members together under Eliot's protection, Waban was able to "establish a community at Natick that survived for more than a century."[32] Yet, as Waban's testimony in his conversion narrative accounts indicates, he was also motivated by fear. As he tells the ministers who have gathered to judge the authenticity of his narrative, "Sometime I thought if we did not pray, the English might kill us." Waban, like Wequash, may also have been drawn to Christianity as a powerful spiritual practice that he turned to in a time of imbalance. As he writes, his desire to get to "the Heavenly Kingdom" meant that he "gave his self and his soul to God."[33] The reasons for Waban's participation in the mission were a combination of his desire for survival, his attempts to protect his community, the coercion of the missionaries, and perhaps, Christian conviction. Thus Waban's writing of the codes does not necessarily signal his complete approval of their content or function. However, Waban's central role in the code's formation indicates the extent to which the missionaries were at the behest of Native people for the progression of their mission.

After the codes were written, Waban and his fellow Praying Indians were tasked with enforcing them. In 1647 the Massachusetts authorities "authorized" Waban and Tahattawan to "hear minor civil cases in monthly sessions, to appoint constables, and to rule on criminal cases referred to them by English magistrates."[34] In many ways, this was a perfunctory assignment because as leaders Waban and Tahattawan had already been determining communal justice for years.[35] In his first meeting with Waban, Eliot describes him to the English readers as "the chief minister of Justice" at Nonantum.[36] As the mission progressed, the Praying Indian judiciaries were accorded more formal powers. According to the English court records, Indigenous judges were eventually given the right to "determine all such matters that do arise among themselves, as one magistrate may do among the English." As Richard Cogley explains, "This provision presumably meant that Indian commissioners, like Puritan magistrates, were empowered to hear civil suites under 20 shillings and to punish minor criminal infractions such as drunkenness, Sabbath-breaking, and petty theft." While the Indigenous judges determined smaller cases, Gookin held quarterly sessions to hear larger cases that were referred to him. However, Gookin's schedule meant that he was not able to spend extensive time adjudicating Indigenous cases.[37] Many, if not most, of the judicial rulings among the residents of the mission towns were made by Waban, his relatives, and other community members.

In a transcript from one of the court sessions, we can see the close working relationship between Gookin, Waban, and the Indigenous community. Of course, while Gookin relied on Indigenous judges for many of the minor judicial decisions, he still retained final authority as the English colonial representative. He was also the one who transcribed the cases, thereby giving him narrative authority as well. Nevertheless, Gookin's transcripts give us a glimpse into how the judicial systems in the mission communities may have worked. In 1668 Gookin transcribed the case of Sarah Ahhaton, a Massachusett woman accused of adultery by her husband, William Ahhaton. Both Sarah and William were under the jurisdiction of the Praying Indian town at Punkapoag. William, also known as Quaanan, was the son of Tahattawan, making him Waban's brother-in-law. In addition to being part of a leadership family, William also served as a teacher, minister, and community leader at Punkapoag.[38] As Gookin indicates, the case started in Waban's court. In 1666, "around planting time," or late spring, Sarah appeared before Waban after her husband "chardged her that shee loved other men." The two had been in a partnership for ten years. Specifically, the transcript explains that William claimed that Sarah "did sometimes speak alone with Joseph a married man of Packemit."[39] Not content to verbally accuse her, Gookin explains that William "did beat [Sarah] severall times, as som other Indians of the place do know." The case itself is at the intersection between English gender codes and existing Massachusett practices. Among the Massachusett, women could choose their own partners. Because women owned the wigwams and longhouses, in marriage a man would move into a woman's dwelling. However, among both the Wampanoag and under the Nonantum codes, adultery was taboo.

Yet in the transcript, performance of Sarah's adultery is not clearly evident. Rather, it seems William's accusations about Joseph and Sarah may have been motived by William's desire for vengeance. William's ire seems to have been raised after Sarah was warned by Joseph's mother, aunt, and another woman that William "did love, and keepe company with other women." The mothers and aunts who warned Sarah of her husband's infidelity were tasked with maintaining order and balance among the Massachusett community. Some of them may have even been clan mothers, a group of elders who held high authority among the Wampanoag. A largely internal affair, Waban's court relied on the existing organizational structures in the community. It was friends and relatives who testified to Sarah's beatings, and it was also Indigenous women who were themselves long-standing arbitrators of communal justice, who informed Sarah that her husband was cheating. Though we don't know all the details of the case, it seems that Waban made the decision in favor of William. Perhaps he sided with his relative, perhaps he was attempting to enforce English gender codes, or perhaps for another reason, Waban "did then chardge [Sarah] that she should not at any time after bee alone in company of the said Joseph."[40] William seems to have gone unpunished.

This was not the end of the case. A few months later, "about weeding time," Sarah and William found themselves in court again. As Gookin recounts, they were present at "an indian court kept at pakemitt at the house of squamock the Ruler." Pakemitt, also known as Punkapoag, was the home of Joseph and his family. It was also the community headed by William's father, Old Hahawton.[41] The fact that this court was held in William and Joseph's home community seems to have influenced the court's proceedings. Though the text is unclear, it is possible that the reason Sarah and William were back in court for the same charge may have been that the community wanted to have its own hearing regarding their members' affairs. The courts' ties to the community also allowed Sarah to escape punishment because Joseph, her purported paramour, had inside knowledge of the court's deliberation. As Gookin explains, Joseph's "uncle William" told him that Sarah was going to be "whipt erelong" for "wch shee was before Waban." Attempting to protect her, Joseph sent her to his mother's wigwam to hide. After three days, Sarah went to her own home "nere Pawtuckett, wher her father and mother lived." When Sarah's family heard her about situation, they also took matters into their own hands. As Gookin writes, "Her father & mother wth some other friends came downe wth her to Packemit, & by their endevors a reconciliation was made between her and her husband."[42] This peace continued, but only for a short time—"about seven or 8 weeks until about hilling time."

By that time, the beatings and suspicions from William had taken their toll on Sarah: they "did weaken and alienate her former affections to him." Actualizing her husband's accusations, Sarah finally "lay" with Joseph, who came "to her wigwam" while William was "at the Sea Side." As Gookin explains, in this instance it was Joseph's mother who worked to protect Sarah by insisting that she "withdraw herselfe & go to Philip's wigwam Sachem of mount hope neare Secunck, wheare shee should bee entertained."[43] Not long after her departure, Joseph joined Sarah, and the two carried on as a couple. Up to this point in Gookin's transcript of the case, the primary mechanisms of justice are communal and internal. As Ann Marie Plane points out, "the English-style magistrates Sarah Ahhaton faced in the Indian court were probably members of the original elite families, who largely continued pre-Christian roles in the new enclaves."[44] The Indigenous courts and the Praying Indian communities in which Sarah found herself were connected. As the narrative explains, the court at Punkapoag intended to punish her because she broke the ruling she had received in Waban's courtroom. Further, Sarah and Joseph's family members in Natick, Punkapoag, and Pawtucket worked with (and at times against) one another. At the second hearing, Joseph's kinship networks trumped the judicial rulings; Sarah escaped the court's sentence because of Joseph's uncle and mother. Kinship may also have been a reason she was sent to Metacom, or Philip, as Joseph's family likely had kinship ties to the Pokanoket who could offer Sarah and Joseph protection. Attempting to resolve the case internally, the residents in the mission community used a mix of both formal and informal mechanisms.

It is only when Sarah finally turned herself in to the Punkapoag court that she received judicial punishment from the English. Leaving Joseph, Sarah first returns to Punkapoag, where "from thence [she] was carried to Natick before Wabun." Perhaps realizing that the English rules could not overcome kinship ties, or perhaps for some other reason, Waban sent the case to Gookin, who finally meted out Sarah's punishment. Gookin "committed her to prison." In Gookin's narrative, the punishment was divinely ordained because it was Sarah's choice to turn herself in after it "pleased God to smite her hart wth the Sence of her Sinne."[45] Plane explains that after lingering in prison for at least a month, Sarah was "finally sentenced by the Massachusetts General Assembly to stand on the Boston gallows with a noose around her neck for one hour on a Sabbath day and to be 'severly' whipped at Natick by the Indian constable."[46] In the trial transcripts, it seems that Sarah and William had a sort of reconciliation: when asked if her husband had "layne wth her since her returne," she responded, "yea, once in prison." William also "manifested himself to her as willing againe to receve her if the Court please to pardon her." Made a public example by both Waban and Gookin, Sarah endured a severe punishment, while William got away unscathed.[47]

Despite the clear imposition of colonial justice upon Wampanoag practice, the case of Sarah Ahhaton also illustrates the fact that Gookin was dependent on Indigenous people to enforce any judicial rulings. When making his ruling, Gookin presumably heard the facts of the case from Waban, and later from Sarah herself using an Indigenous interpreter, Andrew Boughow.[48] Even Gookin's transcription seems to carry traces of Indigenous narrative conventions, as the events of the case are recounted using local agrarian markers. Moving from "planting time," to "weeding time," to "hilling time," the story of Sarah's case proceeds alongside the yearly corn planting cycle. Not present at any of the events save the final court hearing, Gookin has to rely on the memories of Native participants as the testimony of the case was related to Gookin almost two years after Sarah first appeared in Waban's court. Despite Sarah's eventual treatment in the English courts, the actions of her family and Joseph's family show how kinship ties and Indigenous communities played a substantial role in determining communal justice even after the arrival of the English.[49]

Though clearly influenced by the imposition of English Christianity, the Praying Indian judicial systems retained Algonquian social and spiritual beliefs as well. In the same way that manitou guided Wequash's actions and determined Cutshamekin's relationship with colonial leaders, it also determined the actions of the subsequent Praying Indians. Manitou was an "impersonal force that permeated the world, observable in anything marvelous, beautiful, or dangerous." As a force, manitou was "not uniformly distributed in the world" and while it could inhabit "natural phenomena, objects or people," it was "not necessarily a permanent quality."[50] Judicial rulings, alongside treaties, and ceremonies, worked to redistribute, balance, or maintain manitou to ensure societal flourishing. The "notion of *manitou* in all things was at the center of coastal practices for marking agreements and building political order."[51] In participating in the practices and structures of northeastern Algonquian communities, colonists like Gookin and Eliot became part of the common pot. As such, they were beholden to and influenced by Algonquian spiritual practices. As Brooks writes, "Europeans were in the common pot, whether they knew it or not, and they had brought with them ideas, behaviors, and materials that could potentially disrupt or destroy it."[52]

Competing Narratives of King Philip's War

Gookin's consideration of Indigenous systems is not limited to his judicial rulings but extends to his defense of the Praying Indians recounted in *Doings and Sufferings*. In defending the actions of the mission town residents, Gookin relies on descriptions of Indigenous words and deeds. As such, *Doings and Sufferings*, like the Praying Indian judicial system, intertwines Indigenous beliefs and practices with missionary motivation. Written in 1677, *Doings and Sufferings* was Gookin's attempt to respond the accounts of the war promulgated by other Bay Colony leaders, namely the two most popular histories of the war, Increase Mather's *A Brief History of the War with the Indians in New England* (1676) and William Hubbard's *Narrative of the Troubles* (1677). As Gookin explains in his introduction, the problem with Mather and Hubbard's "historical narratives" was that they said "very little" about "the Christian Indians, who, in reality, may be judged to have no small share in the effects and consequents of the war."[53]

More than just an attempt to vocalize the Praying Indian experience during the war, Gookin's narrative attempts to justify and defend the residents of the mission communities, whom Hubbard and Mather have largely dismissed. Like many in the Bay Colony, Hubbard's and Mather's narratives are largely suspicious of Praying Indian motivation in the war as these authors are convinced that the Praying Indians would inevitably choose kinship over conversion. Their suspicions extended to Gookin and Eliot as well. Wary of the missionaries' claims that the Indigenous converts were "civilized," most of the English colonists assumed that "the entire Indian population, regardless of prior allegiances or protestations of friendship, had risen against the colonies."[54] In their attempts to give significance to the war, Mather and Hubbard folded the inscrutability of Indigenous conversion into their larger providential renderings of the war's significance.

In Mather's *Brief History* the attack on the Puritan mission is somewhat subdued. As Mather explains, *A Brief History* was his attempt to "methodize

Treaties, Reciprocity, and Providence   139

such scattered Observations" as he had about King Philip's War.[55] In Mather's estimation, King Philip's War was divine punishment for the degradation of New England's second generation. As Anne Kusener Nelsen points out, Mather did not view the war as an exceptional occurrence but rather as a "scourge in a succession of scourges."[56] One impetus for the divine scourging was the Bay Colony's failure to grow its Indigenous mission. As Mather suggests, "the Lords Holy design in *Warr*" was "(in part) . . . to punish us for our too great neglect in [converting the Indians]." For Mather, the missionary project was not a complete failure. He acknowledges the efforts of the first generation of founders, particularly the "Reverend Mr. *Eliot*" who "hath taken most indefatigable pains" in his efforts to preach to the Indians. However, the second generation did not follow in Eliot's footsteps and "It cannot be long, before that faithful, and now aged Servant of the Lord rest from his labours." Once Eliot was gone, "sad will it be for the succeeding Generation."[57] For Mather, the missionary project, like the rest of the New England colony, had lost its way. The second and third generations could not live up to the faithfulness of the first. Though Mather does not reference Gookin directly, as Eliot's successor, Gookin may have seen Mather's words as dismissive of the continuing efforts he was making in growing the Puritan mission.

As the first of the three histories of the war that was published, Mather's account was in print before Hubbard's. However, Mather had heard the content of Hubbard's forthcoming account during Hubbard's 1676 election sermon.[58] As Nelsen explains in her oft-cited account of the dispute, Hubbard and Mather differed greatly on the war's providential meaning. While Mather saw the war as providential punishment for New England's sins, Hubbard blamed the war on individual actors—namely "Satans Instruments" or Indigenous people, whose "shew of . . . Religion" is "no doubt . . . learned from the *Prince of Darkness*."[59] Like Mather, Hubbard also provides his opinion on the New England missionary project. However, where Mather praises Eliot as the product of a dying generation, Hubbard dismisses Eliot and instead sets himself up as Eliot's successor. In the prefatory poem printed with Hubbard's account, poet Benjamin Thompson makes a direct contrast between Eliot, who he terms the Indians' "grand Apostle" who writes of "their return," and Hubbard, who writes about "how they burn, / Rob, kill and Roast, lead Captive, flay, blaspheme."[60] As Lepore explains, the poem suggests that Eliot's writing "had been rightly replaced by Hubbard's account of the Indian's barbarity."[61] The claim that Hubbard was attempting to replace Eliot as the spokesperson for Indian affairs was not ill founded. While Mather's account is dismissive of the Praying Indians, Hubbard's stands out in its attempts to create a calculated argument against the authenticity of Indigenous conversion.

Like Mather, Hubbard's account also contains an indirect indictment of Gookin, albeit a much more pointed and personal one. On the final pages of his narrative, Hubbard addresses the Praying Indian question directly for any who may be wondering "what is become of the *Conversion of the Natives*, so much *famed abroad*." Employing Mather's rhetoric of divine inscrutability, Hubbard acknowledges the possibility of Indigenous conversion. As he writes, "it is supposed that there are some that do make *a serious profession* of the Christian Religion." Yet, while this statement suggests the possibility of true conversion, his account quickly forecloses this suggestion. Relying on a discourse of civility versus savagery, Hubbard argues that "never any notable work of Religion was known to take much place, where some kind of Civility, and *Culture of good manners*, had not gone before." In Hubbard's historical view, "we rarely find any *Gentill Nation* turned *Christian* before they became *Humane*."[62]

Making the connection explicit, Hubbard describes the efforts that have been made to "civilize" Indigenous people in New England as clearly unsuccessful as evidenced by the events of King Philip's War. For Hubbard, the New England mission has failed because the missionaries have taken too gentle of an approach. As he writes, "The Civility that is found amongst the *Natives* of this Country; hath hitherto been *carried on* and obtained, only by the gentle means of *Courtesy, Familiarity*, and such like *civil behaviour*, which in other places was never yet attended with any *eminent Success* that way." To illustrate his claims that Indigenous people cannot be truly converted, much less civilized, Hubbard ends his narrative with a story about previous English missionary attempts among the Powhatan confederacy in Virginia. In his final pages, he reminds his readers of the 1622 military attacks in Virginia by the Powhatan sachem Opechancanough. In the battles, Opechancanough and his followers defended their homelands by attacking English plantations and in the process killed a number of settlers. The attacks came after the Powhatans had repeatedly attempted to persuade the English settlers to leave their territory.

Among the dead was the English missionary George Thorpe, an enthusiastic proselytizer who had attempted to befriend Opechancanough and had even built the sachem an English-style house.[63] In Hubbard's version of the events, Thorpe's ardent defense of the Powhatan made him blind to the threat they posed. In a description almost certainly aimed at the defenders of the Bay Colony mission, Hubbard writes that Thorpe, "out of his good meaning was so full of Confidence and void of Suspicion, that he would never believe *any hurt* of [the Powhatan], till he *felt their cruel hands imbrued in his own blood.*" Hubbard then explains that "the geneality of the Indians in New England are in their manners and natural disposition, not much unlike those in Virginia, living much in the same clime."[64] In this parallel, Hubbard not only points to the inherent contradiction of a Christian Indian; he also critiques anyone who defends them.

Interestingly, the particular story that Hubbard chose to illustrate the impossibility of conversion seems to have been a veiled attack on the Gookin family.[65] The 1622 uprising occurred four months after Daniel Gookin Sr. arrived in Virginia to set up his cattle trade. Though only recently arrived, Gookin Sr.'s plantation Marie's-Mount at Newport News was one of the few not attacked by Opechancanough's forces.[66] While it is hard to determine why Marie's-Mount was not attacked, it may have been that Gookin's status as a merchant and trader gave him some sort of value to the tribal leaders.[67] While we have limited evidence of Gookin Sr.'s Indigenous trading networks, we do know that Daniel Gookin himself regularly established ties with Native people through trade. In 1632 English captain Henry Fleet encountered the younger Gookin while he was looking to trade beaver pelts with Indigenous traders on the upper Potomac River. As Luke Pecoraro explains, "Fleet describes Gookin Jr. as an 'interpreter,' and learned from Gookin about a powerful tribe called the Massawomecks whose chiefdom was at the head of Chesapeake Bay, with whom he might be able to trade."[68] Though trade may not have been the sole reason why the Gookin family was not attacked in 1622, Hubbard's decision to include the story reminds his readers that the Gookin family has a long history of relationships with Indigenous people and insinuates that the Gookin family's ties to Indigenous communities may challenge their loyalty to the English settlers. As Hubbard seems to be saying, Gookin is, and always has been, too trusting of Native people.

Hubbard's personal jab at Gookin alongside his larger critique of Gookin's missionary work was reason enough for Gookin to feel the need to defend himself. However, the timing of Gookin's text in relation to Hubbard's further suggests that *Doings and Sufferings* was a direct response to *A Narrative of the Troubles*. As Gookin's epistle dedicatory indicates, *Doings and Sufferings* was written for an English audience. Like Winthrop's "Of Maiz," *Doings and Sufferings* was specifically addressed to Robert Boyle. However, rather than writing to Boyle as the head of the Royal Society, Gookin addressed his tract to Boyle in his capacity as leader of the Corporation for the Propagation of the Gospel in New England. Though Gookin clearly intended to update the corporation on the state of their mission, the fact the narrative was written to an English audience in late December 1677 suggests that Gookin also hoped his account would counter Hubbard's. Having already received the official sanction of the Bay Colony for his original publication in March of 1677, Hubbard traveled to England in early 1678 to "superintend" the publication of *Narrative of the Troubles* for an English audience.[69] His trip was taken only a few weeks after Gookin's narrative was written, and Gookin's narrative may have traveled to England on the same boat as Hubbard himself. Though Gookin's account was never published, its timing suggests that Gookin was hoping to mitigate the effects of Hubbard's account and maintain the favor of his English benefactors by providing them with an "impartial" account from one "well acquainted with that affair."

Reconfiguring the Diplomatic Relation

When read as a rebuttal to other accounts of the war, Gookin's narrative format begins to make sense. As part of his strategic response to Hubbard, Gookin retains the general form and order Hubbard used, though Gookin puts his account in service to a very different end. Both *A Narrative of the Troubles* and *Doings and Sufferings* are written in a form that literary scholar Jeffrey Glover terms a "diplomatic relation," a genre that captured "both official acts of ratification and the many behaviors and negotiations that surrounded them." Its intent was to provide Europeans readers with "potential evidence of [Indigenous] consent." Glover explains that "the English crown and its colonists sought to demonstrate possession of foreign territories" by detailing the treaties they had made with Native people. Native treaties were not intended to showcase Indigenous sovereignty but were rather reprinted to provide

Treaties, Reciprocity, and Providence   143

evidence that the English colonists were "carrying out a supposedly peaceful conquest"—in this light, the majority of colonial authors only emphasized treaties when they aligned with European aims.[70] In Hubbard's account, descriptions of Native treaties provide evidence to English readers that the Bay Colony has performed its colonial conquest "correctly" and thus is now justified in attacking Metacom and his followers.

In *Doings and Sufferings*, Gookin employs the diplomatic relation form in order to provide English readers with evidence that the Indigenous residents of the mission towns are trustworthy. Gookin's account revisits and revises many of the same events that Hubbard describes in *A Narrative of the Troubles*, which allows him to provide a new interpretation of the events of the war. Using eyewitness testimony and documentary evidence, Gookin verifies his claims, and indeed the claims of the larger New England Puritan mission—that the Praying Indians are true converts and as such deserve the rights accorded to them in previous treaties and negotiations. Gookin's commitment to mirroring Hubbard's narrative structure makes Gookin's account difficult to follow at times. As relatively minor players in a war between the English and the Wampanoag, the Praying Indians' actions during the war fail to fit into the same narrative structure as the one Hubbard employs for the war's larger events. Nevertheless, Gookin's focus on the Praying Indians strategically disrupts one of Hubbard's primary ends—that of justifying English actions during the war. As Gookin shows, in failing to differentiate between Indigenous people and abandoning their past treaties, the English have not only turned their back on their allies but have also forsaken their "covenant with our King, in our charter, to use our best endeavours to communicate the Christian religion to the Indians."[71]

Gookin not only reinterprets Hubbard's narrative of the war; he also reinterprets Hubbard's visual elements. Both *A Narrative of the Troubles* and *Doings and Sufferings* start by locating their readers within the physical spaces where the events of the war unfurled. Hubbard takes his readers to New England using an inserted map. Intent on justifying English conquest, Hubbard's map defines the terrain of the battle using English names and prioritizing English villages. Hubbard's naming conventions are part of his larger strategy to identify the space upon which King Philip's War takes place as English space. As Hubbard's caption to the map suggests, the intent of the map is to mark the English villages that "have been assaulted by the *Indians*," supporting his larger narrative in which the English are victims attacked in their own lands.[72] The figures in Hubbard's map reinforce his narrative aims. The map marks the English towns using tiny houses and church buildings while the locations of the Narragansett, the Pocasset, the Pequot, and the Nipmuc are indicated by trees or blank spaces. As Lepore notes, the trees and blank spaces invoke the larger logic of *vacuum domicilum*, the idea that Indigenous people did not "properly" use the land and therefore held no claims to it.[73] Hubbard's map is not merely a political statement, but it also reinforces his claims that the war is a spiritual one between the forces of evil and the forces of light. Hubbard's map positions the colonists as attacked in their own lands, "religious martyrs" who are justified in their treatment of the "savage" Indians.[74]

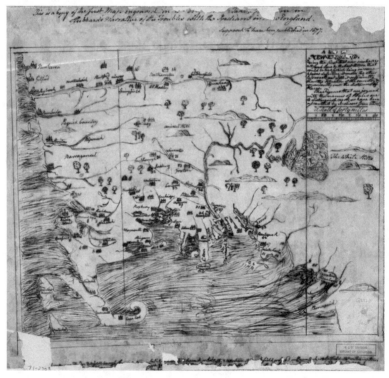

FIGURE 5. "A map of New-England, being the first that ever was here cut, and done by the best pattern that could be had, which being in some places defective, it made the other less exact: Yet doth it sufficiently show the situation of the country & conveniently well the distances of places." William Hubbard, 1677. Courtesy of the Library of Congress, Geography and Maps Division.

Not surprisingly, the Praying Indians have no place in Hubbard's map—an omission that Gookin's account seeks to rectify. As part of his attempts to counter Hubbard and retell the war as an event focused on Praying Indians, Gookin follows his own epistle dedicatory with a map as well—albeit a verbal and not a visual one. Gookin map fills in Hubbard's blank spaces. Explaining that before he can give a "particular and real account of this affair," he must first "premise some things necessary to be understood for the better clearing of our ensuing discourse," Gookin begins by introducing the of Christian Indians in terms of their location, history, leaders, and the members' public performances of Christianity.[75] Gookin starts by describing the mission work on Nantucket and Martha's Vineyard (Wampanoag), then moves on to talk about the Cape Indians in New Plymouth (Nauset, Wampanoag) and the Praying Indians in Connecticut Colony (Mohegan). Finally, he ends with the Praying Indians who live in the Bay Colony (Nipmuc, Penacook, Wampanoag), explaining that these are the people on whom his account focuses because they "have felt more of the effects of this war than all the rest of the Christian Indians."[76] By mapping the Praying Indian villages throughout the New England colonies, Gookin defines the entirety of New England as being anchored by Praying Indian towns, thereby setting the stage for his larger narrative. It is important to note that Gookin is not focused on mapping the location of Indigenous people as a whole. Rather, his focus is on those who have performed conversion and moved to the Praying Indian communities.

After mapping out the names and locations of the mission communities, Gookin continues to mimic Hubbard's narrative form. Once they have strategically defined the space of New England for their readers—for Hubbard, it is an exclusively colonized space, for Gookin, it is a colony peopled with Indigenous converts—both Hubbard and Gookin describe the backstory of the war by moving through a number of past legal agreements between Indigenous people and English settlers. Following his map, Hubbard reinforces his claims that the English have "properly" obtained the land by presenting a brief history of colonial land transactions. Starting with the English crown, Hubbard explains that the first settlers in New England "obtained a Patent, under the great Seal from King James." It was from this "grand and Original Patent" that "all other Charters and grants of Land from Pemmaquid to Delaware Bay, along the Sea coast, derive their Linage and Pedigree."[77] First establishing the authority of the English crown, Hubbard then chronologically lists the English patents and treaties up through the commencement of King Philip's War to show his readers that the English had faithfully and authoritatively conducted their colonial project. At the same time, Hubbard abdicates the English from blame for the war by using his history to place blame on Indigenous nations.

Intertwined with Hubbard's history of English patent claims is another narrative of Indigenous perfidy. While Hubbard's describes the English as having scrupulously kept their end of the deal, his shows Indigenous people as incapable of keeping theirs. Drawing a line between Miantonomi's breaking of the 1638 Treaty of Hartford through his attack on the Mohegan and Metacom's failure to keep both the 1621 treaty that his father, Massasoit, made with Plymouth settlers, as well as Metacom's 1671 treaty with the English, Hubbard establishes King Philip's Was as the result of the sachems' inability to keep their promises. Using the examples of Massasoit, Miantonomi, and Metacom, Hubbard argues that both the Narragansett and the Wampanoag have been led by inherently warlike sachems who have rejected all English attempts at peace. In Hubbard's version of events, King Philip's War was the natural result of the English attempting to make political agreements with Indigenous sachems whose hearts, he claims, are filled only with "inveterate hatred" and "malice."[78]

In *Doings and Sufferings*, Gookin also employs Hubbard's discourse of political agreements to characterize the war's events, but crucially, Gookin's account show that it is not always Indigenous leaders who break their agreements and not only the English who keep them. Maintaining his desire to differentiate between Indigenous people who have performed conversion and those who have not, Gookin devises a philosophy of treaties based on a biblical principal of covenants. In Gookin's rendering, there is a difference between a covenant and a political agreement. The former is an agreement made between spiritual equals, while the latter is a civil agreement. In contrast to civil agreements, which can be broken, Gookin explains that "a covenant . . . is a very binding thing, and the breach of it sorely punished by the Lord." Covenants, or spiritual agreements, can be made with those outside of one's nation or group. Condemning the English (and Hubbard's) inability to differentiate between "one Indian and another," Gookin turns to biblical precedent. He lists several biblical references in which the Israelites make and keep covenants with their "heathen" neighbors. As he explains, "the Scriptures do record that sundry of the heathen in Israel's time, being proselyted to the Church, proved very faithful and worth men and women; as Uriah the Hittite, Zeleg the Ammonite, Ithmah the Moabite . . . and Rahab the harlot, and Ruth the Moabitess, and divers others, men and women."[79] In all these examples, the "heathen" participants in the treaty kept both their spiritual and social obligations to the Israelites, despite the fact that the Israelites (like the English) did not always keep their own promises. For Gookin, covenants are not merely political agreements but are also spiritual acts and concurrently entail spiritual obligations.

Countering Hubbard's localized history of political agreements and patents with a larger spiritual and typological history, Gookin moves the war out of the colonial context and into a larger history of Christian engagement with outsiders in which he typologizes the English settlers as the nation of Israel forging ahead in the New England wilderness. However, in contrast to the typical New England Puritan typology in which the English settlers are "God's chosen people" and Indigenous people are "the enemies of the Lord," Gookin formulates a typological reading of history that weaves the Praying Indians into the larger "city on a hill." Indigenous leaders who make covenants with the English have become as deserving of God's favor as the English themselves. Grafted into the English Christian community, the Praying Indians are now covenanted community members and are thus deserving of all the political rights and spiritual protection that the other members enjoy. And as Gookin illustrates throughout the rest of *Doings and Sufferings*, the Praying Indians' inclusion in the English community cannot be undone.

Gookin's distinction between covenants as agreements with spiritual implications and patents or other agreements which are solely political undergirds the entire logic of *Doings and Sufferings*. On one hand, Gookin's conception of covenants allows him to justify the English's broken treaties with the Narragansett, the Wampanoag, and the Pokanokets because, as Gookin reasons, these tribes as a whole have not honored the spiritual obligations of their covenants. When listing the providential reasons for the war, Gookin echoes Hubbard as he posits that one intended end of the war was "the punishment and destruction of many of the wicked heathen," especially the "Pakanahats [Pokanokets] and the Narragansetts."[80] Yet while Gookin agrees with Hubbard that retaliation is justified, his reasoning is different. For Hubbard, Indigenous people in general, and the Wampanoag in particular, are so full of "Subtilety, malice, and Revenge" that they seem "to be as inseparable from them, as if it were part of their *Essence*."[81] Hubbard believes that Metacom's followers have an inherently vengeful nature, which justifies English warfare. However, for Gookin, English warfare is the consequence of the sachems' decision to reject Christianity. As evidence, Gookin refers to a 1675 agreement between the Bay Colony and the Narragansett in which the "their chief Sachems malignantly rejected and opposed [the gospel]." By rejecting Christian instruction, Gookin believes that the sachems have made a conscious decision to forgo the spiritually binding element involved in a covenant. For Gookin, the only spirituality that is binding is that practiced by the English. Yet, while Gookin's logic both is inseparable from his English Puritanism and also produced devastating consequences, his thinking acknowledges that Indigenous people have a choice in their spiritual practice. Rather than being intractably evil as Hubbard claims, Gookin sees the sachems as having made a choice to reject Christian instruction—a choice not dependent on their identity as Native people or some form of inherent "savagery" but one made through reason and, more importantly for Gookin, a choice that they can change.

Making Sense of the War

To illustrate the covenanted relationship that the English have with the Praying Indians, Gookin begins the story of the war with Waban. Beginning in April 1675, two months before any battles had taken place, Gookin explains to his readers that when Waban "came to one of the magistrates on purpose, and informed him that he had grounds to fear that Sachem Philip and other Indians . . . intended some mischief shortly to the English and Christian Indians."[82] The magistrate ignored Waban, so, a month later, Waban once again warned the authorities of an impending attack. Ignored a second time, Gookin records that six weeks later, Waban came a third time to plead with the English to prepare for the attack. From the beginning of the war, Gookin shows Waban prioritizing his loyalty to the English above his ties to his relatives.

Detailing Waban's actions allows Gookin to show his English readers that the Praying Indians keep their promises and provides him with an opportunity to illustrate the unique value that the Praying Indians bring to the English war efforts. Waban's warning about the attack's timing is derived from his Indigenous knowledge. As Gookin explains, Waban and the other Christian Indians entreated the magistrates to take preemptive action immediately, because "when the woods were grown thick with green trees then it was likely to appear." On June 20, only a short time after Waban's third warning, the first battle of the war began as Metacom's forces attacked Plymouth Colony. And, as Waban had predicted, Metacom's followers attacked when the summer growing season was at its height, and the English could "see no enemy to shoot at" because of "the thick bushes."[83]

Emphasizing Waban's persistent warnings to the Bay Colony about the Wampanoag attack not only establishes Waban as an English ally but also allows Gookin to counter Hubbard's claims that Indigenous people are unable to keep their promises. As Gookin shows, Waban acted in response to a specific agreement that the Massachusett had made with the Bay Colony—the 1644 treaty between Cutshamekin and Governor John Winthrop. As the language of the 1644 treaty states, the Massachusett agreed "to give speedy notice of any conspiracy, attempt, or evill intention of any which wee shall know or hereof against the same."[84] Warning the magistrates of the impending attack, Waban and his relatives at once display their loyalty to the English and act out of their covenant agreement, proving to Gookin's readers that Indigenous people can be trusted to keep their promises.

The 1644 treaty that the Bay Colony made with Cutshamekin, Masconomet, Squa Sachem, Nashoonon, and Wassamequin is central to Gookin's defense of the Praying Indians in *Doings and Sufferings*. Following his description of Waban's warnings, Gookin lists a number of other examples showing that the Praying Indians have kept their covenant with the Bay Colony by acting as guides and interpreters and generally aiding in the English war efforts. After these descriptions, Gookin reprints the entirety of the 1644 treaty.[85] Following the treaty, Gookin also includes the question-and-answer session with Cutshamekin's amended responses. As Gookin suggests, both the Praying Indians' actions in the war as well as their willingness to "be instructed in the knowledge of God" are derived from their commitment to keeping the 1644 treaty with the Bay Colony. In return for their compliance the Praying Indians were supposed to receive governance and protection.

Gookin illustrates how, rather than the mutual protection promised, the colonial authorities have treated the Praying Indians with contempt and suspicion. In late October of 1675, as winter was just beginning, colonial authorities rounded up about two hundred Natick residents, with more to follow, and removed them to Deer Island, a small, isolated island with scarce resources. On the island, "confined Natives were forbidden from unauthorized trade and contact with mainland colonists or Indigenous relations." They were also "cut off from their customary hunting ranges and supplies," meaning that they faced a brutal winter with little food and inadequate shelter.[86] Ensuring that his readers are aware of the connection he is making, Gookin explicitly follows his printing of the treaty and its signatories by clearly connecting the treaty provisions with the contemporary situation of the mission residents. As he writes:

> The praying Indians, *confined to Deer Island, are the people with whom the above written agreements were made*, wherein subjection and mutual protection are engaged; and these Indians, as is before declared, made discovery of what they knew of the plottings and conspiracy of the enemy, before the war began; also most readily and cheerfully joined with, and assisted the English in the war; as is before in part touched, and will more clearly appear in the sequel of this discourse; also they submitted themselves to the laws of God and the English government, and desiring themselves and children to be taught and instructed in the Christian religion; *and have in all other points, so far as I know, (for the body of them,) kept and performed the articles of their covenant above expressed.* (emphasis added)[87]

In reprinting the 1644 treaty with the Praying Indians, Gookin explains the legal reasons behind Praying Indian loyalty at the same time as he drives home a point he has been making throughout the narrative: while the residents of the mission towns have held up their end of the bargain, the English colonists have failed to keep theirs.

Treaties, Reciprocity, and Providence   151

FIGURE 6. Gookin's manuscript of *Doings and Sufferings* (1677), showing the names of the English present at the signing of the 1644 treaty. Courtesy of the Newberry Library.

By pointing out the Bay Colony's failure to keep its word, Gookin again challenges Hubbard's providential interpretation of the war. Whereas Hubbard claims that the English are martyrs being unjustly attacked by vengeful Indians, Gookin shows that the English are culpable for the war's events because in failing to protect the Praying Indians they have failed in God's calling. English culpability goes beyond their lack of protection for the Praying Indians and extends into their active attempts to attack and destroy the mission town residents' homes and bodies. As Gookin shows, "through the harsh dealings of some English," the Praying Indians have been falsely accused of setting barns on fire, unfairly charged with aiding the enemy, and unjustly imprisoned as well. Eventually, as he writes, "the animosity and rage of the common people increased against [the Praying Indians]" to the extent that the General Court further broke its agreements with the Praying Indians when it forced the converts onto Deer Island—a clear failure of its covenant. The war, as Gookin claims, is punishment for the English' treatment of the Praying Indians, breaking a covenant is a breech that will be "sorely punished by the Lord."[88]

Below the reprinted treaty, Gookin also reprints the names of all of the signatories, both Indigenous and English. His inclusion of these names was strategic. Listed among the names of the English signatories are many members of the colonial leadership who were spearheading the attacks against the Praying Indians Gookin was defending. Among the English signatories of the 1644 treaty that Gookin lists in *Doings and Sufferings* are Samuel Symonds, Daniel Dennison, William Hawthorne, Simon Willard, and Edward Tyng. These six men were among the magistrates who had given the orders to "dispose" "all the Naticke Indians" to "Deare Island."[89]

Another listed magistrate, Simon Bradstreet, husband of poet Anne Bradstreet, had served with Gookin and William Hawthorne in a 1675 trial in which eleven Indigenous men affiliated with the mission communities were tried for murder. Among those arrested, bound with ropes, and marched at gunpoint to jail was James Printer, the Nipmuc man who in 1663 had facilitated the printing of the Bible in Wampanoag. Printer was held in confinement for several weeks. Eventually he was released. As Brooks explains, after "Gookin's incessant advocacy . . . the court found James Printer and nearly all the men not guilty." The accused men had been telling the truth. They had been hunting game to feed their families, not attacking the English. Released to Waban's custody, they joined their relatives in home confinement. However, not all of the accused men were released: "two were convicted, one was sold into slavery, and one executed."[90] Those who returned to their families were only home a short while before being forced to Deer Island.

While Gookin could not stop the forced removal of Indigenous people to Deer Island, he did use his authority as a magistrate to try to stop their further persecution. As Gookin notes in *Doings and Sufferings*, he not only reprinted the 1644 treaty in his treatise but he also had the treaty read aloud in the General Court at a special session in February 1676.[91] One of the aims of the session was to determine what to do with those still being held on Deer Island. Gookin explains that at the session "there were several motions and applications made to them touching the poor Christian Indians at Deer Island. Some would have them all destroyed; others, sent out of the country; but some there were of more moderation." In a bid to convince those "of more moderation," Gookin reminds the court of its preexisting covenant relationship with the Praying Indians and insists that they reread the 1644 treaty aloud. In this instance, Gookin's efforts seem to have been mildly successful.

As he writes, "When the General Court had read and considered this agreement, it had this effect (through God's grace) in some degree to abate the clamors of many men against the Indians."[92] Gookin is likely referring to the court's decision to send provisions to their Indigenous allies that they had confined "so as to prevent their perishing by any extremity that they may be put unto for want of absolute necessaries" and to allow "meet persons to visit them from time to time."[93] Though still held against their will, after four months of confinement, they were now at least being allowed a few provisions.

In both printing a copy of the treaty for his metropolitan readers and physically bringing a copy of the treaty before the General Court, Gookin illustrates the central role treaties played in determining Indigenous-English relations. His multilayered narrative allows Gookin to emphasize the efficacy of his argument. By "showing" his English readers that the General Court was convinced by his argument that the Praying Indians were indeed following their legal obligations, Gookin reinforces the argument's efficacy. At the same time, Gookin's reading of the treaty before the court provided an opportunity for the colonists to change their ways. Though they had been misguided in their treatment of the Praying Indians, Gookin allowed for the magistrates to revisit their treaties in the hopes that they would keep the legal covenants they had made with the Praying Indians. As part of his larger missionary aims, Gookin attempted to reassure his English benefactors that King Philip's War was only a minor detour for a missionary project that had and would continue to create loyal and faithful Indigenous converts.

Tracing Indigenous Influence in *Doings and Sufferings*

On February 28, 1676, only five days after Gookin read the 1644 treaty in court, Massachusetts private Richard Scott was brought before the court for a tirade against Gookin. As the records indicate, Scott had barged into the Blue Anchor Tavern in Cambridge and loudly derided Gookin as "an Irish dog" who was "never faithful to his country, the sonne of a whoare, a bitch, a rogue" and "the devil's interpreter."[94] Though Gookin had been defending the Praying Indians since the start of the war, his argument in front of the General Court came at the height of antipathy toward the

Praying Indians during the war. As the fighting between Metacom's forces and the colonists was heating up, and as the colonists worked to tighten their borders and prosecute anyone that they deemed to be suspicious, they grew increasingly suspicious of all Indigenous people. The intensity of Scott's response suggests that Gookin's argument posed a clear threat to those who wanted to remove or destroy all Indigenous people, allies or not.

It is possible that Gookin's decision to use the 1644 treaty in defense of the Praying Indians may have been inspired by his long career as a politician. However, it is also possible that Gookin's decision to use the treaty came from another source—Waban and the residents of the mission communities themselves. In 1644, when the original treaty was made, Gookin had just arrived in the Bay Colony and was not yet a member of the General Court, meaning he may have been unfamiliar with the treaty's particulars. By contrast, as a leader of the Massachusett, Waban would have been intimately aware of the treaty's details and its implications. Waban was in his early forties when the treaty was signed, and his leadership role among the Massachusett may have meant that Waban had even attended the formal court session. One of the signatories of the 1644 treaty, Squa Sachem, had been an ally of Waban's father-in-law, Tahattawan. When Waban later became sachem of the Praying Indians after Cutshamekin died, he was responsible for knowing the terms of the treaty and maintaining the relationships necessary to abide by its agreements. As a tribe diminished by disease and war with surrounding Indigenous nations, Waban and the other mission residents saw the treaty's promise of protection as one of their primary recourses for communal survival.

In agreeing to the 1644 treaty with the Bay Colony, Cutshamekin and his fellow signatories were attempting to facilitate new kinship ties. Essentially, they were trying to find a way to bring the Bay Colony missionaries into the common pot. Long before the Europeans arrived, Native societies employed treaties as a central means of organizing and stabilizing their societies. As Colin Calloway points out, treaties were associated with "rituals of respect and reciprocity, that allowed, indeed required, [Native people] to resolve conflicts, establish mutual trust, and come together in peace." Not only a means of maintaining intertribal ties, treaties also defined intratribal relations as well. Through treaties, Calloway explains, "Native peoples extended or replicated kinship . . . to include people with whom

Treaties, Reciprocity, and Providence 155

they were not related by birth or marriage, bringing them into community by adoption, alliance, and ritual."[95] Signing the treaty created new ties between the Massachusett and the English. Despite several failures on the part of the English, Cutshamekin, Waban, and the other Praying Indians took their agreement with the English seriously.

Gookin's interpretation of both the 1644 treaty and his relationship with the Praying Indians that he describes in *Doings and Sufferings* points to the fact that on some level, Gookin had been instructed in northeastern Indigenous treaty-making practices. Throughout his text, Gookin attempts to convince English missionary supporters of their responsibility to the Praying Indians using the language of spiritual kinship. In his opening letter, Gookin addresses Boyle and his fellow members of the Corporation for the Propagation of the Gospel in New England as "nursing fathers" to the Indigenous converts. Following his letter of introduction, Gookin includes a letter of endorsement from Eliot. Eliot's letter repeats the language of spiritual kinship by addressing the corporation members as "foster father[s]" who, like "natural fathers," are "pleased to hear well of their children."[96] Later in the text, Gookin reaffirms the parent-child relationship by referring to John Eliot as the "spiritual father in Christ" of Nipmuc mission resident Joseph Tuckapawillin.[97] As Gookin indicates, in signing the treaty and following its dictates, the Praying Indians have become part of the English family. For Gookin, as for Waban, the treaty between the Praying Indians and the English facilitated the formation of new kinship ties.

As scholars such as Laura Stevens and Abram Van Engen have convincingly indicated, Puritan missionary writings often invoked sentimental bonds between English and Indigenous communities. Authors like Eliot and Gookin employed sentimental terms in their descriptions of Indigenous people in order to invoke the pity of British supporters and increase support for their missionary work. As Stevens explains, British missionary texts "linked Britain's imperial self-image to the compassion its people felt for heathens and used that emotion to encourage donations."[98] In describing the Praying Indians as the needy children of the English benefactors, Gookin uses patriarchal language to invoke a clear power-dynamic between the colonial "fathers" and the Indigenous "children" that require his aid and instruction. Though Gookin's use of kinship language has clear colonial aims, when read in the context of his larger account, it also implies binding obligations. For Gookin, the residents of the mission communities were not merely objects of pity; rather, the existing treaties between the English and the Praying Indians necessitated concrete and deliberate political action on the part of both parties. The Indigenous converts had performed the actions necessary to ensure a proper relationship, while the English had not.

Alongside the language of kinship, Gookin also uses the language of English law to defend the rights of the mission residents. In *Doings and Sufferings* he recounts his own appeal to the Bay Colony magistrates on behalf of the Praying Indians a few weeks before they were sent to Deer Island. As Gookin explains, "the General Court then sitting at Boston" was "vigorous[ly]" debating "for removing the praying Indians from their plantations." In response, Gookin offered a sevenfold defense of the Praying Indians before the magistrates. After reminding the court of the time and resources that have been put into the Indian mission, Gookin turns to legal arguments. Not only has the Bay Colony made a legal promise to protect the Praying Indians, but, as Gookin explains, "the General Court hath granted those Indians lands and townships, and thereby confirmed and settled them therein as the English; so that, besides their own natural right, they have this legal title, and stand possessed of them *as the English are*" (emphasis added).[99] As Gookin's words imply, by conferring land upon mission residents, the court itself gave clear evidence that the Praying Indians were capable of entering into reciprocal agreements and, by virtue of the 1644 treaty, had legal rights on par with those of English citizens.

Gookin's decision to use the language of treaties as the basis for legal rights and obligations may have been another concept he had learned from Waban and the other residents of the mission towns. Indeed, for the northeastern Algonquian nations as for many other Indigenous communities, one's ability to make and keep treaties was a marker of one's civility. Treaties defined civil order at the same time as they identified Indigenous citizenship. As Ojibwe Heidi Kiiwetinepinesiik Stark explains, an Indigenous nation's ability to make a treaty was the basis of international law: "Treaty making was the primary apparatus utilized among nations to recognized each other's national character. International law—defined through the colonial enterprise of territorial expansion and land acquisition—was predicated upon the recognition of treaties as diplomatic agreements between nations."[100] Using northeastern Algonquian concepts of kinship and diplomacy, Gookin attempts to convince his readers that the Praying Indians' treaty-making with the English regarding land claims was clear evidence of civility.

Figuring Civility

In *Doings and Sufferings*, Gookin depicts events beyond the scope of King Philip's War and includes examples of other Indigenous people showing loyalty to the English both before and during the war. Essentially, Gookin populates his narrative with examples of Indigenous people fulfilling obligations to the English. One of these vignettes is of Penacook sachems Passaconaway and Wannalancet, his son. Like the rest of *Doings and Sufferings*, Gookin's inclusion of the two sachems was a direct response to Hubbard. In *A Narrative of the Troubles*, Hubbard uses Passaconaway to show that it was not just Metacom and Miantonomi who failed to keep treaties but numerous other sachems and saunkskwa had failed to keep their promises with the English as well. His depictions of the Indigenous leaders reinforce his narrative claims that all Indigenous people partake in "perfidious Treachery, and falsehood in breaking Covenant with the English."[101] In taking Passaconaway as an example, Hubbard attempts once again to dismiss the effectiveness of the Bay Colony's missionary attempts. Passaconaway was a well-known sachem and an important powwaw, or spiritual leader, whom John Eliot claimed to have converted sometime in the mid-1640s. A clear source of pride for the missionary. Eliot explains that his attempts to convert Passaconaway were part of his aim to "engage the *Sachims* of greatest note to accept the Gospel, because that doth greatly animate and encourage such as are well-affected, and is a damping to those that are scoffers and opposers."[102]

In Hubbard's rendering, Passaconaway has clearly not been "engage[d]" to the gospel but rather only acted interested because he was fearful of English reprisal. Quoting a 1660 speech of Passaconaway, Hubbard explains that the sachem counseled his followers, "take heed how you quarrel with the English, for though you may do them much mischief, yet assuredly you will be destroyed and rooted off the earth if you do."[103] For Hubbard,

Passaconaway's words are evidence that the sachems "intimat[e] some secret awe of God . . . although they bare no good affection to their religion." Making a biblical analogy, Hubbard compares Passaconaway to Balaam, the Moabite prophet whom an angel prohibited from prophesying against the Israelites.[104] Like Balaam, Passaconaway's treaty with the English was the result of him being "under the awful power of divine illumination, yet when left to himself, was as bad an enemy to the Israel of God as ever before."[105] In using Passaconaway as an example, Hubbard claims that any favor that the sachems and saunkskwa show to the English is only the result of their fear of a powerful English God and thus lacks sincerity. His example conveniently reinforces the spiritual superiority of the English God, while cautioning English readers not to misread the actions of Indigenous leaders.

In a direct challenge to Hubbard, Gookin rereads the story of Passaconaway using his philosophy of Praying Indian trustworthiness. Establishing his authority for his readers, Gookin emphasizes the fact that his knowledge of the sachem comes from his own experience, whereas Hubbard's information came from a secondhand source—someone Hubbard claims was "much conversant with the Indians about *Merimack* river." As Gookin explains, he is a better source than Hubbard as he himself "saw [Passaconaway] alive at Pawtucket, when he was about 120 years old." Acknowledging Hubbard's analogy between Passaconaway and Balaam, Gookin writes that Passaconaway "possibly might have such a kind of spirit upon him as was upon Balaam." However, he then provides an alternative explanation. For Gookin, God's sending an angel to Passaconaway (as he did to Balaam) is only further evidence that God was preparing the important Indigenous leader for conversion. Providing context, Gookin reminds his readers that in 1644, ten weeks after Cutshamekin and his fellow sachems treated with the English, Passaconaway also "agreed to 'such articles as Cutshamekin and others have formally accepted.'" [106] For Gookin, the sachem's willingness to sign a treaty with the English is evidence of his civility. Drawing an intertwined relationship between civility and conversion, Gookin also indicates that Passaconaway's signing of the treaty signals his interest in English Christianity. For Gookin, the speech that Hubbard records in *Narrative of the Troubles* is evidence not of malevolence but rather of Passaconaway's "peace and good correspondency" with the English. In cautioning his followers against warfare, Passaconaway manifested his desire to "keep and maintain amity and friendship with the English" by teaching his followers to "never engage with any other Indians in a war against them."[107]

Echoing Indigenous ideas about the relationship between treaties and kinship, Gookin also shows Passaconaway's civic leadership through the actions of his son, Wannalancet. Like his father, Wannalancet maintained the treaty his father had made with the English. In Gookin's estimation, the leadership of the father had transferred to the son, and Wannalancet's ability to keep his father's treaties was evidence of his readiness for Christianity. As Gookin writes, "about four or five years since," Wannalancet "embrace[d] the Christian religion, after some time of very serious consideration." Again, Gookin can speak with authority about Wannalancet's performance of conversion because he and Eliot were present at its occurrence. As Gookin explains in *Historical Collections*, in May 1674, he and Eliot visited Wannalancet's Pawtucket home. It was at this visit, which came after many years of attempts by Eliot and Gookin, that the sachem finally decided to "pray to God." As Gookin explains, Wannalancet described his conversion as a change of allegiance. The sachem explains that "all my days, used to pass in an old canoe . . . and now you exhort me to change and leave my old canoe, and embark in a new canoe, to which I have hitherto been unwilling: but now I yield up myself to your advice, and enter into a new canoe, and do engage to pray to God hereafter."[108]

Much like Wequash, Wannalancet's performance of conversion has a diplomatic function. Gookin recognizes this and approves—for Gookin, creating Christians is good not only spiritually but politically as well. Although Hubbard saw Passaconaway and his son as a threat, Gookin shows that during the war Wannalancet remained loyal to the treaty his father had signed with the English. As Gookin writes, when the English were attacking his village, despite having "advantage and opportunity enough in ambushment, to have slain many of the English soldiers, without any great hazard to themselves," Wannalancet "restrained his men, and suffered not an Indian to appear or shoot a gun." As he continues, "They were very near the English, and yet though they were provoked by the English, who burnt their wigwams and destroyed some dried fish, yet not one gun was shot at any Englishmen. This act speaks much for them." In contrast to Hubbard, Gookin demonstrates that Praying Indians make good allies because they have "principles of Christianity to fix them to the English."[109]

Despite the narrative interpretations of both Gookin and Hubbard, the actions of Passaconaway and Wannalancet were likely the result of their sachem obligations coupled with their fear of English reprisal. As Delucia writes, like many other sachems, Passaconaway sought "ways to advocate for [his] home community['s] interests while attempting to fashion workable relations with the increasingly populous colonizers." Passaconaway was known throughout his life as attempting to maintain "stable relations" with the English to avoid communal destruction.[110] And while Gookin sees Passaconaway's request to have Eliot visit as the result of his thirst for the Christian God, that request was also tied to his sachem responsibilities. Richard Cogley suggests that Passaconaway desired an English missionary presence 1) to "prevent the loss of subjects through a Christian secessionist movement" and 2) "to increase English settlement in the area as a way of discouraging marauders."[111] However, in his rereading of Passaconaway and Wannalancet, Gookin presents the two sachems as beholden to their treaty obligations. Alluding to the power of kinship ties, Gookin shows how the treaty Passaconaway signed brought him into a long-lasting alliance with the English. As Gookin shows, Passaconaway and Wannalancet invited the English into their space and at the same time allowed for English teaching. The treaty Passaconaway signed initiated relational ties between the English and the Penacooks. These ties, Gookin insinuates, are binding.

While *Doings and Sufferings* presents a kinder portrait of mission residents than Hubbard promoted, Gookin's image of the Praying Indians remains rooted in his own aims to defend and advance the colonial mission. Rather than concern for Indigenous communities as a whole, he is single-mindedly focused on defending the authenticity of Indigenous conversion to his English readers. The disconnect of Gookin's narrative strategy comes into focus in his final vignette of *Doings and Sufferings*. In attempting to translate Algonquian kinship and treaties into a form of Christian civility recognizable to his English readers, Gookin has created an idealized vision of an English–Praying Indian community in which neither the Christian Indians nor the English colonists want to take part. Recounting a court session he and Eliot had held among the mission town residents after the war ended, Gookin again turns to Waban, this time recounting a speech

Waban had given to encourage his relatives. In the speech, Waban explains that despite their being "hated" by the "enemy Indians" and cut off from the English, God has still shown his goodness to the Praying Indian followers. The goodness Waban cites came from "many godly persons in England, who never saw us, yet showed us kindness and much love, and gave us some corn and clothing, together with other provision of clams, that God provided for us."[112]

Waban's words create a personal link between Boyle and the members of the corporation. With a quote clearly cherry-picked for his English readers, Gookin implicitly uses Waban's words to reinforce the strong bond that he claims exists between the Praying Indian children and their "English fathers." At the same time, however, Waban's words point to the imagined nature of the relationship. As he explains, the supporters in England "never saw us." Conversely, the Praying Indians have never seen their English benefactors. The ties between the two groups are imagined. Furthermore, the poor treatment Waban and the other members of the mission community received during King Philip's War shows that the good feelings of the English in the metropole, if they exist, do not translate to their English counterparts in New England. The English community of Christians that Gookin has promised the Praying Indians does not materialize in the colonies. Rather, for the Praying Indians, it is a community that only exists in Gookin's words.

Attempting to explain the discrepancy between the corporation members and the colonists, Gookin tells Waban: "You know all Indians are not good; some carry it rudely, some are drunkards, others steal, others lie and break their promises, and otherwise wicked. So 't is with Englishmen; all are not good, but some are bad, and will carry it rudely."[113] In these words, Gookin excuses the English from the accusations he leveled at them in the beginning of the text. In attributing the harsh treatment of the Praying Indians to the failure of individuals, Gookin creates a double standard as he moves away from a discourse of kinship. While Waban and the Praying Indians have "endeavour[ed] to do all we could to demonstrate our fidelity to God and to the English, and against their and our enemy," the English could choose to be loyal or not without facing a threat to their perceived civility.

The difference between the standards for English civic actions and Indigenous ones come into play again in the text's final lines. Addressing his

English readers, Gookin closes with an image that his English readers would recognize as the epitome of Christian practice—the image of a martyr. As Gookin writes, "these poor, despised sheep of Christ" are the "first professors, confessors, if I may not say martyrs, of the Christian religion among the poor Indians in America."[114] For the English Puritans, martyrdom was the highest form of Christian practice, as it represented complete identification with one's Christian self, to the disregard of one's body. Collectively identifying the Praying Indians not only as loyal Christians but as martyrs, Gookin claims them as the ultimate profession of Christian faith. He also exonerates them from the violence that Hubbard attributes to the rest of the war's Indigenous participants. As Adrian Chastain Weimer muses, "a martyr was, by definition, not a persecutor."[115] Yet, in claiming them as martyrs "of the Christian religion among the poor Indians in America," Gookin maintains a status of difference between the Praying Indians and their English counterparts. Gookin describes them as a collective rather than as individuals, reinforcing the inscrutability of the Praying Indian to English readers. Furthermore, in claiming their martyrdom rather than affirming their continued existence, Gookin absolves English readers from any responsibility toward the Praying Indians. Instead of being accorded the legal rights and responsibilities they deserve, the mission residents are to be mourned as part of a tragic past.

EPILOGUE

Remembering and Forgetting

—\(\mathcal{W}\)—

D espite Gookin's attempts to show that the Praying Indians were valuable members of the English Christian community, *Doings and Sufferings* was not widely read by the seventeenth-century English readers Gookin was attempting to convince. The manuscript was never published. It doesn't even seem to have been given a place in the archives of the Corporation for the Propagation of the Gospel. Rather, Gookin's manuscript was lost to posterity until a clergyman in England found it and passed it onto the Reverend Mr. Campbell of Pittsburgh sometime in the 1820s.[1] Campbell alerted the historian and Unitarian minister Jared Sparks, who then had the manuscript printed for the American Antiquarian Society in 1836. The fact that there seems to have only been one missing copy of Gookin's work seems to confirm that few, if any, members of Gookin's intended audience read his work.

Its publication history makes *Doings and Sufferings* a good fit for this book, which is filled with texts in which Indigenous people and Indigenous influence were largely ignored or misread by their intended audiences. Like *Doings and Sufferings*, the prescriptions in Eliot's *Christian Commonwealth* fell on deaf ears. While *A Key into the Language of America* and *New Englands First Fruits* garnered more readers, the Native presence in these texts remained largely overlooked. In the case of John Winthrop Jr.'s "Of Maiz," the tract has stayed tucked among other documents in the Royal Society Archives, rarely accessed by readers or researchers. While there are many reasons these particular texts were largely ignored, one reason lies with the rhetoric of colonization. These narratives challenge long-standing claims of Indigenous absence and instead testify to English settlers' lasting obligations to Indigenous people—obligations that subsequent generations have desired to forget. Not only do these texts chronicle obligations of friendship and care, but they bring to the fore obligations regarding land exchange and legal protections as well. After being instructed in the proper ways to act, relate, and govern within Indigenous spaces, the English leaders and their descendants were expected to follow through—to enact what they had been taught, to uphold and maintain the relationships necessary to maintain balance.

While the texts I chronicle in this book may have not garnered large readerships in their time, the teachings of Wequash, Cutshamekin, Cassacinamon, and others have lived on in other texts written by the colonial authors and in the genres that resulted from these encounters. As prolific chroniclers of their missionary efforts, both Thomas Shepard and John Eliot would go on to write several accounts describing and interpreting their time in New England's colonies. In these later writings, both men would develop the genres initiated in their earlier experiences with Wequash and Cutshamekin. After writing about Wequash, Shepard would continue to record accounts of conversion. In these narratives, he built upon his past experience using the performances of earlier converts to assess those of future converts. Following Shepard's lead, subsequent chroniclers of the New England mission recorded and circulated Indigenous conversion narratives throughout the eighteenth and nineteenth centuries. Likewise, question-and-answer sessions like those derived from Cutshamekin and Eliot's dialogues peppered the pages of Eliot's missionary accounts and inspired subsequent missionary practices. In the years since the authors' deaths, the writings of Shepard and Eliot have been staple texts for those interested in the early American colonies and have inspired countless books, articles, and discussions.

Likewise, the writings of John Winthrop Jr. and Daniel Gookin have served as important primary source texts, anchoring our understanding of the events of the early colonial years. Winthrop's scientific treatises not only helped contemporary readers understand the development of empirical thought in colonial America but served to frame how members of the Royal Society made sense of colonial empiricism—ways of thinking developed from Cassacinamon himself. More recently, both Winthrop Jr. and Gookin have received increased attention for their role in developing colonial systems and creating frameworks of understanding for colonial experience. In 2019 the Tomaquag Museum published its own version of Roger Williams's *A Key into the Language of America* that puts Williams's words back into an Indigenous context. These early works are being made available for future readers through classroom editions and new scholarly attention to their texts, thus ensuring that the lessons of the Indigenous leaders continue to be taught.

While the influence of Indigenous leaders is present in colonial authors' writings, their memories and teachings are active in the writings and practices of their relatives. The larger public may have forgotten the names of leaders like Wequash, Cutshamekin, and Cassacinamon, but their descendants have not. For centuries, their children, grandchildren, and great-grandchildren have been reminding the English of their treaty obligations. This process of remembering started early. In 1676, as part of an ongoing colonial dispossession of his lands, Wequash's brother, Wequashcook, wrote to the Connecticut court demanding that it honor its treaties and agreements with him and return his lands. As part of his argument, the aging sachem reminded the court of his family's past alliances with the English. Harkening back to the Pequot War, Wequashcook writes that he "can see no reason" why his lands should be "condemned as conquered land" because "his father [Wepitanock] was the English's friend and entertained Major Mason and his company at his wigwam when going against the Pequots upon pain of death. And also he and Harman Garret and his men then faithfully assisted the English, and never did the English wrong."[2] Invoking the family history of alliance, Wequashcook calls out the English for their treatment of the Pequot. For Wequashcook, the instructions, guidance, and communal care his brother and father provided to English leaders were evidence of a reciprocal relationship intertwined with obligation—namely, that the English must honor the treaties, keep their word, and respect the governing structures that had existed before their arrival and upon which they had built their own colonial systems.

In the years since, Indigenous people have continued to try and remind America of its promises. In his 1836 speech "Eulogy on King Philip," Pequot minister William Apess reminds the English settlers turned American citizens of their obligations to the seventeenth-century sachems who sustained their colonial forefathers during the early years of settlement. Apess himself was a descendant of Metacom, or King Philip. As he writes, without the support and care of Indigenous people, "every white man would have been swept from the New England colonies." Written as Andrew Jackson's removal policies were nullifying long-standing land treaties in the

Southeast, Apess's speech pointed out the many ways in which the English settlers failed to uphold their treaties throughout American history. In his speech, Apess turns back not only to Metacom but also to Masconomet, the Pawtucket sachem who met Governor Winthrop upon his arrival to North America. As Apess reminds his audience, it was Masconomet, "a benevolent chief," who "bid the Pilgrims welcome to his shores."[3]

In recent years, Indigenous people continue to return to these early encounters between colonists and Indigenous leaders to plead for recognition and make the case for their own right to survival. At the same time, the descendants of Wequash, Cutshamekin, Cassacinamon, and others have continued trying to teach settlers about how to interact in our now shared space. In courtrooms, classrooms, protests, museums, community outreach centers, and elsewhere, Indigenous people remind the United States that it was, and is, located upon Indigenous land and is thereby deeply intertwined with Indigenous people, places, and concepts.

In many ways, the questions with which I started this book were inspired by my own experiences of remembering and forgetting. Growing up in the Black Hills of South Dakota, the Očhéthi Šakówiŋ, I always knew that I lived in an Indigenous place. Not only was there a large and visible Lakota presence in my hometown, but we also had Lakota speakers in our classroom, Native American day celebrations, powwows, basketball tournaments, and other community events in which Indigenous and settler communities encountered one another. While Native people and places had always been a part of my life in Rapid City, it wasn't until I left that I began to understand the ways in which my hometown had been deliberately shaped by the local Indigenous community. As I began to study Native literature and talk with Indigenous people about my hometown, I recognized that Lakota and Dakota teachers had been actively shaping the curriculum, the landscapes, and the communal practices of the community in which I had been raised. However, like the New England colonists whose texts populate this book, knowledge of a people and their practices did not always, or even often, equate to compassion or equity. Recognizing the presence of Indigenous people is not enough. America has a long way to go. Despite continued challenges, Indigenous people are still present, active, and instructing. The first step is to listen.

NOTES

INTRODUCTION: Indigenous Kinship, Colonial Texts

1 John Winthrop, "Entries for June 12–13, 1630," in John Winthrop, *The History of New England from 1630 to 1649*, vols. 1 and 2, ed. James Savage (Salem, NH: Ayer, 1825), 27.

2 Annawon Weeden, "Salem Ancestry Days," April 30, 2021, Pioneer Village, Salem, MA, https://vimeo.com/543768038.

3 Winthrop, "Entries for June 12–13, 1630," 27.

4 The area around Naumkeag was also home to the Massachusett. Early accounts claim that the sachem was in charge of the areas around Salem as well. "Mosconomo's possessions extended from the Merrimac River to Salem on the south, and from the sea to Cochicewick, now Andover, on the west." Cyrus Mason Tracy, *Standard History of Essex County, Massachusetts: Embracing a History of the Country from Its First Settlement to the Present Time, with a History and Description of Its Towns and Cities* (Boston: C.F. Jewett, 1878), 200.

5 Jean O'Brien, *Firsting and Lasting: Writing Indians Out of Existence in New England* (Minneapolis: University of Minnesota Press, 2010), 55, 6, xv.

6 Jeffrey Glover, *Paper Sovereigns: Anglo-Native Treaties and the Law of Nations, 1604–1664* (Philadelphia: University of Pennsylvania Press, 2014), 3–4.

7 For more on Winthrop's rhetoric of disease, see Cristobal Silva, "New England Epidemiology," in Cristobal Silva, *Miraculous Plagues: An Epidemiology of Early New England Narrative* (New York: Oxford University Press, 2011), 1–48.

8 John Winthrop to Sir Simonds D'Ewes, July 21, 1634, in *The Winthrop Papers*, vol. 3, *1631–1637* (Boston: Massachusetts Historical Society, 1943), 172–73.

9 John Winthrop to John Winthrop Jr. December 12, 1634, in *Winthrop Papers*, 3:176–78.

10 Francis J. Bremer, *John Winthrop: America's Forgotten Father* (Oxford: Oxford University Press, 2003), 191. In his extensive biography of Winthrop, Bremer only makes passing mention to the colonial governor's encounter with Native people instead claiming that disease had "all but eliminated the native people in many areas." This is just one of many accounts of absence in scholarship.

11 *A Copy of the Kings Majesties Charter for Incorporating the Company of the Massachusetts Bay in New-England in America, 1628* (Boston: Printed for S. Green, for Benj. Harris at the London Coffee House, 1689), 22.

12 Kristina Bross, *Dry Bones and Indian Sermons: Praying Indians in Colonial America* (Ithaca, NY: Cornell University Press, 2002), 6.

13 Laura Stevens, *The Poor Indian: British Missionaries, Native Americans, and Colonial Sensibility* (Philadelphia: University of Pennsylvania Press, 2004), 3.

14 Alyssa Mt. Pleasant, Caroline Wiggington, and Kelly Wisecup, "Materials and Methods in Native American and Indigenous Studies: Completing the Turn," *William and Mary Quarterly* 75, no. 2 (2018): 207.

15 Lisa Brooks, *The Common Pot: The Recover of Native Space in the Northeast* (Minneapolis: University of Minnesota Press, 2008), 5, 7.

168   NOTES TO PAGES 9–18

16   Kathleen Donegan, *Seasons of Misery: Catastrophe and Colonial Settlement in Early America* (Philadelphia: University of Pennsylvania Press, 2014), 2.

17   Betty Booth Donohue, *Bradford's Indian Book: Being the True Roote and Rise of American Letters as Revealed by the Native Text Embedded in Of* Plimoth Plantation (Gainesville: University Press of Florida, 2011), xv.

18   Sarah Rivett, *The Science of the Soul in Colonial New England* (Chapel Hill: University of North Carolina Press, 2012), 126.

19   Joshua David Bellin, *The Demon of the Continent: Indians and the Shaping of American Literature* (Philadelphia: University of Pennsylvania Press, 2001), 4.

20   Jean O'Brien and Chris Andersen, introduction, in *Sources and Methods in Indigenous Studies*, ed. Chris Andersen and Jean M. O'Brien (New York: Routledge, 2016), 2.

21   Kathleen Bragdon, *Native People of Southern New England, 1500–1650* (Norman: University of Oklahoma Press, 1996), 168.

22   Michael Witgen, *An Infinity of Nations: How the Native New World Shaped Early North America* (Philadelphia: University of Pennsylvania Press, 2012), 75.

23   Lisa Brooks, *Our Beloved Kin: A New History of King Philip's War* (New Haven, CT: Yale University Press, 2018), 59.

24   Colin Calloway, *Pen and Ink Witchcraft: Treaties and Treaty Making in American Indian History* (New York: Oxford University Press, 2012), 12.

CHAPTER ONE: Kinship, Captivity, and Diplomacy

1   Hugh Peter and Thomas Weld, *New Englands First Fruits*, in *The Eliot Tracts: With Letters from John Eliot to Thomas Thorowgood and Richard Baxter*, ed. Michael P. Clark (Westport, CT: Praeger, 2003), 58. Though Peter and Weld are attributed as the authors of the tract, they never take individual credit. Rather the tract is often addressed as collectively authored by the Bay Colony leadership. For this reason, I alternate between "Bay Colony authors" and "Weld and Peter" when describing the tract's authorship.

2   *A Copy of the Kings Majesties Charter for Incorporating the Company of the Massachusetts Bay in New-England in America, 1628* (Boston: Printed for S. Green, for Benj. Harris at the London Coffee House, 1689), 22.

3   Much of the failure of New England colonies was that they couldn't produce profitable crops like Virginia's tobacco or, later, Caribbean sugar. See Susan Dwyer Amussen, *Caribbean Exchanges: Slavery and the Transformation of English Society, 1640–1700* (Chapel Hill: University of North Carolina Press, 2007), 27–28. The lack of profit led many investors in New England to shift to the West Indies. See Raymond Phineas Sterns, "The Weld-Peter Mission to England," *Publications of the Colonial Society of Massachusetts* 32 (1937): 189.

4   Kristina Bross, *Dry Bones and Indian Sermons: Praying Indians in Colonial America* (Ithaca, NY: Cornell University Press, 2002), 2–3.

5   By 1643 Weld was developing a reputation as a defender of the colonies. Only a few years before publication of *New Englands First Fruits*, Weld had played a large part in defending the Antinomian Controversy. As Abram Van Engen writes, "Weld

NOTES TO PAGES 18–25   169

turned the Antinomian Controversy into one of New England's earliest and most prominent seduction plots" by emphasizing that the Puritans had been "seduced by heretics" (*Sympathetic Puritans: Calvinist Fellow Feeling in Early New England* [Oxford: Oxford University Press, 2015], 112).

6   Weld and Peter, *New Englands First Fruits*, 61, 64, and 67.

7   Weld and Peter, 60.

8   Weld and Peter, 61, 62, 58.

9   Roger Williams, *A Key into the Language of America*, ed. John J. Teunissen and Evelyn J. Hinz (Detroit: Wayne State University Press, 1973), 88. Williams's description of Wequash's death is also significant in that it is "perhaps the first dying speech recorded by a Protestant missionary of a North American native"—a genre that would get significantly more popular as the missionary project developed (Rivett, *Science of the Soul*, 186).

10   Laura Stevens, *The Poor Indian: British Missionaries, Native Americans, and Colonial Sensibility* (Philadelphia: University of Pennsylvania Press, 2004), 186; Drew Lopenzina, *Red Ink: Native Americans Picking Up the Pen in the Colonial Period* (Albany: State University of New York Press, 2012), 80. See further analysis on the rhetorical importance of Wequash's account in Bross, *Dry Bones*, 190–92. For more information on the metropolitan significance of the two accounts of Wequash, see Jonathan Beecher Field, *Errands into the Metropolis* (Hanover, NH: Dartmouth College Press, 2009), 37; and Richard Cogley, *John Eliot's Mission to the Indians before King Philip's War* (Cambridge, MA: Harvard University Press, 1999), 18–20.

11   Particularly helpful is the work being done by the Mashantucket Pequot Museum and Research Center.

12   Shepard likely recorded more conversion narrative accounts, but we have about sixty-seven in extant. As Lori Rogers-Stokes points out, there are two sets of manuscript records that have been transcribed (*Records of Trial from Thomas Shepard's Church in Cambridge, 1638–1649: Heroic Souls* [Cham, Switzerland: Palgrave Macmillan, 2020], 2). See also Michael McGiffert, "Preface: God's Plot Revisited," in *God's Plot: Puritan Spirituality in Thomas Shepard's Cambridge*, rev. ed., ed. Michael McGiffert (Amherst: University of Massachusetts Press, 1994), xi.

13   For discussion of the conversion narrative within a colonial American context, see Patricia Caldwell, *The Puritan Conversion Narrative: The Beginnings of American Expression* (New York: Cambridge University Press, 1985), 87; Sarah Rivett, *The Science of the Soul in Colonial New England* (Chapel Hill: University of North Carolina Press, 2012), 77; and Meredith Neuman, *Jeremiah's Scribes: Creating Sermon Literature in Puritan New England* (Philadelphia: University of Pennsylvania Press, 2013), 184–86.

14   For a good write up of Shepard's morphology of conversion, see Van Engen, *Sympathetic Puritans*, 13.

15   Weld and Peter, *New Englands First Fruits*, 62.

16   *A Copy of the Kings Majesties Charter*, 22; Cogley, *John Eliot's Mission*, 5.

17   For more on the relationship between the tract and the missionary project see Bross, *Dry Bones*, 7.

18   When the term "first fruits" is used in the Eliot tracts, it is primarily used typologically, to connect English colonial missionary projects with the actions of the early

170   NOTES TO PAGES 25–29

Christian church. Interestingly enough, is not limited to colonial New England but also used to describe missionary work in India; see John Eliot, *A Further Accompt of the Progress of the Gospel amongst the Indians in New England*, in Clark, *Eliot Tracts*, 358; and Henry Whitfield, ed., *Strength Out of Weaknesse*, in Clark, *Eliot Tracts*, 217–18.

19   The practice of giving first fruits to religious leaders was also practiced among the Romans and the Greeks.

20   The Office of First Fruits and Tenths continued to operate until 1704, when the revenues from first fruits and tenths were granted to Queen Anne's Bounty.

21   Deuteronomy 26:1–2, 1599 Geneva translation.

22   Jean O'Brien, *Firsting and Lasting: Writing Indians Out of Existence in New England* (Minneapolis: University of Minnesota Press, 2010), xii.

23   Melissa Jayne Fawcett, *Medicine Trail: The Life and Lessons of Gladys Tantaquidgeon* (Tucson: University of Arizona Press, 2000), xv.

24   Daniel Heath Justice, *Why Indigenous Literatures Matter* (Waterloo, Ontario: Wilfrid Laurier University Press, 2018), 73.

25   Lisa Brooks, *The Common Pot: The Recover of Native Space in the Northeast* (Minneapolis: University of Minnesota Press, 2008), 2; Lisa Brooks, *Our Beloved Kin: A New History of King Philip's War* (New Haven, CT: Yale University Press, 2018), 29, 17.

26   Wepitanock was alternatively known as Momojoshuck, Seepocke, and Aquawoce. Ninigret is also referred to in some sources as Yanemo or Jannemo. I would place the year of Wequash's birth sometime between 1605 and 1615, as he was acting as an adult in aligning with the Narragansett and serving as a Pequot guide by the 1630s. For claims that Weptimock was Wequash's father, see John William De Forest, *History of the Indians of Connecticut* (Hartford: W. J. Hamersley, 1853), 179–80; *Narragansett Tribe of Indians: Report of the Committee of Investigation; A Historical Sketch and Evidence Taken, Made to the House of Representatives, At Its January Session, A.D. 1880* (Providence: E. L. Freeman, 1880), 12n; *Collections of the Rhode-Island Historical Society*, vol. 3 (Providence: Marshall, Brown, 1835), 65. Ninigret's first wife was also Wequash's sister; Julie Fisher and David Silverman, *Ninigret, Sachem of the Niantics and Narragansetts: Diplomacy, War, and the Balance of Power in Seventeenth-Century New England and Indian Country* (Ithaca, NY: Cornell University Press, 2014), 7.

27   Wepitanock remained the sachem of the Niantic until his death in the early 1650s, at which time Ninigret took over.

28   The Eastern Niantic did not pay tribute to the Narragansett and were largely treated as equal partners in trade and diplomacy. See Fisher and Silverman, *Ninigret*, 17–18.

29   Quaiapin was also known as Matantuck or Magnus. For more on Quaiapin, see Brooks, *Our Beloved Kin*, 44.

30   Nineteenth-century historian John William De Forest suggests that "it seems probable that [Wequash's] mother was a woman of the Pequot race" (*History of the Indians*, 181).

31   Brooks, *Our Beloved Kin*, 17.

32   Among the New England Algonquian, matrilineal ties were just as significant as patrilineal ones in establishing lineages and "determining inheritance of office"

NOTES TO PAGES 29–32   171

(Kathleen Bragdon, *Native People of Southern New England, 1500–1650* [Norman: University of Oklahoma Press, 1996], 158). Lisa Brooks provides a case study on Indigenous female leadership during this time period in her discussion of Weetamoo throughout *Our Beloved Kin.*

33 Wequashcook was also known as Wequash Cook, Cushawashet, or Harmon Garret. The sources on the relationship between Wequashcook and Wequash are quite scant and difficult to decipher. As several contemporary scholars have noted, the two men, though often confused, are not the same man. In Governor Winthrop's account of Wequash's conversion, he incorrectly refers to Wequash as "Wequash Cook." However, my investigation indicates that Wequashcook (or Harmon Garret) and Wequash were brothers—both the sons of Wepitanock. Several sources claim that Wequash (the convert) referred to himself as Wequashcook and that his brother, Harmon, took on the name after Wequash's death, becoming Wequashcook II. For example, see Richard A. Wheeler, *The Pequot Indians: An Historical Sketch* (Westerley, RI: G. B. & J. H Utter, 1879), 9; De Forest, *History of the Indians*, 181; and "Harman Garrett," in *The Native Northeast Research Collaborative* (New Haven, CT: Yale Divinity School), https://nativenortheastportal.com/node/7603.

34 Weld and Peter, *New Englands First Fruits*, 63. For more information on the development of benevolent conquest see Ken MacMillan's "Benign and Benevolent Conquest? The Ideology of Elizabethan Atlantic Expansion Revisited," *Early American Studies* 9, no. 1 (2011): 32–72.

35 Weld and Peter, *New Englands First Fruits*, 63, 74.

36 Lopenzina, *Red Ink*, 83.

37 In *Red Ink*, Lopenzina lists some of the references to Wequash as a traitor (83). However, there are a number of other accounts as well. A longer list of references to Wequash as traitor or "renegade" includes Increase Mather, *A Relation of the Troubles Which Have Hapned in New-England, by Reason of the Indians there; From the Year 1614 to the Year 1675* (Boston: John Foster, 1677), 31; Catherine Maria Sedwick, *Hope Leslie, or Early Times in Massachusetts* (1827), ed. Carolyn L. Karcher (New York: Penguin, 1998), 50; Samuel Gardner Drake, *The Book of the Indians, or Biography and History of the Indians of North American from Its First Discovery to the Year 1841*, vol. 2 (Boston: Benjamin B. Mussey, 1841), 96nn; Alfred Cave, *The Pequot War* (Boston: University of Massachusetts Press, 1996), 146, 148. Cave's claim that Wequash was a "renegade Pequot" is often cited in contemporary scholarship.

38 Roger Williams, "For his much honored Mr Governor, and Mr. Winthrop, Deputy Governor of the Massachusetts, these. New Providence, this 2d of the week [May, 1637]," in *The Letters of Roger Williams, 1632–1682*, ed. John Russel Bartlett (Providence, RI: Printed for the Narragansett Club, 1874), 18.

39 Bragdon, *Native People of Southern New England, 1500–1650*, 142.

40 See Cave, *Pequot War*, 106.

41 Legal historian Adam J. Hirsch points out that the meeting between Williams and Miantonomi reflected a prewar negotiation process common to seventeenth-century Indigenous warfare. English leaders such as Winthrop were operating with a European conception of warfare in which most wars were waged over land rights and with the intent to turn enemies into subjects. By contrast, Algonquian

172   NOTES TO PAGES 32–34

like Miantonomi were not driven to warfare for land scarcity, and Algonquian governing structures did not require full subjugation of an enemy tribe in order to obtain allegiance. Instead, Indigenous leaders often met to describe the terms of a battle and the conditions of success before a battle or skirmish took place. See Hirsch, "The Collision of Military Cultures in Seventeenth-Century New England." *Journal of American History* 74, no. 4 (1988): 190. For Miantonomi's war incentives see Michael Oberg, "' We Are All the Sachems from East to West': A New Look at Miantonomi's Campaign of Resistance." *New England Quarterly* 77, no. 3 (2004): 483–84.

42   Williams, *Letters*, 18–19.

43   The report produced by archaeologists Kevin McBride and the Mashantucket Pequot Museum and Research Center confirms the centrality of Narragansett practices to the battle's success explaining that the Pequot were a much more formidable enemy than has been assumed. English success was the result of "intelligence gathering, careful planning, logistics, prior military experience, and tactical adjustments based on previous encounters." For a more detailed account of the battles and the war see Kevin McBride, Douglas Currie, David Naumec, Ashley Bissonnette, Noah Fellman, Laurie Pasteryak, and Jacqueline Veninger, *Battle of Mistick Fort: Site Identification and Documentation Plan, Public Technical Report* (Native Park Service American Battlefield Protection Program, GA-2255-09-017, 2013), 8, http://pequotwar.org /wp-content/uploads/2011/05/MPMRC_-NPS_ABPP_PublicReportMistick Fort.pdf.

44   Michael Leroy Oberg, *Uncas: First of the Mohegans* (Ithaca, NY: Cornell University Press, 2003), 72.

45   Wequash was facilitating the gathering and transferring of Pequot captives before he took part in the Mystic Massacre. As Williams explains to Winthrop in a second May 1637 letter, Wequash had been tasked to bring captured Pequot women to Canonicus and Miantonomi. These women were possibly ones that had come with Wequash to the Narragansett seeking protection before the ensuing battle; see Williams, *Letters*, 23.

46   In 1633 Dutch traders were angry that the Pequot would not allow other Algonquian tribes access to the Dutch trading fort. As a result, they captured and executed Tatobem, despite the Pequots' willingness to cooperate with Dutch demands for ransom. In response, Pequot warriors and their Western Niantic allies murdered English trader John Stone in 1634, mistaking him for a Dutch trader. The English often referenced Stone's death, and the later death of English trader John Oldham, as justification for war with the Pequot.

47   Oberg cites Wequash as an "important rival to Sassacus" (*Uncas*, 47). Cave cites him as "an unsuccessful contender for the grand sachemdom" (*Pequot War*, 66).

48   According to Oberg, an unknown sachem briefly led the Pequot after Tatobem's death and before Sassacus's succession. However, this interim sachem was killed quickly after he took over leadership responsibilities. Oberg also suggests that Sassacus was a "weak[er] and less effective leader" than his father had been (*Uncas*, 42–43, 48).

49   The challenge could come if a sachem "fell short in their public responsibilities or in their character" (Fisher and Silverman, *Ninigret*, 16).

NOTES TO PAGES 34–39   173

50   Neal Salisbury, *Manitou and Providence: Indians, Europeans, and the Making of New England, 1500–1643* (New York: Oxford University Press, 1982), 210.

51   This shift of alliances reflected the larger tensions growing between the Pequot and Narragansett. The formerly close allies were at odds with one another and preparing for potential conflict. As Kevin McBride notes, in 1634 the Pequot constructed two military posts, Mistick and Weinshauks, in preparation for an "anticipated conflict" with the Narragansett. See McBride et al., *Battle of Mistick Fort*, 34.

52   McBride et al., 10.

53   "Petition of Cassinamon and Obachickwood," July 1647, Connecticut State Library, Connecticut Archives Series I (1647–1789), Vol. I, Doc. I, https://nativenortheastportal.com /digital-heritage/petition-cassasinamon-and-obachickwood. For more details on the setting in which Cassacinamon produced the petition, see Sean Wiemann, "Lasting Marks: The Legacy of Robin Cassacinamon and the Survival of the Mashantucket Pequot Nation" (PhD diss., University of New Mexico, 2011), 151–52.

54   Mashantucket Pequot Museum, "Pequot War Timeline," *Battlefields of the Pequot War*, 2010, http://pequotwar.org/about/timeline/.

55   John Mason, *A Brief History of the Pequot War* (1736), ed. Paul Royster, http://digital commons.unl.edu/etas/42.

56   See Katherine A. Grandjean, "The Long Wake of the Pequot War," *Early American Studies: An Interdisciplinary Journal* 9, no. 2 (2011): 384.

57   John Underhill, *Newes from America; Or, A New and Experimentall Discoveries of New England* (London: Printed by J.D. for Petere Cole, 1638), 43. Lopenzina suggests that it may have been Wequash himself whom Underhill was quoting in this passage (*Red Ink*, 79).

58   Grandjean, "Long Wake," 384.

59   Weld and Peter, *New Englands First Fruits*, 61.

60   Richard Mather, *A Farewel-Exhortation to the Church and People of Dorchester in New-England* (Cambridge, MA, 1657), 3.

61   Weld and Peter, *New Englands First Fruits*, 61.

62   As O'Brien writes, "for Indians as well as the English, a society in crisis constituted concrete evidence of spiritual relationships out of order" (Jean O'Brien, *Dispossession by Degrees: Indian Land and Identity in Natick, Massachusetts, 1650–1790* [New York: Cambridge University Press, 1997], 55].

63   Evan Haefeli, "On First Contact and Apotheosis: Manitou and Men in North America," *Ethnohistory* 54, no. 3 (2007): 421.

64   Brooks, *Our Beloved Kin*, 75.

65   Kathleen Bragdon, *Native People of Southern New England, 1650–1775* (Norman: University of Oklahoma Press, 2009), 31–32; O'Brien, *Dispossession by Degrees*, 55.

66   Lopenzina makes the helpful comparison of Wequash's actions to that of a condolence ceremony. As Lopenzina writes, Wequash may be "attempting to reinstate a process not unlike the diplomatic rituals of wampum exchange in which all parties offer their narratives in an attempt to clear the path of bloodshed and bad feelings" (*Red Ink*, 83).

67   As Lopenzina suggests, in this portrait of Wequash, we see a figure who is "sick at heart, standing in traumatic relation to the imposition of Christian values, both knowing and not knowing God" (*Red Ink*, 81).

68 Thomas Shepard, *The Sound Believer*, 125, 146, quoted in Charles E. Hambrick-Stowe, *The Practice of Piety: Puritan Devotional Disciplines in Seventeenth-Century New England* (Chapel Hill: University of North Carolina Press, 1986), 36.

69 For an example of Pequot grief in the early colonial time period, see the Mashantucket Pequot Museum's "Pequot Village," diorama display 26. For a discussion about the death of children, see Brooks, *Our Beloved Kin*, 281–82.

70 Thomas Shepard, "The Sum of Christian Religion: In Way of Question and Answer (1647)," 18, quoted in Van Engen, *Sympathetic Puritans*, 13.

71 Weld and Peter, *New Englands First Fruits*, 62.

72 For more details on the land dispute and the uses of the tracts to authorize land claims, see Jeffrey Glover, *Paper Sovereigns: Anglo-Native Treaties and the Law of Nations, 1604–1664* (Philadelphia: University of Pennsylvania Press, 2014), 187–93. Also see J. Patrick Cesarini, "The Ambivalent Uses of Roger Williams's *A Key into the Language of America*," *Early American Literature* 38, no. 3 (2003): 469–94.

73 Williams, *A Key*, A7.

74 In May of 1637, Williams sent Wequash directly to Winthrop with a message detailing a recent skirmish between Wequash and another Pequot (Williams, *Letters*, 21). In an August 14, 1637, letter to Winthrop, Israel Stoughton explains that Wequash was almost killed when he went with Stoughton on an expedition to capture the remaining Pequot in the final days of the war. Edward Elias Atwater, *History of the Colony of New Haven to Its Absorption into Connecticut History of the Colony of New Haven to Its Absorption into Connecticut* (New Haven: Printed for the Author, 1881), 343.

75 Roger Williams to John Winthrop, July 1637, in Williams, *Letters*, 35.

76 English soldier Lion Gardiner records his encounter with Wequash in the days before the Mystic Massacre. Attempting to tract down missing Pequot, Gardiner asks Wequash, "how many of the pequits wear yet alive that had he[l]ped to kill English men?" In response, Gardiner explains that Wequash "write them downe as may apeare by his own hand." By giving the English the names of the few Pequot who had murdered English soldiers, the sachems hoped to protect themselves and the other Pequot who had not killed English soldiers. In Gardiner's account, Wequash's strategy pays off, and he is rewarded for revealing the hidden captives with some sort of trade deal. Lion Gardiner, "Relation of the Pequot Warres," *Early American Studies: An Interdisciplinary Journal* 9, no. 2 (Spring 2011): 481–82.

77 For more details on the captive trade, see Andrea Cremer, "Possession: Indian Bodies, Cultural Control, and Colonialism in the Pequot War," *Early American Studies* 6, no. 2 (2008): 295–354.

78 Wequash played a similar role as a negotiator in 1640, when he revealed to Thomas Stanton that "one of the petty Sachems of Nayantick was aboard Mr. Oldham's pinnance, and that some goods and gold are at Nayantick." The exchange is recorded in Roger Williams July 21, 1640, letter to Governor Winthrop. Coincidentally, this is also the last mention of Wequash in Williams's letters. Williams, *Letters*, 139.

79 Williams, 67. In later years, Wequash's brother, Hermon Garrett, or Wequashacook, would confirm Wequash's status as a sachem among the Pequot. J. Hammond Trumball explains that, "after the death of Wequash, Hermon Garrett assumed his name and claimed to succeed him as Sachem. But his right was contested by

NOTES TO PAGES 42–47   175

Ninigret, (a younger brother of Momojoshuck who had married Hermon Garrett's sister) on the ground that the sons of Momojoshuck were not of the whole blood. In a deed given by Herman Garrett in 1672, he describes himself as 'Sachem or prince and rightful owner of' certain lands within the reputed bounds of Stonington (east of Pawcatuck River,) which lands were 'given to his eldest brother Wequashcooke by his father Wettamozo and at his brother Wequashcook's death given to him, the said Hermon Garrett, or alias Wequashcook, as the next brother and heire'" (Hammon J. Trumball, *The Public Records of The Colony of Connecticut from 1666 to 1678: With the Journal of the Council of War, 1675 to 1678: Transcribed and Edited, In accordance with a Resolution of the General Assembly, with notes and an appendix* [Hartford: F. A. Brown, 1852], 57n).

80   Oberg, *Uncas*, 74.
81   Weld and Peter, *New Englands First Fruits*, 61.
82   Weld and Peter, 62.
83   O'Brien, *Dispossession by Degrees*, 32.
84   Thomas Shepard, *The Clear Sun-Shine of the Gospel Breaking Forth upon the Indians in New-England*, in Clark, *Eliot Tracts*, 138.
85   Weld and Peter, *New Englands First Fruits*, 62.
86   Williams, *A Key*, 88. This is where Wequash was residing at the time of his death, though he may have lived in other areas around Connecticut. In 1642 John Winthrop confirms Wequash's location, writing that Wequash, "an Indian, living about Connecticut river's mouth, and keeping much at Saybrook with Mr. Fenwick, attained to good knowledge of the things of God and salvation by Christ, so as he became a preacher to other Indians, and labored much to convert them, but without any effect, for within a short time he fell sick, not without suspicion of poison from them, and died very comfortably" (*The Journal of John Winthrop, 1630–1649*, ed. Richard S. Dunn, James Savage, and Laetitia Yeandle [Cambridge, MA: Harvard University Press, 1996], 208).
87   Brooks, *Our Beloved Kin*, 172, 271.
88   Williams, *Letters*, 92.
89   Williams, *A Key*, 88.
90   Weld and Peter, *New Englands First Fruits*, 62.
91   Ralph Dunning Smith includes Wequash's deed with Whitfield and also includes a history of the lands (*The History of Guilford, Connecticut, from Its First Settlement in 1639* [Albany, NY: J. Munsell, 1877], 69). In the same deed, Dunning Smith refers to Quaiapin as "the sachem squaw of Quillipiag."
92   In Dunning Smith's copy of the deed, Wequash refers to himself as being "of Pasquishunk," or of the lands around the mouth of the river (Dunning Smith, *History of Guilford*, 66–67).
93   Jill Lepore, *The Name of War: King Philip's War and the Origins of American Identity* (New York: Knopf, 1998), x.
94   Thomas Shepard, "The Autobiography," in McGiffert, *God's Plot*, 56.
95   For the reference to Wequash's son, see De Forest, *History of the Indians*, 180.
96   Williams, *A Key*, A7v.
97   Brooks, *Our Beloved Kin*, 78.
98   Williams, *A Key*, 88.

176 NOTES TO PAGES 48–53

99 Weld and Peter, *New Englands First Fruits*, 62.

100 Williams, *A Key*, A7r.

101 Bross, *Dry Bones*, 190.

102 Williams, *A Key*, A7v.

103 Weld and Peter, *New Englands First Fruits*, 62.

104 Winthrop, *Journal*, 208.

105 John Winthrop, "A Declaration of former Passages and proceedings betwixt the English and the Narrowgansets, with their confederates wherein the grounds and justice of the ensuing warre are opened and cleared" (Cambridge, MA, 1645), 3.

106 Native Northeast Research Collaborative, "Sequassen," *Natives of the Northeast Portal*, 2019, https://nativenortheastportal.com/bio/bibliography/sequassen.

107 Oberg, *Uncas*, 100–107. In 1659 Wyandanch, the Montauckett sachem and friend of Lion Gardiner, who served with the English in the Pequot War, was also killed by poisoning. Though it occurred quite a few years after Wequash's death, it illustrates that poisoning deaths were not unique among the Algonquian. Gardiner claims, "it was by poyson also 2 thirds of the Indeans upon long Iland died" (Gardiner, "Relation of the Pequot War," 487). For a good overview on Algonquian knowledge of poisons and use of poison in warfare and death, see David E. Jones, *Poison Arrows: North American Indian Hunting and Warfare* (Austin: University of Texas Press, 2009).

108 McGiffert, "The Journal," in McGiffert, *God's Plot*, 118.

109 McGiffert, "Preface," ix.

110 Thomas Shepard, *The Sincere Convert Discovering the Paucity of True Beleevers and the Great Difficulty of Saving Conversion* (London: Printed by T.P and M.S. for Humphrey Blunden, 1641), 144–45.

111 Andy Dorsey, "Rhetoric of American Experience: Thomas Shepard's Cambridge Confessions and the Discourse of Spiritual Hypocrisy," *Early American Literature* 49, no. 3 (2014): 631.

112 Thomas Shepard, "The Journal," in McGiffert, *God's Plot*, 119.

113 Weld and Peter, *New Englands First Fruits*, 62.

114 Adrian Chastain Weimer, *Martyr's Mirror: Persecution and Holiness in Early New England* (New York: Oxford University Press, 2011), 3.

115 Weimer explains that "the historical imagination of martyrdom was a shared repertoire of images, actions, and language for seventeenth-century English Protestants." "The shared ideal of holy suffering . . . allowed visible piety to break through social and theological boundaries" (*Martyr's Mirror*, 151–52). By the time of Wequash's death, Thomas Shepard already had publicly debated the authenticity of martyrdom claims in New England. Shepard and other Massachusetts Bay leaders had worked to discredit Anne Hutchinson's claims of martyrdom; see Weimer, 68. Hutchinson may have been back in Shepard's mind at the time he wrote his description about Wequash because she was killed at the hands of Siwanoy warriors in August 1643.

116 Rivett, *Science of the Soul*, 78.

117 Bruce D. Hindmarsh, *The Evangelical Conversion Narrative: Spiritual Autobiography in Early Modern England* (Oxford: Oxford University Press, 2005), 53; Rivett, *Science of the Soul*, 70–71.

118 Caldwell, *Puritan Conversion Narrative*, 157.

119 Dorsey, "Rhetoric of American Experience," 633.

NOTES TO PAGES 54–60   177

120 McGiffert, "Introduction," in McGiffert, *God's Plot*, 3.
121 Shepard, "Autobiography," 28, 31, 64.
122 Caldwell, *Puritan Conversion Narrative*, 34. Lori Stokes-Rogers has pointed to the form of the narratives as the source of their anxiety. As she explains, the narratives were "records of trial sessions," and not finished accounts of conversion. Thus, the anxiety in them was the inherent result of the "cycle of preparation" and not necessarily inherent to the individual. Lori Stokes-Rogers, *Records of Trial from Thomas Shepard's Church in Cambridge, 1638–1649: Heroic Souls* (Cham, Switzerland; Palgrave Macmillan, 2020), 2, 13.
123 McGiffert, "Introduction to the Autobiography," in McGiffert, *God's Plot*, 140.
124 Rivett, *Science of the Soul*, 31.
125 Brooks, *Common Pot*, 5.
126 As Bross points out, *Tears of Repentance* was immensely popular with English readers. In 1658 it was listed by bookseller William London as one of "the most vendible Books in *England*" (*Dry Bones*, 1).
127 Rivett, *Science of the Soul*, 151.
128 George Denison and Daniel Gookin, "Report to the Massachusetts General Court on the Laying out of Land for the Pequot, June 16, 1664," New England Indian Papers Series, Yale Indian Papers Project, Massachusetts Archives, http://hdl.handle.net/10079/digcoll/3656.
129 Harman Garrett, "Will of Harman Garrett, February 1, 1678," Yale Indian Papers Project, http://images.library.yale.edu:8080/neips/data/html/1678.02.01.00/1678.02.01.00.html.

CHAPTER TWO: Questions, Answers, and Treaty-Making

1 "4 November 1646," in *Records of the Governor and Company of the Massachusetts Bay in New England*, vol. 2, *1642–1649*, ed. Nathaniel B. Shurtleff (Boston: William White, 1853), 178–79.
    Cogley points out that Eliot's positioning as the first minister to the Algonquian was likely circumstantial rather than deliberate. He writes that Eliot was "distinctive only in the sense that he was the first minister to take his turn" (Richard Cogley, *John Eliot's Mission to the Indians before King Philip's War* [Cambridge, MA: Harvard University Press, 1999], 49).
2 Eliot explains that his journey to Cutshamekin took place "six weekes before" his meeting with Waban, which he dates as October 28, 1646 (Thomas Shepard, *The Day-Breaking, if not the Sun-Rising of the Gospell with the Indians in New England*, in *The Eliot Tracts: With Letters from John Eliot to Thomas Thorowgood and Richard Baxter*, ed. Michael P. Clark [Westport, CT: Praeger, 2003], 83–84). William Wallace Tooker suggests that Cockenoe, a Pequot War captive, may have been taken into an English household rather than sold into slavery in Barbados because he was not Pequot but only an ally of the Pequot. Margaret Ellen Newell explains that Cockenoe was a Long Island Montauket Indian who was visiting Pequot relatives when he was captured in 1638 and placed into the service of Richard Callicott. See Mary Ellen Newell, *Brethren by Nature: New*

178 NOTES TO PAGES 60–66

England Indians, Colonists, and the Origins of American Slavery (Ithaca: Cornell University Press, 2015), 94–95.

3 Shepard, *Day-Breaking*, 83.

4 Thomas Shepard, *The Clear Sun-Shine of the Gospel Breaking Forth upon the Indians in New-England*, in Clark, *Eliot Tracts*, 124.

5 Governor Winthrop terms Waban "a new sachem near Watertown mill" (John Winthrop, *The History of New England from 1630–1649*, edited by James Savage [Boston: Phelps and Farnham, 1825], 303) and Eliot calls him "the chief minister of Justice" (Shepard, *Day-Breaking*, 83).

6 Shepard, *Day-Breaking*, 84.

7 Henry Whitfield, ed., *Strength Out of Weaknesse*, in Clark, *Eliot Tracts*, 228.

8 See Neal Salisbury, "Red Puritans: The 'Praying Indians' of Massachusetts Bay and John Eliot," *William and Mary Quarterly* 31, no. 1 (1974): 36; Cogley, *John Eliot's Mission*, 55. Several other scholars refer to Cutshamekin as a "reluctant" convert, including Harold W. Van Lonkhuyzen, "A Reappraisal of the Praying Indians: Acculturation, Conversion, and Identity at Natick, Massachusetts, 1646–1730," in *New England Encounters: Indians and Euroamericans, ca. 1600–1850*, ed. Alden T. Vaughan (Boston: Northeastern University Press, 1999), 210; Jean O'Brien, *Dispossession by Degrees: Indian Land and Identity in Natick, Massachusetts, 1650–1790* (New York: Cambridge University Press, 1997), 43.

9 Kristina Bross, *Dry Bones and Indian Sermons: Praying Indians in Colonial America* (Ithaca, NY: Cornell University Press, 2002), 85.

10 See Kathryn Gray, *John Eliot and the Praying Indians of Massachusetts Bay: Communities and Connections in Puritan New England* (Lewisburg, PA: Bucknell University Press, 2015); James P. Ronda, "'We Are Well As We Are': An Indian Critique of Seventeenth-Century Christian Missions," *William and Mary Quarterly* 34, no. 1 (1977): 66–82; and Van Lonkhuyzen, "A Reappraisal of the Praying Indians," 205–32.

11 Shepard, *Day-Breaking*, 88.

12 Bross, *Dry Bones*, 111; Richard Coe and Aviva Freeman, "Genre Theory: Australian and North American Approaches," in *Theorizing Composition: A Critical Sourcebook of Theory and Scholarship in Contemporary Composition Studies*, ed. Mary L. Kennedy (Westport, CT: Greenwood, 1998), 138.

13 O'Brien, *Dispossession by Degrees*, 48.

14 Paul Royster, preface to John Eliot, *The Christian Commonwealth, or The Civil Policy of the Rising Kingdom of Jesus Christ* (1659), ed. Paul Royster (Faculty Publications, Libraries at University of Nebraska–Lincoln), https://digitalcommons .unl.edu/libraryscience/19.

15 Lisa Brooks, *The Common Pot: The Recover of Native Space in the Northeast* (Minneapolis: University of Minnesota Press, 2008), 5.

16 See Thomas Morton, *New English Canann, or New Canaan* (London: Printed for Charles Greene, 1632), book 3, chapter 3. For more details on the significance of the event in terms of cross-cultural signification, see Erik R. Seeman, *Death in the New World: Cross-Cultural Encounters, 1492–1800* (Philadelphia: University of Pennsylvania Press, 2010), 146–53. The Bay Colony and the Massachusett leadership ties remained strong until Chickatawbut's death in 1633, as evidenced by their reciprocal willingness to prosecute community members who disregarded

NOTES TO PAGES 66–68   179

the established alliance between the two parties. See *The Journal of John Winthrop, 1630–1649*, ed. Richard S. Dunn, James Savage, and Laetitia Yeandle (Cambridge, MA: Harvard University Press, 1996), 50–51, 57, 78. For more information about their relationship, see Jenny Hale Pulsipher, *Subjects unto the Same King: Indians, English, and the Contest for Authority in Colonial New England* (Philadelphia: University of Pennsylvania Press, 2005), 21.

17 Chickatawbut attempted to retaliate militarily but he was thwarted when colonists were tipped off to his approach by the Wampanoag sachem Massasoit. See Morton, *New English Canann*, book 3, chapter 3.

18 See Winthrop, *Journal*, 101.

19 Neal Salisbury, *Manitou and Providence: Indians, Europeans, and the Making of New England, 1500–1643* (New York: Oxford University Press, 1982), 214.

20 Oldham was killed not by the Pequot but by the Manisses of Block Island. Though the Manisses had at one time been tributaries of the Pequot, at the time of Oldham's death, they seem to have been tributaries of the Narragansett. See Kevin McBride, Douglas Currie, David Naumec, Ashley Bissonnette, Noah Fellman, Laurie Pasteryak, and Jacqueline Veninger, *Battle of Mistick Fort: Site Identification and Documentation Plan, Public Technical Report* (Native Park Service American Battlefield Protection Program, GA-2255-09-017, 2013), 11, http://pequotwar.org/wp-content/uploads/2011/05/MPMRC_-NPS_ABPP_PublicReportMistick Fort.pdf; Matt Cohen, "Lying Inventions: Native Dissimulation in Early Colonial New England," in *Native Acts: Indian Performance, 1603–1832*, ed. Joshua David Bellin and Laura L. Mielke (Lincoln: University of Nebraska Press, 2011), 36.

21 Kathleen Bragdon, *Native People of Southern New England, 1500–1650* (Norman: University of Oklahoma Press, 1996), 153.

22 Robert Williams Jr., *Linking Arms Together: American Indian Treaty Visions of Law and Peace, 1600–1800* (New York: Oxford University Press, 1997), 36, 99.

23 Winthrop, *Journal*, 189.

24 Cutshamekin's actions also potentially signaled to Canonicus that the English had decided to assign the blame for Oldham's murder to the Pequot, and not the Narragansett. The murder itself was wrapped up in the complicated kinship ties among the Algonquian, as it had been committed by the Manisses of Block Island, a one-time tributary of both the Pequot and the Narragansett. At the time of Oldham's death, though, they seem to have been tributaries of the Narragansett: see McBride et al., *Battle of Mistick Fort*, 11; and Cohen, "Lying Inventions," 36.

25 Winthrop, *Journal*, 186.

26 For more on southern New England Algonquian kinship ties, see O'Brien, *Dispossession by Degrees*, 16–17.

27 Lisa Brooks, *Our Beloved Kin: A New History of King Philip's War* (New Haven, CT: Yale University Press, 2018), 29. Neal Salisbury explains that the Pequot saw Cutshamekin's killing of a Pequot as the event that started the war: "Until then [the Pequot] had carefully refrained from violence despite repeated English efforts to humiliate and otherwise provoke them. But with the blood of a Pequot shed and no alternative means of obtaining reparation available, they had no choice" (*Manitou and Providence*, 218).

28 Cogley reads Cutshamekin's actions here as those solely undertaken in his role

180   NOTES TO PAGES 68–71

under the authority of Massachusetts Bay. He writes that in sending the scalp to Canonicus, Cutshamekin "symbolically reaffirmed the alliance of the Narragansett and Massachusett, but the latter, acting for Massachusetts Bay, were now calling the shots" (*John Eliot's Mission*, 34).

29   As Cave explains, Cutshamekin's gesture was "particularly effective in stirring up long-standing Narragansett animosity toward the Pequots" (Alfred Cave, *The Pequot War* [Boston: University of Massachusetts Press, 1996], 125). For details of the treaty between the parties, see Winthrop, *History of New England*, 190–92.

30   See the formal petition of the sachems in "22 June 1643," in Shurtleff, *Records of the Governor*, 2:40.

31   Jeffrey Glover describes the shared tactics used by Williams and Gorton in their attempts to undermine Bay Colony land claims through alliance with the Narragansett in *Paper Sovereigns: Anglo-Native Treaties and the Law of Nations, 1604–1664* (Philadelphia: University of Pennsylvania Press, 2014), 189–91.

32   Winthrop, *Journal*, 459.

33   Cutshamekin was one of several sachems who were moving to gain English ties at the same time. See Pulsipher, *Subjects unto the Same King*, 26–27.

34   Among the sachems who aligned with Cutshamekin were his nephew and future successor, Josias Wompatuck; Masconomet, the Agawam sachem whom Governor Winthrop had met on his first night in Salem harbor; Passaconaway, a Pennacook sachem; the "Squa Sachim," a Pawtucket woman sachem and wife of Nanepashemet; and Nashowanon and Wossamegon, two Nipmuc sachems (Cogley, *John Eliot's Mission*, 36, 34–35). Those these leaders aligned with Cutshamekin; they were not all present at the courthouse for the 1644 submission.

35   Shurtleff, *Records of the Governor*, 2:55.

36   Cogley terms the signing of these treatise "the submission of the sachems" (*John Eliot's Mission*, 23).

37   Salisbury, "Red Puritans," 36.

38   Winthrop, *Journal*, 494. Dennis Connole explains that this area included several tribes and accounts for the whole of Massachusett territory at the time: "The Indians of 'Wachusett' included the Nashaways and the Quabaugs, two Nipmuck tribes that inhabited the area to the south and west of Wachusett Mountain. Both happened to be, at the time the submissions were signed, tributaries of the Massachusett tribe" (*The Indians of the Nipmuck Country in Southern New England, 1630–1750: A Historical Geography* [Jefferson, NC: McFarland, 2007], 65).

39   Stephanie Fitzgerald, "' I Wannatuckquannum, This Is My Hand': Native Performance in Massachusett Language Indian Deeds," in *Native Acts: Indian Performance, 1603–1832*, ed. Joshua David Bellin and Laura L. Mielke. (Lincoln: University of Nebraska Press, 2012), 146–47.

40   Winthrop, *Journal*, 499.

41   As the *Records* indicate, the agreement with Soconoco and Pumham was signed "after clear interpretation of every perticuler by their owne interpreter, Benedict Arnold" (Shurtleff, *Records of the Governor*, 2:41).

42   Cogley also makes a note of the sachem's English fluency (*John Eliot's Mission*, 40).

43   In many ways, Cutshamekin here acts as an experienced user in the cross-cultural discourse community that existed among the English and Massachusett leaders.

NOTES TO PAGES 71–76   181

44   Shurtleff, *Records of the Governor*, 2:56. Emphasis added.

45   Brooks, *Our Beloved Kin*, 75.

46   For more on treaties and their spiritual implications, see Williams, *Linking Arms Together*, 99.

47   Winthrop's response seems to be guided by a concept that Cogley terms the "affective model" of Indian-colonial relations, which "taught that Indians would yearn to participate in the English way of life once they had witnessed the virtues of the colonists" (*John Eliot's Mission*, 5).

48   Winthrop, *Journal*, 494. Cogley argues that the colonists saw the submission as a "voluntary action," which led them to "conclude that the local Indians had affected the English virtues," thus providing evidence that they were prepared for Christian instruction (*John Eliot's Mission*, 51).

49   Eliot does not provide extensive details about his approach to his meeting with Cutshamekin, but he does indicate that his second journey to Waban was "in the like" as the one he undertook six weeks earlier. See Shepard, *Day-Breaking*, 83, 84.

50   Cogley, *John Eliot's Mission*, 40.

51   Shepard, *Day-Breaking*, 83.

52   Shepard, 84.

53   Shepard, 84.

54   Bross, *Dry Bones*, 97.

55   Craig White, "The Praying Indians' Speeches as Texts of Massachusett Oral Culture," *Early American Literature* 38, no. 3 (2003), 442.

56   Among many Indigenous tribes, the thunderbird remains a powerful spiritual being: see Basil Johnston, *The Manitou: Supernatural World of the Ojibwe* (New York: Harper Perennial, 1996), 120; and Theresa S. Smith, *The Island of the Anishnaabeg: Thunderers and Water Monsters in the Traditional Ojibwe Life-World*, 2nd ed. (Lincoln: University of Nebraska Press, 2012), 66–91. Images of thunderbirds are also a central part of both traditional and contemporary Indigenous art. See Edward J. Lenik, "The Thunderbird Motif in Northeastern Indian Art," *Archaeology of Eastern North America* 40 (2012): 169.

57   Bragdon, *Native People of Southern New England, 1650–1775*, 187–88.

58   Fitzgerald, "'I Wannatuckquannum,'" 146–47.

59   William Wood, *New England's Prospect* (London: By Tho. Cotes, for John Bellamie, 1634), part 2, chapter 9, 87.

60   Evan Haefeli, "On First Contact and Apotheosis: Manitou and Men in North America," *Ethnohistory* 54, no. 3 (2007): 434.

61   This system of balance was behind the majority of English-Algonquian treaties in the early years of colonization. See Brooks, *Common Pot*, 7.

62   Sarah Rivett, *The Science of the Soul in Colonial New England* (Chapel Hill: University of North Carolina Press, 2012), 128–29.

63   David D. Hall, ed., "A Report of the Trial of Mrs. Anne Hutchinson before the Church in Boston," in *The Antinomian Controversy, 1636–1638: A Documentary History*, 2nd ed. (Durham, NC: Duke University Press, 1990), 381.

64   Michael P. Winship, *The Times and Trials of Anne Hutchinson* (Lawrence: University Press of Kansas, 2005), 111.

65   Repentance and public confession were an integral part of New England Puritan

182 NOTES TO PAGES 76–80

communal and spiritual life. As Hall points out, confession, the ritual of repentance allowed the Puritans "a patterned means of connecting the natural and the social worlds to supernatural power." In her failure to confess, Hutchinson breaks the ritual process and upsets communal order. David D. Hall, *Worlds of Wonder, Days of Judgment: Popular Religious Belief in Early New England* (New York: Alfred A. Knopf, 1989), 168.

66 As Bross notes, during the 1640s, the accounts of the Hutchinson trial transcripts were still circulating among English readers (*Dry Bones*, 102). Bross also writes that Eliot used his questions to present "Praying Indian Christianity and culture . . . as metonymic of colonial Christian and gender practice: a 'native' New England faith is proffered as proof of the efficacy of the New England Way" (110).

67 Fiorella Foscarini, "Diplomatics and Genre Theory as Complementary Approaches," *Archival Science* 12 (2012): 395.

68 Steffi Dippold, "The Wampanoag Word: John Eliot's Indian Grammar, the Vernacular Rebellion, and the Elegancies of Native Speech," *Early American Literature* 48, no. 3 (2013): 548. Sarah Rivett further explains that Eliot viewed Wôpanâak as a "fallen" language that could be "redeemed." As she writes, "By retraining Indian children to read and speak a redeemed version of their mother tongue, [Eliot] imagined that his praying Indians would ultimately generate a sacred space more nearly tailored to their own spiritual aptitude" (*Unscripted America: Indigenous Languages and the Origins of a Literary Nation* [New York: Oxford University Press, 2017], 169–70).

69 Edward Winslow, *The Glorious Progress of the Gospel amongst the Indians in New England*, in Clark, *Eliot Tracts*, 153–54.

70 In this instance, Eliot begins with a disclaimer explaining that he has forgotten the majority of the questions asked over the past year, but he is able to recount a few. While Eliot likely employs this convention to underscore to his readers the sheer number of questions he has been asked by the eager converts, this statement also reminds us of the narrator's influence in the formation and response to the recorded questions.

71 Shepard, *Clear Sun-Shine*, 129.

72 Shepard, 129.

73 Shepard, 129.

74 Winslow, *Glorious Progress*, 152. While Eliot may have included this allusion to Martha's Vineyard out of a sense of rivalry with Mayhew, it is also likely that Cutshamekin's subjects were actually residing in the area. While the area around Martha's Vineyard is not traditionally Massachusett territory, the limited information we have about the extent of Massachusett networks makes it plausible that Cutshamekin had subjects in the area (be they fellow Massachusetts or tributaries).

75 Whitfield, *Strength Out of Weaknesse*, 228.

76 O'Brien, *Dispossession by Degrees*, 32.

77 As Jean O'Brien notes, the founding of Natick was mired in conflicts over English land claims and Indigenous rights for several years. The English inhabitants of Dedham, the nearest English village, were particularly upset, and there were several legal cases against Eliot for his founding of Natick. See O'Brien, *Dispossession by Degrees*, 34–39.

78 O'Brien, 39.

79 Henry Whitfield, *The Light Appearing More and More towards the Perfect Day*, in Clark, *Eliot Tracts*, 202.

80 Whitfield, 203.

81 Whitfield, 203.

82 Whitfield, 203.

83 Whitfield, *Strength Out of Weaknesse*, 228. While Eliot does not tell us the exact nature of the strife, Eliot's reference to Gorton's Plantation makes it likely that Cutshamekin was again working on the continued land dispute between the Narragansett, the Pawtuxet, the Shawomet, and the English that had helped lead to the 1644 treaty between the Massachusett and Massachusetts Bay in the first place. Eliot mentions the fact that Cutshamekin and the other sachems met with Gorton after their proceedings, writing that during his journey "some of those bad *Indians* and *Cutshamoquin* with them did buy much strong Water at *Gortons* Plantation, and had a great drinking." Cutshamekin seems to have drunk with them but refrained from getting drunk (228). Cutshamekin's drinking may have been a part of the treaty-making process. According to the *Narragansett Historical Record*, among other sources, the dispute over land that had contributed to the 1644 treaty between the Massachusett and Massachusetts Bay flared up again in the summer of 1651, when Massachusetts Bay received word back from an English court that their claims to Gorton's land (via the Pawtuxet and Shawomet sachems) had been dismissed (234).

84 Whitfield, *Strength Out of Weaknesse*, 226, 228.

85 Whitfield, 226, 228.

86 O'Brien, *Dispossession by Degrees*, 11.

87 Cogley, *John Eliot's Mission*, 116.

88 As Kathryn Gray notes, "Eliot sent *The Christian Commonwealth* to England as early as 1652 (or even 1651) when he asked Jonathan Hanmer and Ferdinando Nicolls for their comments on the manuscript," (*John Eliot and the Praying Indians*, 9).

89 Eliot, *Christian Commonwealth*, vi.

90 Eliot, vii.

91 Natalie Spar, "Reading Eliot's *The Christian Commonwealth* at Natick: An Origin Story," *Early American Literature* 53, no. 1 (2018): 35.

92 Paul Royster, among others, celebrates the tract as the first "American" political treatise (preface to Eliot, *Christian Commonwealth*). James Holstun describes Eliot's tract as "the single most ambitious utopian project within the larger Puritan utopia of New England" (*A Rational Millennialism: Puritan Utopias of Seventeenth-Century England and America* [New York: Oxford University Press, 1987], 103). Relatedly, Theodore Dwight Bozeman celebrates the work as a "remarkable sketch of millennial polity" (*To Live Ancient Lives: The Primitivist Dimension in Puritanism* [Chapel Hill: University of North Carolina Press, 1988], 266). Kathryn Gray notes that the "treatise is, or should have been, part of a debate which took place in reading communities and church congregations across New and Old England . . . [about] toleration and separatism and as such sits in dialogue with other equally radical voices" (*John Eliot and the Praying Indians*, 12).

93 Eliot, *Christian Commonwealth*, iii.

94 Spar, "Reading Eliot's *The Christian Commonwealth*," 34.

95 Eliot, *Christian Commonwealth*, iv.

184   NOTES TO PAGES 85–90

96   Eliot, viii.

97   John Eliot, September 18, 1633, Letter to Sir Simonds D'Ewes, in *Letters from New England: The Massachusetts Bay Colony, 1629–1638*, ed. Everett Emerson (Amherst: University of Massachusetts Press, 1976), 105.

98   Spar, "Reading Eliot's *The Christian Commonwealth*," 47.

99   Eliot, *Christian Commonwealth*, 2, 5–6. Spar also notes Eliot's expanded voting rights: "*The Christian Commonwealth* is clear that the vote should be more inclusive than it was in Massachusetts Bay" ("Reading Eliot's *The Christian Commonwealth*," 47).

100   Eliot, *Christian Commonwealth*, 19.

101   Holstun, *A Rational Millennialism*, 154. Cogley summarizes the existing scholarship on this point: "James Holstun notes that the settlement's nearly universal adult male suffrage departed from the Bay Colony's current practice of restricting the vote to communicant men, and Dwight Bozeman observes that Eliot's *Christian Commonwealth* 'not only ignored New England institutions, but also implied a severe critique' of them. Thus, the implications of Eliot's political program at Natick were that Massachusetts Bay should broaden its franchise and also replace selectmen, deputies, and assistants with rulers of tens, fifties, and hundreds. His extant sources, however, contain no explicit evidence that he hoped such would become the case" (*John Eliot's Mission*, 113–14).

102   Spar also notes this connection: "Eliot's order of tens bears more resemblance to Wampanoag kinship networks than European territory-based politics" ("Reading Eliot's *The Christian Commonwealth*," 41).

103   See Bragdon, *Native People of Southern New England, 1500–1650*, 142; Michael Leroy Oberg, *Uncas: First of the Mohegans* (Ithaca, NY: Cornell University Press, 2003), 22.

104   This scenario played out during the Pequot War as increasing numbers of Pequot left and joined other tribes or formed new kinship groups after the appointment of Sassacus.

105   In Exodus 18:21–22 (KJV) Jethro tells Moses to "select capable men from all the people . . . and appoint them as officials over thousands, hundreds, fifties and tens." These selected men would "serve as judges for the people at all times."

106   Eliot, *Christian Commonwealth*, 11, 12.

107   Whitfield, *Strength Out of Weaknesse*, 226. See also Spar, "Reading Eliot's *The Christian Commonwealth*," 43–44.

108   Bragdon, *Native People of Southern New England, 1650–1775*, 153.

109   Cogley, *John Eliot's Mission*, 96. For more on the publication history, see J. F. Maclear, "New England and the Fifth Monarchy: The Quest for the Millennium in Early American Puritanism," *William and Mary Quarterly* 32, no. 2 (1975): 254.

110   Shurtleff, *Records of the Governor*, 2:5–6.

111   The first two are *Tears of Repentance* in 1653 and *A Further Accompt of the Progresses of the Gospel amongst the Indians in New-England* (Part 1) in 1659.

112   Rivett, *Science of the Soul*, 126.

113   As O'Brien notes, "seven of the eighteen confessing Indians attributed their eventual conversion either to leaders Waban or Cutshamekin" (*Dispossession by Degrees*, 53).

114   John Eliot, *A Further Accompt of the Progress of the Gospel amongst the Indians in New England*, in Clark, *Eliot Tracts*, 379.

115   Pulsipher, *Subjects unto the Same King*, 137.

116   Eliot, *Further Accompt*, 379.

NOTES TO PAGES 91–94   185

CHAPTER THREE: Corn, Community, and Cassacinamon

1 Samuel Pepys, "July 29, 1662," in *The Diary of Samuel Pepys: A New and Complete Transcription*, vol. 3, *1662*, ed. Robert Lathan and William Matthews (Berkeley: University of California Press, 1979), 149; John Winthrop [the Younger] to Robert Boyle, August 6, 1662, signed July 27, 1662.

2 The original envelope with the red sealing wax is in the Royal Society Archives. "John Winthrop Jr. to Mr. Henry Oldenburg," July 27, 1662, RBO, 21, 19, Royal Society Archives, London.

3 The treatise is known by a number of names. The original document does not have a title. However, it is catalogued in the Royal Society archives as "'Of maiz' by Mr. Winthorp" and published in the transaction records as "The description, culture and use of maiz. Communicated by Mr. Winthrop.' Royal Society Archives, CLP/10i/3. In his 1937 transcription of the treatise, Fulmer Mood titles the tract "Indian Corne" in "John Winthrop Jr., on Indian Corn," *New England Quarterly* 10, no. 1 (1937): 121–33. Alternatively, the *Electronic Enlightenment* database categorizes the treatise as "Report on 'Indian Corn' by John Winthrop [the Younger]," August 6, 1662, *Electronic Enlightenment Scholarly Edition of Correspondence*, ed. Robert McNamee et al., University of Oxford, https://doi-org.ezp3.lib.umn.edu/10.13051/ee:doc/boylroPC0020032a1d. In this chapter, I've referred to the treatise as "Of maiz" because that is the earliest title referenced.

4 A note on terms: In the seventeenth century, *corn* was a categorical term that referred to the staple crop of a region. When referring to the *Zea mays* plant, colonists termed it "turkie corn," "Indian corn," or "maize." I will use all these three terms within this text to refer to the *Zea mays* plant, depending on the terms employed by the various authors whose works I discuss.

5 Winthrop requests that Boyle not read the document to the larger society but rather only "pick out what may be pertinent to the matter of the discourse, & the rest, or anything unsutable wilbe fit to be obliterated." John Winthrop [the Younger] to Robert Boyle, August 6, 1662, signed July 27, 1662, RBO, 21, 19, Royal Society Archives.

6 The charter defines the society as intended to "encourage philosophical studies, especially those which by actual experiments attempt either to shape out a new philosophy or to perfect the old" (Translation of the First Charter, granted to the President, Council, and Fellows of the Royal Society of London, by King Charles the Second, A.D. 1662, https://royalsociety.org/-/media/Royal_Society _Content/about-us/history/Charter1_English.pdf?la=en-GB&hash=EE2FF8F 0745DE30775F7EBD6F9A7A1E5).

7 Walter W. Woodward, *Prospero's America: John Winthrop, Jr., Alchemy, and the Creation of New England Culture, 1606–1676* (Chapel Hill, NC: University of North Carolina Press, 2013), 269, 263–64, 270.

8 The Charter for Connecticut was signed on April 23, 1662—a few months before Winthrop sent "On Indian Corn."

9 John Gerard, *The Herball, or Generall historie of plantes*, ed. Thomas Johnson (1633), 83.

10 I use the term in accordance with Sarah Rivett's concepts as developed in her work *The Science of the Soul in Colonial New England* (Chapel Hill: University of North Carolina Press, 2012).

11 Susan Scott Parrish, *American Curiosity: Cultures of Natural History in the Colonial British Atlantic World* (Chapel Hill: University of North Carolina Press, 2006), 117.

186   NOTES TO PAGES 95–102

12   Samantha Majhor, "We Are All Related: Contemporary Native American Literature and the Nonhuman Turn" (PhD diss., University of Minnesota, 2019), 13, https://hdl.handle.net/11299/224591.

13   Michael Blake, *Maize for the Gods: Unearthing the 9,000 Year History of Corn* (Berkeley: University of California Press, 2015), 23.

14   Robin Wall Kimmerer, "Corn Tastes Better on the Honor System," *Emergence Magazine* 3 (October 31, 2018), https://emergencemagazine.org/feature/corn-tastes -better/.

15   Woodward, *Prospero's America*, 30, 27.

16   As Harriot explains, while his expedition was among the Powhatans, the English used corn to make "mault, whereof was brued as good ale as was to bee desired. So likewise by the help of hops therof may bee made as good Beere" (Thomas Harriot, *A Briefe and True Report on the NewFound Land of Virginia: The Complete 1590 Theodor de Bry Edition*, ed. Paul Hulton [New York: Dover, 1972], 13).

17   Neither Harriot nor Gerard were the first to write about maize in a European context. In 1542 German herbalist Leonhart Fuchs "was the first herbalist to describe American introductions like maize" in his *De Historia Stirpium*. Brent Elliott, "The World of the Renaissance Herbal," in "Gardens and Horticulture in Early Modern Europe," special issue, *Renaissance Studies* 25, no. 1 (2011): 26.

18   Melissa L. Rickman, "Making the Herball: John Gerard and the Fashioning of an Elizabethan Herbarist" (PhD diss., University of Oklahoma, 2011), 77, 1.

19   Gerard, *The Herball*, 82.

20   The term was first used in Richard Haklut's 1588 account *Divers Voyages*.

21   Richard D'Abate, "On the Meaning of a Name:'Norumbega' and the Representation of North America," in *American Beginnings: Exploration, Culture, and Cartography in the Land of "Nurumbega,"* ed. Emerson W. Baker, Edwin A Churchill, Richard S. D'Abate, Kristine L. Jones, Victor A. Konrad, and Harald E. L. Prins (Lincoln: University of Nebraska Press, 1994), 85.

22   Gerard, *The Herball*, 83.

23   The ship is also recorded as *The Lion* in various sources.

24   Jennifer Mylander, "Early Modern 'How-To' Books: Impractical Manuals and the Construction of Englishness in the Atlantic World," *Journal for Early Modern Cultural Studies* 9, no. 1 (2009): 124–25.

25   Woodward, *Prospero's America*, 111.

26   John Winthrop to John Winthrop Jr., March 28, 1631, in *The Winthrop Papers*, vol. 3, *1631–1637* (Boston: Massachusetts Historical Society, 1943), 20–22. For an inventory of the goods shipped aboard the Lyon by Winthrop Jr., see Invoice of Goods Shipped on the Lion, in *Winthrop Papers*, 3:41–43 and 44–47.

27   John Winthrop Jr. to John Winthrop. London, April 30, 1631, in *Winthrop Papers*, 3:31–32.

28   Clayborne is alternatively spelled Claiborne or Cleyburne. Clayborne would later go on to be the colonial governor of Virginia and was a trader who primarily exchanged goods with the Susquehannocks.

29   Eventually the agreement was reduced to "fourty tunne" of maize—of which twenty was for Winthrop Sr. and twenty was to be saved for Winthrop's brother-in-law Emmanuel Downing, who would collect the maize upon his arrival in New England.

NOTES TO PAGES 102–110   187

30 Jane Mt. Pleasant, "The Paradox of Plows and Productivity: An Agronomic Comparison of Cereal Grain Production under Iroquois Hoe Culture and European Plow Culture in the Seventeenth and Eighteenth Centuries" *Agricultural History* 85, no. 4 (Fall 2011): 400.

31 William Bradford, *History of the Plymouth Settlement, 1608–1650*, ed. Valerian Paget (New York: John McBride, 1909), 69.

32 Betty Booth Donohue, *Bradford's Indian Book: Being the True Roote and Rise of American Letters as Revealed by the Native Text Embedded in* Of Plimoth Plantation (Gainesville: University Press of Florida, 2011), 6.

33 Donohue, 11, 9.

34 John Winthrop, "March 23, 1630," in John Winthrop, *The History of New England from 1630–1649*, edited by James Savage (Boston: Phelps and Farnham, 1825), 48.

35 Sean Wiemann, "Lasting Marks: The Legacy of Robin Cassacinamon and the Survival of the Mashantucket Pequot Nation" (PhD diss., University of New Mexico, 2011), 44.

36 John Winthrop to Margaret Winthrop, July 23, 1630, in Papers of the Winthrop Family, vol. 2, Winthrop Family Papers Digital Edition, Massachusetts Historical Society, www.masshist.org/publications/winthrop/index.php/view/PWF02d278.

37 John Winthrop to Margaret Winthrop, November 29, 1630, in Papers of the Winthrop Family, vol. 2, http://www.masshist.org/publications/winthrop/index .php/view/PWF02d294.

38 Martha L. Finch, "'Civilized' Bodies and the 'Savage' Environment of Early New Plymouth," in *A Centre of Wonders: The Body in Early America*, ed. Janet Moore Lindman and Michele Lise Tarter (Ithaca: Cornell University Press, 2001), 46–47.

39 Kimmerer, "Corn Tastes Better."

40 John Winthrop [the Younger], "Report on Indian Corn, Sunday, 6 August 1662," Electronic Enlightenment Scholarly Edition of Correspondence, ed. Robert McNamee et al., vers. 3.0., University of Oxford, 2018.

41 Agreement of the Saybrook Company with John Winthrop Jr., in *Winthrop Papers*, 3:198.

42 Woodward, *Prospero's America*, 50.

43 July 1635 Articles of the Saybrook Company with John Winthrop Jr., in *Winthrop Papers*, 3:198.

44 John Winthrop Jr. to John Winthrop Sr., April 7, 1636, in *Winthrop Papers*, 3:246.

45 Winthrop, "On Indian Corn."

46 Lisa Brooks, "Corn and Her Story Traveled: Reading North American Graphic Texts in Relation to Oral Traditions," in *Thinking, Recording, and Writing History in the Ancient World*, ed. Kurt A. Raaflaub (Chichester: Wiley, 2014).

47 Many more details about the agricultural benefits of the Three Sisters planting system can be found in Jane Mt. Pleasant's article "The Science behind the Three Sisters Mound System: An Agronomic Assessment of an Indigenous Agricultural System in the Northeast," in *Histories of Maize: Multidisciplinary Approaches to the Prehistory, Linguistics, Biogeography, Domestication, and Evolution of Maize*, ed. John Staller, Robert Tykot, and Bruce Benz (Walnut Creek: Left Coast, 2009), 529–37.

48 Kevin McBride, "The Legacy of Robin Cassacinamon: Mashantucket Pequot Leadership in the Historic Period," in *Northeastern Indian Lives, 1632–1816*, ed. Robert S. Grumet (Amherst: University of Massachusetts Press, 1996), 79.

188 NOTES TO PAGES 110–117

49 Winthrop, "Of Maiz."
50 Roger Williams to the Governor of Massachusetts, May 13, 1637, in *Winthrop Papers*, 3:410–11.
51 Israel Stoughton to John Winthrop, June 28, 1637, in *Winthrop Papers*, 3:435–36.
52 Hugh Peter to John Winthrop Sr., July 15, 1637, in *Winthrop Papers*, 3:450.
53 Israel Stoughton to the Governor and Council of Massachusetts, August 14, 1637, in *Winthrop Papers*, 3:482.
54 McBride, "Legacy of Robin Cassacinamon," 79, 81, 80.
55 Woodward, *Prospero's America*, 54, 53.
56 McBride, "Legacy of Robin Cassacinamon," 81. Wiemann writes that Cassacinamon voluntary entered into service for the Winthrops ("Lasting Marks," 124).
57 Wiemann, 123–24. Part of their dependence derived from the 1638 Treat of Hartford. In the aftermath of the Pequot War, the colonial government assigned Cassacinamon and the other Nameag Pequot to be tributaries of Uncas and the Mohegan.
58 For details regarding the aftermath of the war and the land disputes over Pequot lands, see Walter Woodward, *Prospero's America*, chapter 4, "Which Man's Land? Conflict and Competition in Pequot Country." Wiemann, "Lasting Marks," 162–75.
59 Wiemann, 133, 135.
60 John Winthrop Jr., "Overland to Connecticut in 1645: A Travel Diary of John Winthrop Jr.," trans. William R. Carlton, *New England Quarterly* 13, no. 3 (September 1940): 504n19. Robin Cassacinamon may have been related to Sacowaen, the brother of the Pequot sachem Sassacus, as the "neck of land in New London," was where Robin returned to and where Sacowaen had lived prior to the Pequot War. James Hammond Trumball, "Mamacock," in *Indian Names of Places, etc., in and on the Borders of Connecticut* (Hartford, CT: Case, Lockwood & Brainard, 1881), 19.
61 Wiemann, "Lasting Marks," 135; Winthrop, "Overland to Connecticut," 505.
62 Winthrop, 505.
63 "In 1646, Nameag had seventy-two men and eight boys listed in the official count done by the English. If women and girls are included in these estimates, as well as the Pequots who moved to the community over the years, the Pequot population potentially reached some three hundred fifty to five hundred people by the mid-seventeenth century" (Wiemann, "Lasting Marks," 195).
64 Stephanie Fielding, *A Modern Mohegan Dictionary* (Prepared for the Council of Elders, Property of the Mohegan Tribe, 2006), 126.
65 Winthrop, "Of Maiz."
66 Darius Coombs, "Wampanoag Life Ways," talk given at "First Contact: Indigenous Peoples & the First English Settlers," July 19, 2019, hosted by the Nantucket Historical Association, https://youtu.be/5DOdK4cpT-1.
67 Winthrop, "Of Maiz."
68 For more on Winthrop's role in the Atherton Company, his manipulations, and the details of the landholding processes, see Brooks, *Our Beloved Kin*, 44–45, 108, 229–31.
69 Kimmerer, "Corn Tastes Better."
70 Woodward, *Prospero's America*, 112; John Arundell to John Winthrop Jr., January 16, 1656, quoted in Harold Jantz, "America's First Cosmopolitan," *Massachusetts Historical Society Proceedings* 84 (1973), 3–25.

NOTES TO PAGES 117–125   189

71 Gerard, *The Herball*, 83.

72 As Walter Woodward writes, "Winthrop's decision of where to settle his new town, his efforts to secure the mine site from its indigenous owners, and his understanding of how to approach intertribal relations in the region were all arrived at in consultation with and with reliance upon the Pequot sachem Robin Cassacinamon" (*Prospero's America*, 105).

73 Wiemann, "Lasting Marks," 135.

74 John Winthrop Jr. to Thomas Peters, Boston, September 3, 1646, in *The Winthrop Papers*, vol. 5, *1645–1649* (Boston: Massachusetts Historical Society, 1947), 100.

75 As Wiemann writes, "Cassacinamon and the Nameag Pequots functioned as the perfect liaison between the colonists at Nameag and the Mohegan. In turn, Cassacinamon's attachment to Winthrop Jr. and Pequot Plantation served as the Pequots' first significant sign of defiance against Uncas in the post-war period" ("Lasting Marks," 137).

76 Adam Winthrop to John Winthrop Jr., March 1649, in *Winthrop Papers*, 5:319.

77 McBride, "Legacy of Robin Cassacinamon," 83–84.

78 Wiemann, "Lasting Marks," 153.

79 Petition of the Inhabitants of New London to the Commissioners of the United Colonies, September 15, 1646, in *Winthrop Papers*, 5:111–12.

80 New London Town Grants to John Winthrop Jr., September 1, 1652, *Winthrop Papers*, vol. 6, *1650–1654* (Boston: Massachusetts Historical Society, 1968), 61; Wiemann, "Lasting Marks," 200–201.

81 McBride, "Legacy of Robin Cassacinamon," 87.

82 Wiemann, "Lasting Marks," 207.

83 Woodward, *Prospero's America*, 273.

84 Kelly Wisecup, *Medical Encounters: Knowledge and Identity in Early American Literature* (Boston: University of Massachusetts Press, 2013), 18–19.

85 Winthrop, "Of Maiz."

86 The Dr. Wilson he references seems to be Dr. Edmund Wilson, brother of the minister John Wilson of Boston. Wilson was also a cousin to Puritan missionary Henry Whitfield. John Wentworth, "Wentworth Genealogy—the Hitherto Unknown Councillor Paul," *New England Historical and Genealogical Register*, vol. 42 (Boston: Printed by David Clapp & Son, 1888), 175–77.

CHAPTER FOUR: Treaties, Reciprocity, and Providence

1 William Hubbard, *The Present State of New England. Being a Narrative of the Troubles with the Indians in New-England, from the first planting thereof, in the year 1607, to this present year 1677: But Chiefly of the late Troubles in the two last years 1675, and 1676. To which is added a Discourse about the War with the Pequods in the year 1637* (London: Printed for Tho. Parkhurst at the Bible and Three Crowns in Cheapside, 1677), 87.

2 The Mohegan, Pequot, and members of the Praying Indians also aligned with the English.

3 Kristina Bross points out that prewar mission literature was itself rife with prejudices against Indians, constantly describing them in bondage and slavery to Satan.

190   NOTES TO PAGES 125–130

During the war, writers who wished to discredit the Praying Indians simply rehashed the missionaries' own rhetoric in service to their claims that Indians could not be converted (*Dry Bones and Indian Sermons: Praying Indians in Colonial America* [Ithaca, NY: Cornell University Press, 2002], 149–50).

4   Hilary Wyss, *Writing Indians: Literacy, Christianity, and Native Community in Early America* (Amherst: University of Massachusetts Press, 2003), 38.

5   Jill Lepore, *The Name of War: King Philip's War and the Origins of American Identity* (New York: Knopf, 1998), xiii.

6   J. Patrick Cesarini, "'What Has Become of Your Praying to God?' Daniel Gookin's Troubled History of King Philip's War," *Early American Literature* 44, no. 3 (2009): 496.

7   Lepore, *Name of War*, 46.

8   Cesarini, "What Has Become of Praying," 490.

9   Kristina Bross writes that the unique tone of Gookin's text "can be used to measure just how thoroughly the image [of the Praying Indian] was discredited by literature created during and just after the war" (*Dry Bones*, 157).

10   Frederick Gookin, *Daniel Gookin, 1612–1687, Assistant and Major General of the Massachusetts Bay Colony: His Life and Letters and Some Account of His Ancestry* (Chicago: Privately Printed, 1912), 38, 42.

11   F. Gookin, *Daniel Gookin*, 65, 66; Luke Pecoraro, "'Mr Gookin, Wholly upon His Owne Adventure': An Archeological Study of Intercolonial and Transatlantic Connections in the Seventeenth Century" (PhD diss., Boston University, 2015), 12.

12   Pecoraro explains that Gookin left Maryland because he found "the political situation in Maryland to be as oppressive as Virginia" ("Mr. Gookin," 13–14). Richard Cogley, on the other hand, seems unsure whether Gookin actually lived in Virginia or just bought land there (*John Eliot's Mission to the Indians before King Philip's War* [Cambridge, MA: Harvard University Press, 1999], 227).

13   Frederick Gookin explains that an assistant was "one of the Council of eighteen magistrate to whom, with the Governor and the Deputy Governor, the government of the colony was entrusted" (*Daniel Gookin*, 82). Gookin was also active in the colonial militia, first as a captain in the Cambridge band and later, in 1676, he was chosen as a sergeant-major in the Middlesex regiment (Cogley, *John Eliot's Mission*, 227).

14   John Frederick Martin, *Profits in the Wilderness: Entrepreneurship and the Founding of New England Towns in the Seventeenth Century* (Chapel Hill, NC: University of North Carolina Press, 1991), 23.

15   Cogley, *John Eliot's Mission*, 226.

16   Henry Whitfield, ed., *Strength Out of Weaknesse*, in *The Eliot Tracts: With Letters from John Eliot to Thomas Thorowgood and Richard Baxter*, ed. Michael P. Clark (Westport, CT: Praeger, 2003), 245.

17   As Cogley points out, the court made the position official in 1658, although Gookin claims in his *Historical Collections* that he began the role of commissioner in 1656, before he left for his English voyage (*John Eliot's Mission*, 224–25).

18   Louise Breen, *Transgressing the Bounds: Subversive Enterprises Among the Puritan Elite in Massachusetts, 1630–1692* (Oxford: Oxford University Press, 2001), 156; F. Gookin, *Daniel Gookin*, 87–88, 93–95.

NOTES TO PAGES 130–133   191

19   Christine M. Delucia, *Memory Lands: King Philip's War and the Place of Violence in the Northeast* (New Haven, CT: Yale University Press, 2018), 44.

20   Martin, *Profits in the Wilderness*, 24. Martin's text also provides a helpful timeline of all of Gookin's land claims.

21   As Delucia writes, "He could not reside simultaneously in all of these places, so he rented, sold, or remained an absentee investor for various acreage over his lifetime. In the 1660s–1670s he fervently supported establishment of a colonial settlement at Quinsigamond, about thirty miles northeast of Tantiusques, in intimate proximity to the inland Nipmuc settlement at Pakachoag" (*Memory Lands*, 44).

22   As Jean O'Brien points out, in Eliot's political system, "The potential for molding the political order remained in the hands of experienced Native leaders, who may have lost some existing institutions to wield power (tribute, which leaders probably adapted to fit tithing schemes), but gained others (legitimized access to colonial officials)" (*Dispossession by Degrees: Indian Land and Identity in Natick, Massachusetts, 1650–1790* [New York: Cambridge University Press, 1997], 49).

23   *Records of the Governor and Company of the Massachusetts Bay in New England*, vol. 2, *1642–1649*, ed. Nathaniel B. Shurtleff (Boston: William White, 1853), 2:55, emphasis added.

24   O'Brien, *Dispossession by Degrees*, 63.

25   See "Tahattawan," Native Northeast Portal, https://nativenortheastportal.com/node/6089.

26   David Ress, "Autonomy, Not Assimilation," *Australian Journal of American Studies* 41, no. 1 (2022): 31. See also Thomas Green's talk, "Thomas Green, a Member of the Massachusett Tribe, Presents a History of the Massachusett from 1600s to the Present," Pioneer Village at Salem, April 29, 2022, https://youtu.be/4lK7cfxQ9Lg.

27   See "Tahattawan," Native Northeast Portal.

28   Ress, "Autonomy, Not Assimilation," 34.

29   Cogley, *John Eliot's Mission*, 52–54.

30   Ress, "Autonomy, Not Assimilation," 35.

31   Cogley, *John Eliot's Mission*, 58.

32   Ress, "Autonomy, Not Assimilation," 29.

33   John Eliot, *A Further Accompt of the Progress of the Gospel amongst the Indians in New England*, in Clark, *Eliot Tracts*, 375, 376. O'Brien also makes note of this moment as significant in *Dispossession by Degrees*, 52.

34   Cogley, *John Eliot's Mission*, 59.

35   Waban's status within the Massachusett community prior to the arrival of the missionaries is unclear. Francis Jennings sees Waban as a pawn of Eliot and the Bay Colony. Cogley also points out the fact that Waban seems to have been chosen apart from the established protocols of Massachusett governance, however, as Cogley points out, "[Waban's] commission as 'chief minister' of justice ... apparently did not constitute a coup d'etat within the ranks of the Massachusett Indians." Ress points out that Waban was married to Tahattawan's daughter and thus was already a person of some status, though not a sachem himself. It seems like that Waban had some established authority also because the likelihood of Eliot being able to transform the social order at the early stage of the mission was unlikely. Eliot himself preferred to work within existing social structures. Francis Jennings, *The Invasion of America: Indians, Colonialism, and the*

192 NOTES TO PAGES 133–139

Cant of Conquest (New York: Norton, 1976), 239–40; Cogley, *John Eliot's Mission*, 54; Ress, "Autonomy, Not Assimilation," 32.

36 Thomas Shepard, *The Day-Breaking, if not the Sun-Rising of the Gospell with the Indians in New England*, in Clark, *Eliot Tracts*, 83.

37 Cogley, *John Eliot's Mission*, 224, 229.

38 "William Ahhaton," Native Northeast Portal, http://nativenortheastportal .com/node/9182.

39 Sarah Ahhaton, "The Examination of Sarah Ahhaton, October 24, 1668," 152, Yale Indian Papers Project, http://hdl.handle.net/10079/digcoll/3641.

40 Ahhaton, 152.

41 Cogley, *John Eliot's Mission*, 257; Ann Marie Plane, *Colonial Intimacies: Indian Marriage in Early New England* (Ithaca: Cornell University Press, 2000), 1.

42 Ahhaton, "Examination of Sarah Ahhaton," 152.

43 Ahhaton, 152, 153.

44 Plane, *Colonial Intimacies*, 77–78.

45 Ahhaton, "Examination of Sarah Ahhaton," 153.

46 Plane, *Colonial Intimacies*, 77.

47 William remained an important leader in his community. After King Philip's War, he led attempts to petition for the return of community members who had been imprisoned or forcibly taken. See "Petition of William Ahaton to the Massachusetts Council Asking for the Release of a Relation (1675)," Yale Indian Papers Project, OID: 10682701, http://hdl.handle.net/10079/digcoll/3635; "Petition from Natick and Punkapoag Indians to the Massachusetts Governor and Council (1676)," Yale Indian Papers Project, OID: 10682698, http://hdl.handle.net/10079/digcoll/3626.

48 Ahhaton, "Examination of Sarah Ahhaton," 153.

49 The language of the transcript is unclear, but Ahhaton explains that the troubles with her husband began "about two yeares since," and she also explains that right after the initial troubles, she "was brought before Waban the Ruler" which was "about planting time last." It seems that the "two years" refers to the date of the transcription, October 1668.

50 Kathleen Bragdon, *Native People of Southern New England, 1500–1650* (Norman: University of Oklahoma Press, 1996), 184–85.

51 Jeffrey Glover, *Paper Sovereigns: Anglo-Native Treaties and the Law of Nations, 1604–1664* (Philadelphia: University of Pennsylvania Press, 2014), 15.

52 Lisa Brooks, *The Common Pot: The Recover of Native Space in the Northeast* (Minneapolis: University of Minnesota Press, 2008), 7.

53 Daniel Gookin, *An Historical Account of the Doings and Sufferings of the Christian Indians in New England in the Years 1675, 1676, 1677*, in *Archaeologia Americana: Transactions and Collections of the American Antiquarian Society*, vol. 2 (Cambridge: Printed for the Society at the University Press, 1836), 433.

54 Bross, *Dry Bones*, 155.

55 Increase Mather, *A Brief History of the Warr with the Indians in New-England* (1676), ed. Paul Royster (Faculty Publications, Libraries at University of Nebraska–Lincoln), http://digitalcommons.unl.edu/libraryscience/31.

56 Anne Kusener Nelsen, "King Philip's War and the Hubbard-Mather Rivalry," *William and Mary Quarterly* 27, no. 4 (1970): 626.

57 Mather, *A Brief History*, 7–8.

NOTES TO PAGES 139–145   193

58 Hubbard first gave his providential interpretation of the war when he was chosen to give the Election Sermon of 1676—a sermon that Mather himself wanted to give. Nelsen, "King Philip's War," 619.

59 Nelsen, "Hubbard-Mather Rivalry," 627–28; Hubbard, *Present State*, iv, 48.

60 Hubbard, ix.

61 Lepore, *Name of War*, 45–46.

62 Hubbard, *Present State*, 85, 86.

63 Eric Gethyn-Jones, *George Thorpe and the Berkeley Company: A Gloucestershire Enterprise in Virginia* (Gloucester, UK: Alan Sutton, 1982), 189–90. Thorpe was also in the process of establishing an Indian school, Henrico College, which Eric Gethyn-Jones describes as "the first major attempt at the civilization and conversion of the Indian" (180).

64 Hubbard, *Present State*, 87, 88; F. Gookin, *Daniel Gookin*, 43–44.

65 Eric B. Schultz and Michael J. Tougias note that Hubbard's book was full of criticisms of colonial officials, however, because his "text needed to pass muster with Massachusetts Bay authorities" and many of its criticisms "are well veiled" (*King Philip's War: The History and Legacy of American's Forgotten Conflict* [Woodstock, VT: Countryman Press, 1999], 396).

66 John Smith, *The Generall Histories of Virginia, New England & the Summer Isles* (Carlisle, MA: Applewood, 2006), 291.

67 Frederick Gookin and others suggest that the Gookin family survived because they had a better defense system in place. This argument seems implausible because they only been there for four months and there were a limited number of people at the plantation to provide defense (*Daniel Gookin*, 43).

68 Pecoraro, "Mr. Gookin," 45.

69 Edward Warren Day explains that Hubbard went over in early 1678 (*One Thousand Years of Hubbard History, 1866 to 1895. From Hubba, the Norse Sea King, to the Enlightenment Present* [New York: HP, Hubbard, 1895], 181–82).

70 Glover, *Paper Sovereigns*, 17, 3, 9.

71 D. Gookin, *An Historical Account*, 468.

72 Hubbard, *Present State*, xiii–xiv.

73 As Lepore explains, "In the first decades of settlement, the Indians' supposed oneness with the woods (and their corresponding lack of ownership of the land) had served the colonists well in claiming New England as a *vacuum domicilium*—during King Philip's War it made those same Indians frightful enemies" (*Name of War*, 85). Adrian Chastain Weimer also discusses how Hubbard and Gookin's accounts redefine the concept of martyr. For Hubbard, the English are martyrs, unfairly attacked, while Gookin employs the concept of martyrdom for the Christian Indians. See Weimer, "'Devilish Enemies of Religion' in King Philip's War," in Adrian Chastain Weimer, *Martyr's Mirror: Persecution and Holiness in Early New England* (New York: Oxford University Press, 2011).

74 Matthew Edney and Susan Cimburek, "Telling the Traumatic Truth: Hubbard's Narrative of King Philip's War," *William and Mary Quarterly* 61, no. 2 (2004): 325.

75 D. Gookin, *An Historical Account*, 433.

76 D. Gookin, 435. Gookin does note that the Mohegan conversion efforts were hindered by "chief Sachem Uncas, and his eldest son, Oineko, not being encouragers of the Christian religion."

194 NOTES TO PAGES 146–157

77 Hubbard, *Present State*, 2.

78 Hubbard, 6, 8, 11.

79 D. Gookin, *An Historical Account*, 468, 454.

80 D. Gookin, 438–39.

81 Hubbard, *Present State*, 29.

82 D. Gookin, *An Historical Account*, 440–41.

83 D. Gookin, 441.

84 Shurtleff, *Records of the Governor*, 2:55.

85 Cogley explains that the sachems were mostly from the Boston area. Chickatawbut was sachem of the Massachusett, the Squa Sachem and Masconomet were Pawtucket sachems, and Nashowanon and Wossamegon were Nipmuc sachems (*John Eliot's Mission*, 36–37).

86 Delucia, *Memory Lands*, 21–22.

87 D. Gookin, *An Historical Account*, 499.

88 D. Gookin, 449, 442.

89 "October 13, 1675," in *Records of the Governor and Company of the Massachusetts Bay in New England*, vol. 5, *1674–1686*, ed. Nathaniel B. Shurtleff (Boston: William White, 1854), 46, 57.

90 Brooks, *Our Beloved Kin*, 199, 200.

91 The session Gookin refers to is likely the special session on February 21, 1676. Shurtleff, *Records of the Governor*, 5:64. In the records, however, there is no note of Gookin's reading the 1644 treaty.

92 D. Gookin, *An Historical Account*, 500.

93 Shurtleff, *Records of the Governor*, 5:64.

94 F. Gookin, *Daniel Gookin*, 153. Louise Breen talks more extensively about the incident in *Transgressing the Bounds*, 145–46. See also "Deposition of Elizabeth Belcher and Martha Remington Testifying that they witnessed Richard Scott Shouting Insults at Captain Daniel Gookin in the Belcher Residence," March 14, 1676, Massachusetts Archive Collection Records, vol. 30, p. 192, Series 2044, Massachusetts Archives, Boston.

95 Colin Calloway, *Pen and Ink Witchcraft: Treaties and Treaty Making in American Indian History* (New York: Oxford University Press, 2012), 12–13.

96 D. Gookin, *An Historical Account*, 431.

97 D. Gookin, 504; Abram Van Engen, *Sympathetic Puritans: Calvinist Fellow Feeling in Early New England* (Oxford: Oxford University Press, 2015), 144.

98 Laura Stevens, *The Poor Indian: British Missionaries, Native Americans, and Colonial Sensibility* (Philadelphia: University of Pennsylvania Press, 2004), 6. Also see Van Engen, *Sympathetic Puritans*, chapter 5.

99 D. Gookin, *An Historical Account*, 469.

100 Heidi Kiiwetinepinesiik Stark, "Marked by Fire: Anishinaabe Articulations of Nationhood in Treaty Making with the United States and Canada," *American Indian Quarterly* 36, no. 2 (2012): 125.

101 Hubbard, *Present State*, part 2, 14.

102 Edward Winslow, *The Glorious Progress of the Gospel amongst the Indians in New England*, in Clark, *Eliot Tracts*, 153–54.

103 Hubbard, *Present State*, 49.

NOTES TO PAGES 158–166   195

104 Numbers 22, KJV.
105 Hubbard, *Present State*, 48.
106 Cogley, *John Eliot's Mission*, 30.
107 D. Gookin, *An Historical Account*, 433.
108 D. Gookin, *Historical Collections of the Indians in New England. Of their Several Nations, Numbers, Customs, Manners, Religion and Government, Before the English Planted There* (Boston: Belknap and Hall, 1792), 47.
109 D. Gookin, *An Historical Account*, 437.
110 Delucia, *Memory Lands*, 46, 297. Cogley also suggests that Passaconaway joined with Eliot as a result of Cutshamekin's influence (*John Eliot's Mission*, 38–39).
111 Cogley, *John Eliot's Mission*, 147.
112 D. Gookin, *An Historical Account*, 522.
113 D. Gookin, 523.
114 D. Gookin, 523.
115 Weimer, *Martyr's Mirror*, 119.

EPILOGUE: Remembering and Forgetting

1 Daniel Gookin, *An Historical Account of the Doings and Sufferings of the Christian Indians in New England in the Years 1675, 1676, 1677*, in *Archaeologia Americana: Transactions and Collections of the American Antiquarian Society*, vol. 2 (Cambridge: Printed for the Society at the University Press, 1836), 428.
2 "The Humble Declaration of Harman Garrett," September 23, 1676, Native Northeast Portal, http://nativenortheastportal.com/annotated-transcription/digcoll4062.
3 William Apess, "Eulogy on King Philip," in *A Son of the Forest and Other Writings*, ed. Barry O'Connell (Amherst: University of Massachusetts Press, 1997), 108, 113.

INDEX

Ahhaton, Sarah, 134–37
Ahhaton, William, 134–37
Andersen, Chris, 12
Antinomian Controversy, 53–54
Apess, William, 165–66

Balaam, 158
Bellin, Joshua David, 11
Boyle, Robert, 91, 121, 126, 142
Bozeman, Theodore Dwight, 84
Bradford, William, 104
Brooks, Lisa, 8–9, 13, 27, 44, 46, 57, 138, 152
Bross, Kristina, 48, 63, 64, 76
Burke, Kenneth, 75

Caldwell, Patricia, 53, 54–55
Calloway, Colin, 14, 154
Canonicus, 29, 31, 67–68, 107
captives (captivity), 22, 32–33, 35–36, 39–42, 49–50, 57, 68, 112
Cassacinamon, Robin, 15–16, 34–35, 93–95, 109–14, 117–21, 123, 165–66
Cesarini, J. Patrick, 40, 125, 126
Chickatawbut, 62, 66, 104
The Christian Commonwealth (Eliot), 65, 83–85, 87–88
clan mothers, 135
Cogley, Richard, 133, 160
Columbus, Christopher, 97, 101
Connecticut Colony, 46, 91–93, 119, 121
Connecticut River, 32, 43–44, 45, 46, 50–51, 107–8, 112
conversion narrative, 19, 21, 23, 25, 39, 40–41, 43, 50, 52–55, 58; Indigenous conversion narrative, 19–21, 22–23, 37, 45, 56, 58–59, 80, 88
Coombs, Darius, 115
Cromwell, Oliver, 18, 65, 84, 88, 121, 130
Cutshamekin, 15–16, 60, 114; and

diplomacy, 62, 64–65, 67–70, 71–75, 77–79; and governance, 65–66, 80–83

D'Abate, Richard, 100, 160
Deer Island, 125, 150–52
Delucia, Christine, 130, 160
diplomatic relation genre, 126, 142–43
Dippold, Steffi, 77
dispossession (land displacement), 11, 20, 165
Donegan, Kathleen, 9
Donohue, Betty Booth, 9, 104
Dorsey, Andy, 53–54

Eliot, John, 15, 62–63, 76–77, 139, 156, 159; as author, 63–65, 83, 88, 164; and colonial governance, 63, 79–82, 84–85; as missionary, 60, 73–77, 79
English Civil War, 17, 30, 65, 121

Fenwick, George, 44, 46–47
first fruits, 25
firsting, 4–5, 23–25
Fitzgerald, Stephanie, 70, 75
four elements, 106

Gerard, John, 93–94, 98–99, 100–103, 117, 122
Glover, Jeffrey, 5, 40, 142
Gookin, Daniel, 16, 126; as author, 126–27, 138, 142–43, 145–50, 154–56, 158–63; family history, 141–42; as politician, 128–30, 134–37, 151–53
Gorton, Samuel, 69
Gray, Kathryn, 84
Green Corn festival, 116

Harriot, Thomas, 97–100
Harvard College, 24

198 INDEX

Haudenosaunee, 109
Holstun, James, 84, 86
Hooker, Thomas, 46
Hubbard, William, 124–25, 127, 138–46, 148, 157–58
Hutchinson, Anne, 54, 76

Indigenous conversion narrative. *See* conversion narrative
Indigenous diplomacy (common pot), 6, 8–9, 10–12, 16, 47, 57, 66, 70, 90, 137–38, 154
Indigenous kinship, 2, 10, 13–14, 22–23, 27–29, 33, 46, 65, 67, 79, 84–86, 111, 136; and English kinship, 20–21, 46, 52, 125, 155–56, 160; and judicial systems, 88, 137–38; as a method, 12–14, 27–28, 31, 33, 41, 52, 56–57; with nonhuman beings, 94–95, 101; and treaties, 67–69, 154–55, 159
Indigenous methodologies, 13, 20, 45
Indigenous science, 15, 93, 97, 123

Justice, Daniel Heath, 27

A Key into the Language of America (Roger Williams), 19, 23, 27, 40, 42, 44, 164
Kidwell, Clara Sue, 12
Kimmerer, Robin Wall, 96–97, 106, 117
King Philip's War (Metacom's Rebellion), 14, 16, 124, 125–27, 129, 138–40, 143, 146, 153

Lakota, 166
Lepore, Jill, 44, 125–26, 139, 144

Maclear, J. F., 84
Majhor, Samantha, 95
manitou, 38–39, 72, 74, 78, 95, 137
martyr (martyrdom), 22, 51–52, 55, 144, 151, 162
Masconomet, 2, 69, 166
Mason, John, 30, 36, 119
Massachusett nation, 60–62, 64–70, 72, 74–75, 79–84, 86–88, 90, 101, 130, 132, 134–35, 149, 154–55

Massachusetts Bay Colony, 17, 18, 31, 45, 60, 85, 92, 105; charter, 17, 24, 56, 143; and land claims, 69; and treaties, 68, 69, 70, 75, 87, 90, 149–50, 152–53
Mather, Increase, 138–39
Mather, Richard, 37–38
McBride, Kevin, 34
McGiffert, Michael, 50, 55
Metacom (Philip), 136, 143, 146, 148–49, 154, 157, 165–66
Miantonomi, 29, 31–33, 36, 49, 69, 146
Mohegan, 22, 27, 30, 33–37, 46–47, 49, 110, 112, 119–20, 145–46
Mystic Massacre (Battle of Mystick Fort), 29–30, 35–36, 38–39

Nameag (New London), 93, 95, 111–18, 119–21
Nameag Pequot, 114–18, 120–23
Narragansett, 6, 28–29, 31–34, 36, 40, 49, 66–69, 107–8, 110–11, 146
Natick, 58, 61, 65, 79–80, 82–84, 86, 89, 128, 130, 132–33, 137, 150, 152
Naumkeag (Salem), 1, 105
Nelsen, Anne Kusener, 139–40
Neponset, 60–62, 66, 73, 75, 80, 82, 89
New Englands First Fruits (Peter & Weld), 17–18, 23–24, 25–27, 30, 37, 39, 42, 45, 47–48, 51, 59
Niantic, 22, 28–29, 33, 35–37, 44, 47, 49, 107, 110
Ninigret, 28, 49
Nipmuck, 69, 80, 101, 124, 130, 144–45, 152, 155
Nishohkou, 89–90
Nonantum, 80, 82, 132
Nonantum Code, 132–34
Norembega, 100

Oberg, Michael, 33
O'Brien, Jean, 4–5, 11–12, 25, 65, 79–80, 131
Opechancanough, 140–41

Passaconaway, 157
Pawtucket, 69, 136
Pecoraro, Luke, 141

Pequot nation, 9, 15–16, 20–23, 27–30, 32–39, 43, 46–47, 49, 57, 59, 66, 68, 93, 95, 109, 110–12, 115–20, 130, 144, 165
Pequot War, 14, 19, 34, 36, 49, 62, 66, 110–12, 165
Peter, Hugh, 17–19, 30, 37–38, 40, 42, 51, 111
Plane, Ann Marie, 136
Powhatan, 140–41
Praying Indian, 6–7, 16, 61, 65, 79–80, 82, 86–87, 89–90, 143, 145, 147–58, 160–62
Printer, James, 152
Pulsipher, Jenny Hale, 90
Pumham, 68–69, 71
Punkapoag, 134–36

Quaiapin, 29, 44

Raleigh, Walter, 97, 99
Ress, David, 132
Rivett, Sarah, 9–10, 58, 76
Royal Society, 91–92

Saccious, 28
Salisbury, Neal, 66, 70
Sassacus, 33–34
Saybrook Company, 107
Saybrook Fort, 32, 41, 43–44, 46, 107
scientific treatise, 10, 123, 164
Scott, Richard, 153
settler colonialism, 20, 56
Shepard, Thomas, 15, 19, 21–23, 42, 45–46, 50–52, 54–56, 164
Soconoco, 68–69, 71
Spar, Natalie, 83–84
spiritual question (question-and-answer genre), 63–64, 66, 70–72, 74, 78, 90
Squa Sachem, 69, 132
Stark, Heidi Kiiwetinepinesiik, 156
Stevens, Laura, 155
Stoughton, Israel, 111

Tahattawan, 132–34, 154
Taino, 97
Tatobem, 33

Tears of Repentance, 58
Thorpe, George, 141
Three Sisters garden, 116–17
Tomaquag Museum, 164
Treaty of Hartford, 36–37, 68, 146

Uncas, 22, 34, 41–42, 44, 49, 111–12, 119–20
Underhill, John, 30, 36
utopia, 18, 84, 88

Waban, 60–61, 128, 148, 154, 160–61
Wampanoag language (Wôpanâak), 1, 27, 77, 84
wampum, 33–34, 68, 105
Wannalancet, 157, 159
Weetamoo, 13–14
Weimer, Adrian Chastain, 51–52, 162
Weld, Thomas, 17–19, 30, 37–38, 40, 42, 51, 55
Wepitanock, 28, 165
Wequash, 15, 18–19, 27, 40, 42, 44, 59, 107; death of, 21–22, 47–49, 51, 56, kinship ties of, 15, 22, 28, 31, 33–34, 41, 43, 56–57; in the Pequot War, 32, 34, 35–36
Wequashcook (Harman Garrett), 59, 165
White, Craig, 74
Whitfield, Henry, 44
Wiemann, Sean, 114
Williams, Robert, Jr., 67
Williams, Roger, 19, 23, 31–32, 40–44, 48, 56–57, 110, 124
Winthrop, John, Jr., 15, 91–97, 100–103, 106–9, 113–15, 117–18, 121–23
Winthrop, John, Sr., 1–3, 5–6, 48–49, 53, 66–67, 73, 101–2, 104–5, 119–20, 122
Wisecup, Kelly, 122
Witgen, Michael, 13
Wompatuck, Josias, 69
Wood, William, 75
Woodward, Walter, 97, 117, 121
Wyss, Hilary, 125

Zobel, Melissa Tantaquidgeon (Melissa Fawcett), 27

MARIE BALSLEY TAYLOR is an assistant professor of literature at the University of North Alabama. She received her PhD in literature from Purdue University and her MA in English from Georgetown University.